FOODSERVICE COST CONTROL
USING MICROSOFT® EXCEL FOR WINDOWS®

FOODSERVICE COST CONTROL USING MICROSOFT® EXCEL FOR WINDOWS®

Warren Sackler, FMP, CHA
Rochester Institute of Technology

Samuel R. Trapani, EE

John Wiley & Sons, Inc.
New York · Chichester · Brisbane · Toronto · Singapore

Trademark Acknowledgments:
Excel, Microsoft, and Windows are registered trademarks of Microsoft Corporation.
IBM, Lotus, and 1-2-3 are registered trademarks of International Business Machines Corporation.
WordPerfect is a registered trademark of Novell, Inc.

The Introduction to *Foodservice Cost Control Using Microsoft® Excel® for Windows* includes material from *Getting Started with Microsoft Excel 5.0 for Windows*, by Babette Kronstadt, copyright © 1995 John Wiley & Sons, Inc., and used with permission.

Lesson 8 includes material from *Menu Engineering, 2nd edition*, by Michael L. Kasavana and Donald J. Smith, copyright © 1990, Hospitality Publications, Inc., P.O. Box 448, Okemos, MI 48805, and used with permission.

Library of Congress Cataloging-in-Publication Data

Sackler, Warren.
    Foodservice cost control using Microsoft Excel for Windows /
Warren Sackler, Samuel R. Trapani.
      p. cm.
     Includes index.
     ISBN 0-471-15274-9 (pbk. : alk. paper)
      1. Food service—Cost control—Data processing. 2. Microsoft
Excel for Windows. 3. Electronic spreadsheets. I. Trapani, Samuel
R. II. Title.
TX911.3.C65S24 1996
647.95'0285—dc20   96-5408

This book is dedicated to our departed mothers, Mollie Sackler and Mary Trapani, for their wisdom and lifelong support, and to our families.

Also, many thanks to the students pursuing their careers in the hospitality industry.

Thanks to all the restaurant and hotel associations that we have been involved with for many years, for their industry support, especially the National Restaurant Association, the Educational Foundation, and the Rochester Chapter of the New York State Restaurant Association. Many thanks to the American Hotel and Motel Association, the local New York State Association, and the Educational Institute, as well as the Council of Hotel, Restaurant, and Institutional Educators.

Thanks to all of our education colleagues that we have worked with over the years.

Thanks to all the people we have had the experience of working with in our restaurant ventures, new and in the past.

Thanks to all of our friends from our college days and current days.

CONTENTS

PREFACE

Experience is the best teacher. That's why *Foodservice Cost Control Using Microsoft Excel for Windows* is the ideal complement to any basic food and beverage cost-control text. Integrating the cost *concepts* presented in your textbook with the spreadsheet *experience* provided in this workbook will help you grasp the essence of foodservice cost control.

After reviewing fundamental cost control topics, each lesson walks you through practical spreadsheet applications using two restaurant scenarios: The Red Woodpecker, a casual, family-style operation, and the Terrace Garden, a fine-dining establishment. You will learn to manipulate and analyze data to make informed management decisions. And you will be encouraged to develop your own critical thinking and decision-making skills while learning to use Microsoft Excel.

What to Expect

Each lesson includes comprehensive instructions for completing the appropriate Microsoft Excel applications. You'll find helpful tips and reminders featured throughout the book. As they are introduced, key terms appear in boldface and are defined. Charts, tables, and screen captures thoroughly illustrate each lesson. In addition, a Microsoft Excel User's Guide Introduction is a handy reference.

Getting Started

Each lesson begins with a list of learning objectives: what you can expect to learn after following the exercises step-by-step. After a discussion of basic theory, the appropriate spreadsheets are introduced and explained.

Having studied this background, you are ready to tackle one or two application problems. You are given background information, specific tasks, and "check your understanding" questions.

You will find *Foodservice Cost Control Using Microsoft Excel for Windows* a useful tool in developing the skills needed to plan and manage in today's competitive restaurant environment—where a *working* knowledge is what works.

WARREN SACKLER

ABOUT THE DISK

Disk Content

Foodservice Cost Control Using Microsoft Excel for Windows includes 2 floppy disks containing 34 Microsoft Excel files. Each lesson in the book provides instructions on how to use the Microsoft Excel worksheets to reinforce cost control concepts. Disk 1 contains exercises for Chapter 1–Chapter 5. Disk 2 contains exercises for Chapter 6–Chapter 9.

Minimum System Requirements

- IBM PC or compatible
- Windows version 3.0 or later
- Microsoft Excel version 4.0 or later (or other spreadsheet software capable of reading Microsoft Excel files)

Files are formatted in Microsoft Excel for Windows version 4.0. To use the worksheets with other spreadsheet programs, refer to the user manual that accompanies your software package for instructions on reading Microsoft Excel for Windows files.

Using the Disk

To use the files on the disk, load Microsoft Excel for Windows (or other spreadsheet software capable of reading Excel files) and open the file you wish to use. Files are named according to each exercise. For example, **Exercise 1-1A** is **EX1-1A.XLS** on Disk 1.

User Assistance and Information

If you need basic installation assistance, or if your disk is defective , please call our product support number at (212) 850-6194 weekdays between 9 A.M. and 4 P.M. Eastern Standard Time.

To place additional orders or to request information about other Wiley products, please call (800) 879-4539.

Introduction: USING MICROSOFT® EXCEL® FOR WINDOWS

■ OBJECTIVES

After completing this Introduction, you should know:

- What a worksheet is used for
- How to start Excel
- The parts of the Excel screen that are common to Windows programs
- The parts of the Excel screen specific to Excel
- Terminology used in worksheets
- How to use the **View** menu to change the appearance of the screen

- How to use the toolbars
- How to select a cell
- How Excel follows Windows procedures for using menus and dialog boxes
- How to use Help
- How to exit from Excel

PURPOSE OF THE INTRODUCTION

This introduction is designed to teach you the basic concepts, terminology, and techniques that you will need to use Excel successfully to complete the lessons that follow. This introduction will quickly review basic Windows concepts and terminology, but it will also indicate areas in which Excel's procedures may differ from those used in other Windows applications.

Most commands that you are to follow are given using the mouse unless a keyboard combination is particularly easy.

The Introduction includes material from *Getting Started with Microsoft Excel 5.0 for Windows* by Babette Kronstadt and David Sachs, copyright © 1995, John Wiley & Sons, and used with permission.

1

WHAT IS MICROSOFT EXCEL 5.0 FOR WINDOWS?

Excel is an electronic spreadsheet or worksheet. Worksheets are essential tools used by all businesses and can be used in your life as a student as well. A worksheet is an organized way to keep track of numeric data. It is used when you need to perform calculations to analyze the data. Often the data in a worksheet change frequently. One of the strengths of a worksheet is that after you create formulas to perform the calculations, they are automatically updated, or recalculated, whenever you update the data.

More importantly, the worksheet can answer questions about the data. What was the company's profit in the last quarter? Did actual revenues and expenses meet budget expectations? What was the total payroll for the week? What is the effect of different interest rates on the amount of money that can be borrowed?

Because worksheets recalculate automatically, they can also be used to make projections into the future. These projections are often called *what-if* analyses. *What* will be the effect on profits *if* the company can hold expenses for materials to 15 percent? What will be the effect on my grade if I get a 95 on the next exam?

GETTING STARTED

Since Excel runs under Windows the appearance of the Excel window and the methods of starting Excel, selecting commands from menus, completing dialog boxes, and performing basic file commands like opening, closing, and saving files are the same as those used for any other Windows application package. This introductory lesson will review these procedures briefly, but it is assumed that you are familiar with Windows and that you know how to use the mouse.

STARTING EXCEL

Since Excel runs under Windows, it is started in the same way as any other Windows application.

The steps for completing each Excel feature introduced in this book are covered in two ways. First, they are described in a *bulleted* list, that can also be used for reference. The steps are used in a hands-on *Activity*. Be sure to wait until the *numbered* instructions in the *Activity* to practice each feature on the computer.

To Start Excel:

- Turn on your computer and start Windows.
- Open the Microsoft Office program group if it is not already open.
- Double-click on the Excel icon.

Activity: Starting Excel

1. Turn on your computer and start Windows.
2. Point to the Microsoft Excel application icon (Figure I–1) and double-click the left mouse button.

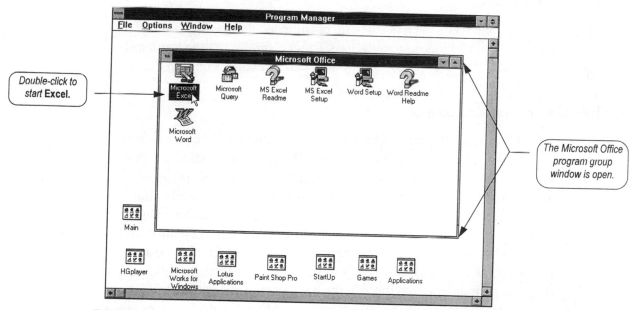

FIGURE I–1

The Microsoft Excel window should be displayed (Figure I-2).

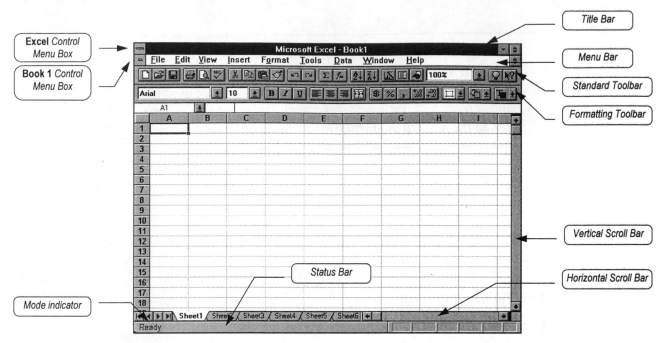

FIGURE I–2

THE EXCEL SCREEN

Most of the Excel screen is made up of components that are familiar to you from other Windows applications. Other elements may be less familiar because they are specific to working with worksheets or with Excel.

Typical Windows Components

Figure I–2 labels the parts of the Excel window that should be familiar to you from using Windows or from other Windows applications. Figure I–2 shows the screen components that appear when Excel is first installed according to a standard setup. As is true with all Windows applications, your screen may look somewhat different from Figure I–3 if someone has changed the default settings. Some of the more common changes and ways of changing the appearance of your screen to match those used in this book will be discussed in this lesson. As you work through this book, if your screen differs from those in the book even after you have tried the techniques described in this chapter, check with your instructor or lab assistant.

The Title Bar

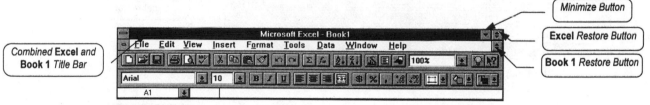

Minimize Button

Excel *Restore Button*

Book 1 *Restore Button*

Combined **Excel** and **Book 1** *Title Bar*

FIGURE I–3

As in all Windows applications, Excel may have two title bars—one displaying the application name (Microsoft Excel), and one displaying the name of the document, or *workbook*, that you are working on. If your screen is using the *default* settings (the settings that are preset by Excel), the two title bars are combined into one (Figure I–3) because the workbook has been maximized.

The right side of the title bar in Figure I–3 contains the *minimize* and the *restore* buttons. The *minimize button* is used to shrink the Excel window to an icon. The presence of the *restore button* indicates that the window is already maximized. The restore button is used to return a maximized window to its previous size and location. Once a window is restored, the restore button is replaced by the *maximize button*. The maximize button is used to enlarge a window to its maximum size. If the title bar on your screen does not resemble Figure I-3, complete the activity below. Otherwise skip to the next section on the menu bar.

Activity: Maximizing the Excel and Workbook Windows

Do this activity if your title bar(s) resemble(s) Figure I–4, Figure I–5, or Figure I–6.

1. If the maximize button appears on the Microsoft Excel title bar, as in Figure I–4 or Figure I–5, then the application is *not* maximized. To maximize it, point to the maximize button on the right side of the Microsoft Excel title bar and click once with the left mouse button.

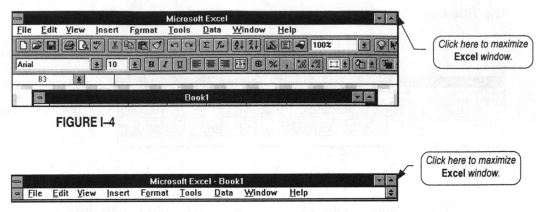

FIGURE I–4

FIGURE I–5

2. If **Book 1** has its own title bar (Figure I–6), point to the maximize button on the right side of the **Book 1** title bar and click once.

The workbook (Book 1) and Excel title bars are now combined and the title bar should resemble Figure I–3.

FIGURE I–6

The Menu Bar

Immediately under the title bar is the menu bar (Figure I–2). The menu bar contains the names of the menus from which you choose Excel commands. If you have used Microsoft Word 6.0, you may notice that all of the menu names except for **Tools** are the same as those in Word.

The Toolbar

Immediately under the menu bar are the *standard* and *formatting toolbars* (Figure I–2), unless the person who previously used Excel on your computer has chosen to hide one or both of them or to display additional toolbars. Excel comes with 13 toolbars, some of which are automatically displayed when you issue certain commands. Additional customized toolbars can be created. You will learn how to display the toolbars of your choice in a few pages. Each toolbar contains a set of buttons that perform related actions more quickly than if you used the **Menu** commands they replace. If you have used Microsoft Word 6.0, you will notice that more than half of the buttons on the standard and formatting toolbars are identical to those used in Word.

Scroll Bars

Excel, like all Windows packages, includes *scroll bars* (Figure I–2), shaded bars along the right and bottom sides of a window, allowing you to move rapidly through a long worksheet.

Status Bar

The *status bar* (Figure I–2) is the shaded bar along the very bottom of the screen that displays information about what you are currently doing. It is very important to get into the habit of looking at the status bar. When you are working with menus or toolbar buttons, the left side of the status bar gives you information on what actions the **Menu** commands or toolbar buttons carry out. At other times the left side of the status bar gives a general description of the *mode* or type of task you are performing, or even instructions for completing a task. The right side of the status bar shows the status of important keys on your computer, such as **NUM LOCK**, **CAPS LOCK**, **SCROLL LOCK**, or **INSERT**.

Workbooks and Worksheets

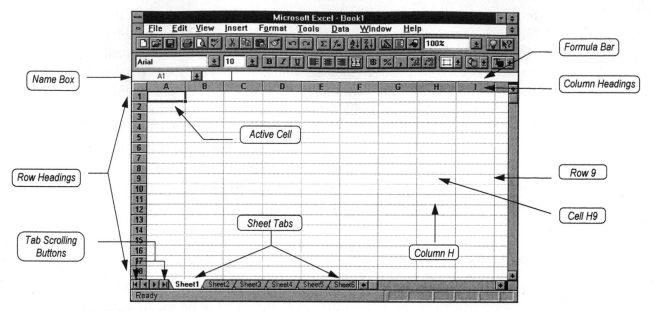

FIGURE I–7

In Excel 5.0 each new file is called a *workbook*. When a new file is created, its default title is **Book 1**, **Book 2**, and so on. A workbook is a container that holds one or more sheets. Each sheet can be a separate worksheet, a chart, or instructions used to automate working with Excel. Figure I–7 shows a worksheet with its main components labeled. If some of the parts of the worksheet are not displayed on your screen, look at Figure I–7 as you read the following descriptions. You will learn how to display missing parts of the worksheet in the section on using the **View** menu.

A worksheet is the main type of sheet used in Excel to store data, perform calculations on data, and otherwise manipulate the data. Most of the terms used to describe parts of the worksheet are described in this section. Unlike the parts of the window previously described, these terms will not be familiar to you unless you have used another worksheet package.

Here is a list of important worksheet terms that will be used in this book:

- *Columns* run vertically down the length of the worksheet; a single worksheet contains 256 columns.
- The *Column heading* is the shaded row at the top of the worksheet, which contains the names for each of the columns. Columns are named by letters (**A** through **Z**, followed by **AA** through **AZ**, **BA** through **BZ**, etc., ending with **IA** through **IV**).

- *Rows* run horizontally across the width of the worksheet. A single worksheet contains 16,384 rows.

- The *Row heading* is the shaded column to the left of the worksheet, which contains the names of the rows. Rows are named by numbers, beginning with **1** and ending with **16,384**.

- *Cells* are the individual locations on the worksheet. A cell is the intersection of a column and a row, so its name is the column name followed by the row name with *no* spaces (e.g. **A1**, **B62**, **BI203**). There are more than 4,000,000 cells on each worksheet. The name of the cell may also be called the *cell address* or the *cell reference*.

- The part of the worksheet that contains the cells is sometimes called a *grid*. The *gridlines* are the horizontal and vertical lines that separate columns and rows. They may be removed from the worksheet, but their presence makes it easier to identify cells.

- The *active* cell is the cell in which your working. It will receive any data you enter and will be acted upon by any commands you choose. It is surrounded by a dark border.

- The *formula bar* is a bar above the worksheet window that is used to enter or edit the contents of the worksheet. The *name box* on the left side of the formula bar usually tells you the location of the active cell. The rest of the formula bar shows you the cell contents.

- *Sheet tabs* are used to switch between the different sheets in a workbook. A workbook may have as many as 256 sheets, but typically only 16 sheets are available when a new workbook is opened.

- The *tab scrolling buttons* appear along the horizontal scroll bar. They are used to move the first, previous, next, and last sheet in the workbook.

THE MOUSE POINTER

As you move the mouse, a mouse pointer moves across the screen. The shape of the pointer changes depending on the part of the screen to which it is pointing. For example, the mouse pointer is an ▧ when you are pointing to items on the menu bar, toolbar, or status bar, but changes to a ✛ when it is pointing to cells on the worksheet grid so that you can select the cell(s).

More importantly, the shape of the mouse pointer may also change to indicate what activity will be performed if you press the mouse button. For example, if you point to certain parts of an already selected cell, the pointer will change from a ✛ to a ▧ or a ✚ . When this happens clicking the mouse button will copy or move the cell contents rather than select the cell. As you follow the activity instructions in this book, look for descriptions of the shape of the mouse pointer and make sure the mouse pointer on your screen is the correct shape!

THE ACTIVE CELL—SELECTING A CELL

Before you can enter data into a cell or perform a command on the contents of the cell, you must select that cell (i.e., make it the *active cell*). The active cell is indicated by the heavy border surrounding it. The name of the active cell can also be seen in the name box on the left side of the formula bar.

To select a cell that is already visible on the worksheet:

- Move your mouse pointer ✛ to the cell and click with the left mouse button, *or*
- Press the **ARROW** keys (← ↑ → ↓) until the heavy border indicating the active cell surrounds the cell of your choice.

Activity: Selecting a Single Cell

1. Point to the cell at the intersection of column **B** and row **3** (cell **B3**) and click with the left mouse button.

    The dark highlight surrounds B3 and B3 appears in the name box on the formula bar (Figure I–8).

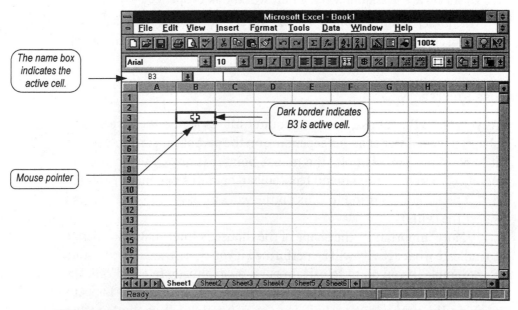

FIGURE I–8

2. Press the **DOWN ARROW** key twice and the **RIGHT ARROW** key once.

C5 should be selected as indicated by the dark border surrounding it, and C5 is indicated in the name box.

GIVING COMMANDS IN EXCEL

Commands in Excel can be given through the use of the main menus (and their related dialog boxes), toolbar buttons, shortcut keys, and shortcut menus. Instructions in this book will focus on the use of menus and toolbar buttons. Shortcut menus will be introduced in Lesson 2 and used in following lessons. Shortcut keys will be mentioned occasionally. The menus and dialog boxes in Excel work the same way as in other Windows packages. Features that may not be common to all Windows packages will be introduced when first used.

To use the menus to give commands:

- Open the menu by pointing to the menu name and clicking the left mouse button.
- Choose a command by pointing to the command name and clicking the left mouse button.
  - If the command name is followed by an ellipsis (...), a dialog box will be displayed. Follow the instructions in Table I–1 to complete the dialog box.
  - If the command name is preceded by a check mark, choosing the command will turn it off.
  - If the command name is followed by a triangle, choosing the command will display a submenu. Choose the submenu command the same way you choose the menu commands.
  - If the command name appears in light print, it cannot be used at that time. Choosing it will have no effect.

KEYBOARD ALTERNATIVES: To open a menu using the keyboard, press the **ALT** key and then type the underlined letter in the menu name. To choose a command from the menu, type the underlined letter in the command name.

KEYBOARD SHORTCUT: Key combinations that appear to the right of a menu command can be used as shortcuts for the command. They must be used, however, before the menu is opened.

To close a menu without choosing a command:

- Point to the menu name or a blank part of the screen outside of the menu and then click the left mouse button.

    KEYBOARD ALTERNATIVE: *Press the **ALT** key to close an open menu.*

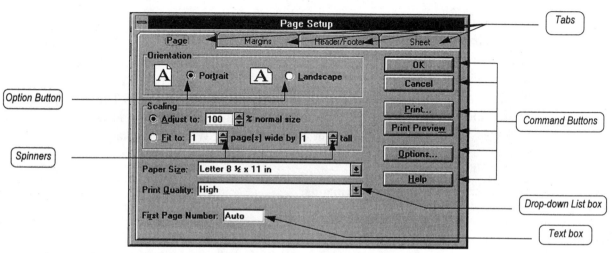

FIGURE I–9

Task	Mouse	Keyboard
Tab (Figure I–9)	Point to the tab and click the left mouse button.	Press **CTRL** and **TAB** until the tab is selected.
Text Box (Figure I–9)	Double-click in the text box; then type the new information.	Press **ALT** and the underlined letter in the text box name; type the new information.
Option (Radio) Button (Figure I–9)	Point to the option button and then click the left mouse button.	Press **ALT** and the underlined letter in the option button name.
Check Box (Figure I–10)	Point to the square preceding the box name and then click the left mouse button to toggle the box on or off.	Press **ALT** and the highlighted letter in the check box name.
List Box (Figure I–10)	Point to the list box item and click the left mouse button. If the item is not visible, click on the scroll arrows to move the list up/down one item at a time; click on the list item once it is displayed.	Press **ALT** and the underlined letter in the list box name; use the **UP** and **DOWN ARROW** keys to select the list item.
Drop-down List Box (Figure I–9 and Figure I–10)	Click the ↓ to the right of the list box and then follow directions for list boxes.	Press **ALT** and the underlined letter in the list box name to open the drop-down list.
Spinner (Figure I–9)	Click the **UP** and **DOWN** arrows to the right of the box until the number you want appears in the box, or type the new number.	Press **ALT** and the underlined letter in the spinner name; press the **UP** or **DOWN ARROW** keys to change the numbers by the default amount or type the new number.
Command Button (Figure I–9)	To execute or cancel the command, or display another dialog box, click on the appropriate command button.	Press **ESC** to cancel a command, **ENTER** to execute a command, or **ALT** and the underlined letter.

TABLE I–1: Using Dialog Boxes

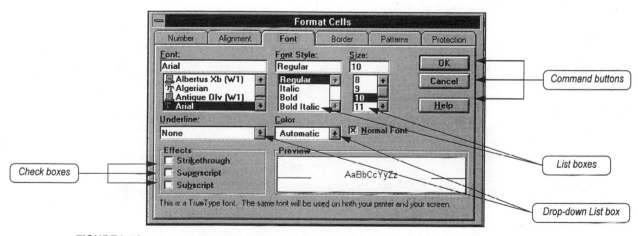

FIGURE I–10

THE VIEW MENU

The **View** menu controls the appearance of the screen. If your screen has not contained all of the components described previously, the **View** menu is the first place to go to change the display.

To display the status bar and formula bar:

- Open the **View** menu by pointing to **View** with the mouse pointer and clicking on **View** with the left mouse button.
- If **Formula Bar** and **Status Bar** are preceded by check marks (✔), they are already selected. If the one that you want displayed is not preceded by a check mark, click on it with the left mouse button.

To display/hide toolbar:

- Open the **View** menu.
- Point to **Toolbars** and click on it with the left mouse button.
- In the **Toolbars** dialog box, a toolbar preceded by a marked check box is displayed. Click on empty check boxes to display additional toolbars; click on marked check boxes to hide already displayed toolbars.

Activity: Using the View Menu to Change the Appearance of the Screen

1. To open the **View** menu, point to **View** in the menu bar and click the left mouse button (Figure I–11).

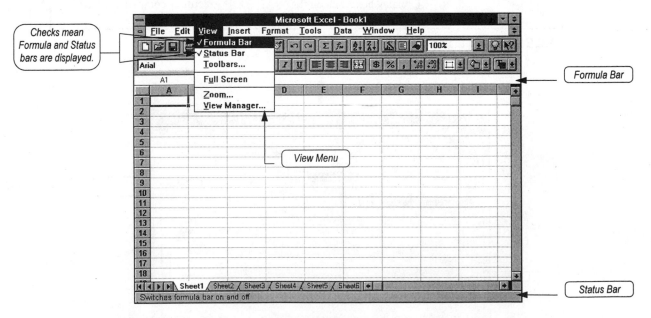

FIGURE I–11

2. In Figure I–11 **Formula Bar** and **Status Bar** are both preceded by check marks indicating that both are displayed. Point to **Status Bar** and click the left mouse button.

Formula Bar and Status Bar work like toggle keys—selecting them changes their state from on to off and vice versa. If the status bar was previously displayed, it will be removed as in Figure I–12. If it was not previously displayed, it will now be displayed.

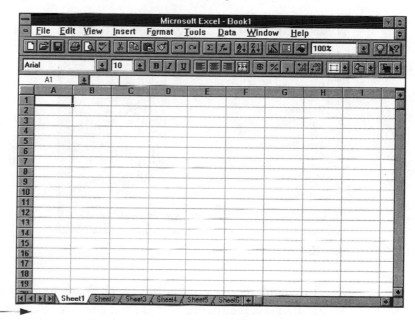

The Status Bar is no longer displayed.

FIGURE I–12

3. Click on **View** again. If the **View** menu resembles Figure I–13 and **Status Bar** is *not* checked, click on **Status Bar**. If **Status Bar** is already preceded by a check mark (as in Figure I–11), click anywhere on the worksheet grid to close the menu.

View	**Insert**	**For**
√ Formula Bar		
Status Bar		
Toolbars...		
Full Screen		
Zoom...		
View Manager...		

FIGURE I–13

PROBLEM SOLVER: *If the title bar, status bar, and other screen parts are not visible on the screen, and the **Full Screen** command on the **View** menu has been selected, click on it again to unselect it.*

4. Choose **View** again.

5. Choose **Toolbars** by pointing to it and clicking the left mouse button.

   *The **Toolbars** dialog box (Figure I–14) is displayed.*

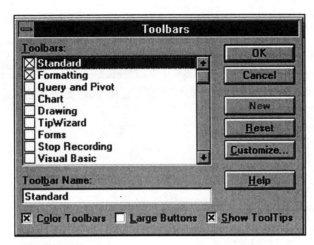

FIGURE I–14

6. The **Standard** and **Formatting** check boxes should be marked as in Figure I–14. If either or both are not checked, click on them to check them. If any other check boxes in the **Toolbars** section of the screen are checked, click on them to unmark them.

7. Compare the **Toolbars** dialog box on your screen with Figure I–14. When it is identical (including the **X**s in the **Color Toolbars** and **Show ToolTips** check boxes) to Figure I–14, click on **OK**.

   *Use the **View** menu throughout this book anytime the status bar, formula bar, or toolbars are missing from your screen.*

USING TOOLBAR BUTTONS

Toolbar buttons can be used to perform many of the commands that the menus perform. While using the toolbars is quicker than using the menus, sometimes your choices are limited or you receive less information about the effects of your command.

One of the improvements Excel made in version 5.0 was the inclusion of **ToolTips**. When you point to a toolbar button, the name of the button appears in a colored box next to the button and a description of the button appears on the status bar. In the previous activity you used the **VIEW/Toolbars** command to make sure **Show ToolTips** would be displayed.

To use a toolbar button:

- Move the mouse pointer to the toolbar button and click the left mouse button.

To find out what a specific toolbar button does:

- Move the mouse pointer until it is on the toolbar button.
- Read the name of the button in the **ToolTips** box that appears next to the mouse pointer. Read a description of the button on the status bar.

GETTING ON-LINE HELP

ToolTips is one of many examples of the help Excel provides. Each of the dialog boxes also contains a **Help** button. Choosing that button displays help about the dialog box that you are currently using. The **Help** menu provides three ways of searching for help on a topic: **Table of Contents**, **Search for Help on**, and an **Index**. In addition, **Quick Preview** and **Examples and Demos** provide tutorials on performing many tasks in Excel. The **TipWizard** button on the standard toolbar 💡 displays the **TipWizard** toolbar, which contains tips on other ways to perform the tasks you have tried since opening Excel. Click on the **Help** button 🗦? and then click on any part of the screen to get help on that part of the screen.

To get Help while working in a dialog box:

- Point to the **Help** command button in the dialog box and click the left mouse button.
- If the Help topic extends beyond the screen, click on the ↓ on the vertical scroll bar to see the rest of the topic.
- Any information on the screen that is green and underlined with a solid line is a *jump term*. If you move the mouse pointer to the jump term, the shape of the mouse changes to a 🖐 . Click the left mouse button to display the Help topic.

- Any information on the screen that is green and underlined with dashes is a *term* for which Excel has a definition. Point to a term and click the left mouse button to display a definition of the term. When you have finished reading the definition, click the left mouse button again.

Activity: Using Help

In this activity you will practice using **Help**.

1. Open the **Format** menu by pointing to **Format** on the menu bar and clicking the left mouse button.

2. Point to **Cells** and click the left mouse button.

3. If the **Font** tab is not on top, point to the **Font** tab and click (Figure I–15).

4. Point to the **Help** command button (Figure I–15) in the **Format Cells** dialog box and click the left mouse button.

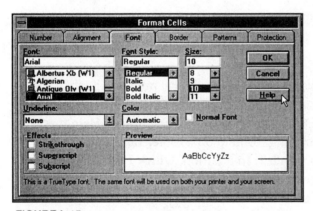

FIGURE I–15

*The **Font Tab, Cells Command (Format Menu)** Help Screen (Figure I–16) is displayed.*

5. Click on the ↓ on the vertical scroll bar until **Normal Style** (in green print underlined) is displayed (Figure I–17).

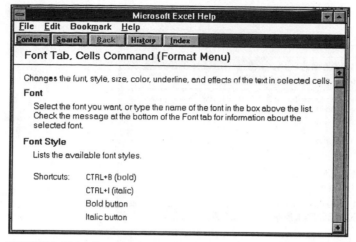

FIGURE I–16

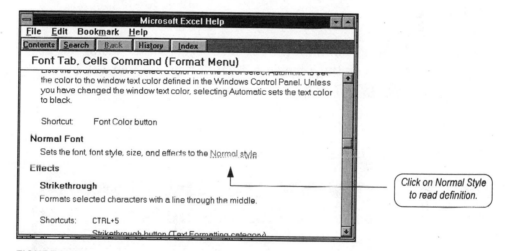

FIGURE I–17

6. Since **Normal Style** is underlined in a green dashed line, it is a defined term. Move the mouse until it is pointing to **Normal Style** and has changed to a hand. Click the left mouse button.

7. Read the definition of **Normal Style** (Figure I–18) and click the left mouse button again to close the definition box.

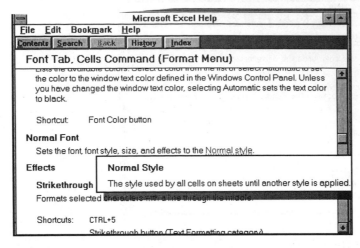

FIGURE I–18

8. Scroll the screen until the **See Also** section of the dialog box appears. Click on the *jump term,* **Bold Button** (Figure I-19).

   *The **Bold Button** Help screen is displayed.*

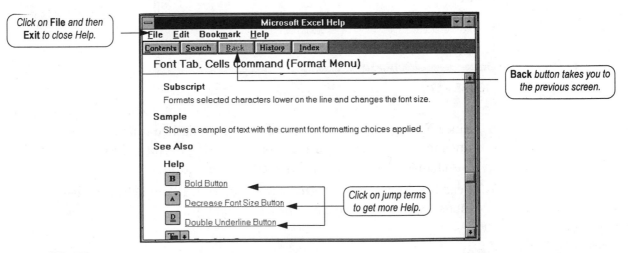

FIGURE I–19

9. Read the **Bold Button** Help screen.

10. To exit from **Help,** click on **File** in the **Microsoft Excel Help** menu bar.

11. Click on **Exit** on the **File** menu.

12. Click on the **Cancel** button in the **Format Cells** dialog box to close it.

ENTERING TEXT AND VALUES

The first steps in creating a worksheet are to enter labels (or titles) that describe the contents of the worksheet, data (which may be either text or numbers), and formulas that perform calculations on the data. All of these cell entries can be classified as *text* or *values*.

Text

A text entry can generally be thought of as any entry made up of letters or letters and numbers. (Excel defines text as any entry that is not a number, formula, data, time, or logical or error value.) Text is used to identify the data that you will be putting into the worksheet. Text can appear anywhere on the worksheet, but is often used across the top of the worksheet as column labels or down the left side of the worksheet as row labels. You will use text in both ways in this lesson. If you accidentally include a text entry in a formula, it has the value of zero.

When you type text it is automatically *left aligned*. This means that the text starts at the left edge of the cell. To center or right align, simply select the cell you wish to align, then click on the center ▤ or right ▤ button on the standard toolbar.

Values

A value is an entry that is a *number or a formula*. Values can be used in all mathematical calculations such as addition, subtraction, multiplication, and division. To enter a value, you typically type the value without any formatting symbols (dollar signs, percents, commas, etc.). Then you use one of Excel's formatting commands to enter these symbols automatically. When entered, values are automatically *right aligned* in the cell. An entry is considered to be a number if it contains only numeric digits and any of the following characters used as described below:

.	to indicate a decimal point
,	to separate the number into thousands; if you type a comma in the wrong place, it makes the entry a label
I	to indicate that a number is positive
−	to indicate that a number is negative
( )	to indicate that a number (not a calculation) is negative
/	to indicate a fraction
$	to display a number as currency
E e	to display a number in exponential format
%	to indicate that a number is a percent

Numbers (e.g., 54, −364) are sometimes also called *constants* because they cannot change unless they are edited or retyped. *Formulas* are used to calculate.

Entering Text or Values

Now you're ready to start creating your worksheet.

To enter text or values:

- Select the cell to contain the data by clicking in the cell or using the **ARROW** keys to move the highlight to the cell.

- Type the data. If you notice any errors while you are typing, press the **BACKSPACE** key until the error is removed and finish typing.

- Press the **ENTER** key or click on the **enter box** to enter the data. Alternatively, you may press an **ARROW** key or click on another cell to both enter the data and move the highlight.

CORRECTING ERRORS

There are several different ways of correcting data entry errors. The best procedure to use depends on when you discover the error and how big the difference is between the data you typed and the correct data.

To correct errors:

- To correct an error that you discover *before* you have entered it into the cell (by pressing an **ARROW** key or the **ENTER** key or by clicking on the **enter box** or a new cell), press the **BACKSPACE** key until you erase the incorrect data. Type the rest of the cell contents and press the **ENTER** key or click on the **enter box**.

  *When you are entering data, you may not use the **ARROW** keys to move the cursor back to an incorrect character. When you press the **ARROW** keys, the data is entered into the current cell and the next cell on the worksheet in the direction of the arrow becomes the active cell.*

- To correct a major error that you notice *after* you have entered the data, select the cell in which you have made the typing mistake. Type the correct cell contents and then press the **ENTER** key or click on the **enter box**.

- To correct an error involving only a few characters, or to add to the cell contents, edit the cell contents using the directions for editing cells.

When only a small part of the cell contents is wrong, it is easier to *edit* the entry rather than erase or retype it. In version 5 of Excel, you may edit directly in the cell. In earlier versions of Excel and in many other worksheets, you may edit only in the formula bar.

To edit cells:

- Double-click the cell containing the data you want to edit.

  *Excel will enter **Edit** mode. There are three changes to the screen: The word **Edit** replaces **Ready** in the far-left side of the status bar; the highlight around the cell changes from a double border to a single border; and the insertion point appears in the cell.*

- Click immediately to the left of the character to be changed or use the **RIGHT** or **LEFT ARROW** keys to move the cursor to the left of the character to be changed.

- To delete characters, press the **DELETE** key once for each character to be deleted. To insert characters, type them. To change characters, press the **INSERT** key. The letters **OVR** will appear on the status bar. Type the new characters.

- When editing is completed, press the **ENTER** key or click the **enter box**.

ALTERNATIVE METHOD: *To edit data in the formula bar, first click in the cell to be edited and then click in the formula bar immediately to the left of the characters to be changed, inserted, or deleted.*

KEYBOARD ALTERNATIVE: *Press **F2** to begin editing. The insertion point will appear in the cell at the end of the data. Move it to the character(s) to be changed and edit the data as described above.*

Clearing Cell Contents

Sometimes you want to erase the entire contents of a cell. The easiest way to do this is to use the **DELETE** key.

To clear the contents of a cell:

- Click on the cell.
- Press the **DELETE** key.

Activity: Clearing the Contents of a Cell

After entering the employee names in the worksheet, you learn that Naomi Gold no longer works for the company.

1. Click on cell **A8**.
2. Press the **DELETE** key.

   Cell A8 should be empty.

Undoing Actions

Excel lets you undo many commands if you realize your mistake immediately after making it.

To undo an action:

• Open the **EDIT** menu.

  The top command on the Edit menu will either indicate the action that you can do (i.e., Undo Clear) or will indicate that you Can't Undo.

• Choose **UNDO (action)**.

Immediately after **EDIT/Undo** or the **Undo** button ⟲ has been selected, Excel changes the **Undo** menu item to **Redo**. That way, if **EDIT/Undo** did not correct your problem, you may undo the undo!

To reverse EDIT/Undo:

• Open the **EDIT** menu.

  If you have used EDIT/Undo and that action can still be reversed, the top menu choice will be REDO (action).

• Choose **REDO (action)**.

ENTERING VALUES

You enter values in the same way that you enter text. However, Excel aligns values on the right side of the cell instead of the left side. In addition, when you type values, you have some additional choices in how you enter them. For example, should you type dollar signs or the commas that separate thousands? Excel gives you the option to type *formatting characters* such as dollar signs and commas when you enter the data, or to wait and add all of these characters at once.

OPENING AN EXERCISE/LESSON

When you are ready to begin working or continue working on an exercise, open the worksheet and begin working or continue working from where you stopped.

To open an Exercise/Lesson:

- Choose **FILE/Open** or click on the **OPEN** button 🖾 on the standard toolbar.

  The Open dialog box will appear on the screen.

- The current drive appears in the list box labeled **Drives**: If you file has been saved to a different drive, click on the ↧ at the right of the list box and click on the name of the drive that contains your data.

- The current directory is highlighted in the list box labeled **Directories**: If your file has been saved in a different directory, double-click on the name of the directory containing your data.

- The file names are listed in alphabetical order in the **File Name** list box. Click on the name of the file you want to open. If the file name is not visible, click on the ↧ on the vertical scroll bar until the file name is visible and then click on it.

- Click on **OK** or press **ENTER**.

SAVING A FILE WITH THE SAME NAME

Every time you make changes to a file, you must save the file again or the changes will be lost when you close the worksheet or exit from Excel. When you save the file using the same name, the current version of the worksheet replaces the previously saved version.

Note: Files are automatically saved when you print using the **Print** button located within the spreadsheet (See "Printing a Worksheet," below).

To save a file again with the same file name:

- Choose **FILE/Save** or click the **Save** toolbar button, 🖫 .

PRINTING A WORKSHEET

Typically, you want to print worksheets so that you can share information with others.

To print a worksheet using the default settings:

- Make sure that the printer is turned on.
- Click on the **Print** button located at the top right side of the spreadsheet.

NOTE: Files are automatically saved when you print using the **Print** button located within the spreadsheet.

Occasionally you want to have a printed copy of the formulas contained in the cells instead of the values. In the business world you can use this copy to document your worksheet, so that you and everyone else can see what formulas you used to obtain your results. If there are errors in the worksheet, a printout containing formulas can help find them. In school instructors often want a printout with formulas displayed to see what formulas were used in constructing the worksheet.

EXITING FROM EXCEL

While you are working, Excel creates temporary files to help it with its work. Therefore, it is always important to exit correctly from a program, rather than to turn off the computer while in the middle of the program.

To exit from Excel:

- Point to **File** on the menu bar and click the left mouse button.
- Point to **Exit** on the **File** menu and click the left mouse button.
- If you have made any changes to the workbook and not saved your work, an alert box containing four choices, **Yes**, **No**, **Cancel**, and **Help** will appear. To save changes to the file, click on **Yes**. To exit without saving changes to the file, click on **No**. To continue working in Excel, choose **Cancel**. To get help on how to use the alert box, click on **Help.**
- If you are finished using **Windows**, choose **FILE/Exit** from the Program Manager menu. When the prompt **This will end your Windows session** appears, click on **Yes**.

SUMMARY

In this introduction you have seen the parts of the Excel screen that are common to all Windows applications and those that are specific to Excel or to worksheet software. You have seen how to use the **View** menu to change the appearance of the screen. You have also reviewed the use of menus and dialog boxes and using **Help**. You completed the basic tasks of entering text, values and formulas, opening, and printing a worksheet. As you work through this book, if you have trouble with basic worksheet terminology or the use of menus and dialog boxes, refer back to this chapter.

INSTRUCTIONS FOR FOOD AND LABOR COST CONTROL EXERCISES

Once you have familiarized yourself with the basics of Excel you may use the following "Quick Guide" to begin working on any particular exercise.

Quick Guide:

1. Click on the **open file** icon.
2. In the open dialog box, click on the down arrow key for drives.
3. Click on the A: drive.
4. Click on **EX1-1A**. Click **OK** if you want the selection highlighted. If you want the next assignment, use the mouse to move to it, then click on that selection and click **OK**. Wait for the assignment to appear.
5. To begin the assignment:

   Type **[CTRL]-D** and fill in the date, for example, '09/20/96.

   Type **[CTRL]-N** and type in your name.

   Use the mouse to move to the "Restaurant Name" field. Next, type the restaurant name you are using and hit **[ENTER]** to insert the name.

   [CTRL]-R will bring the cursor to the top of the page.

   [CTRL]-B brings the cursor to the beginning of the assignment.

   Begin working on the assignment.
6. When complete, use the **Print** button in the spreadsheet to print. Check to see that printing has started.
7. Once printing is complete, you may exit the program.

INCOME STATEMENTS

■ OBJECTIVES

After completing Lesson 1, you should be able to:

1. Explain the income statement and its main uses;
2. Discuss components of the income statement;
3. Explain layout and placement of numeric entries;
4. Explain how to compute and use percentages;
5. List and explain the three basic cost control formulas;
6. Discuss costs, prime costs, and profits;
7. Analyze graphically how sales and costs affect profit;
8. Review industry standard operating results by market segment.

■ KEY TERMS

Income statement	Variable costs
Annual income statement	Directly variable costs
Income	Semivariable costs
Costs	Controllable costs
Profits	Noncontrollable costs
Total sales	Prime cost
Precosting	Arrow game
Fixed costs	Developing a budget

■ CONCEPT REVIEW

An *income statement* is used by the cost controller to monitor the financial condition of the operation. The main functions of the statement are: (1) review historical operating results; (2) compare current operating results with historical results; (3) project future operating results based on historical results. An ***annual income statement*** shows the previous year's financial results in a general way.

Three main categories within a typical income statement are of particular interest to the cost controller: (1) ***income***, (2) ***costs***, and (3) ***profit***. As you'll see later, these categories are used to provide key management control information.

Each category is further broken down into more specific subcategories, as follows:

Category	*Subcategories*
Income	Sales of food
	Sales of beverages
	Total sales
Costs	Cost of food
	Cost of beverages
	Total cost of food and beverages
	Cost of payroll
	Cost of overhead
Profit	Net profit

For each subcategory on an income statement, there are usually two numeric entries listed in a columnar format on the respective line. In the first column, dollars are listed; in the second column, percentages are listed. Dollar amounts are important, but the percentage figures are more important to the cost controller. Because dollar volumes vary, it is difficult to determine whether costs are in line unless percentages are used for the comparative calculations.

COMPUTING COST PERCENTAGES

When computing cost percentages, you must reference the dollar amount of the line item to a standard amount—usually, the amount listed for the category labeled ***total sales***. The exception to this rule occurs when determining the percentages for cost of food and cost of beverages. These percentages are determined by referencing the amounts to the totals for food sales and beverage sales respectively. This example will clarify:

■ To determine the labor cost percent, relate the cost of labor to the total sales:

$$\text{Labor cost percent} = \frac{\text{Cost of labor}}{\text{Total sales}} \times 100\%$$

■ To determine the food cost percent, relate the cost of food to the food sales:

$$\text{Food cost percent} = \frac{\text{Cost of food}}{\text{Food sales}} \times 100\%$$

The statement shown in Figure 1-1 is a typical layout for an income statement. The Red Woodpecker Grill used the format for the year ending December 31, 1995.

COST CONTROL FORMULAS

Three basic cost control formulas are frequently used in the foodservice industry when reviewing and planning: (1) past costs percent; (2) present costs; (3) future sales.

FIGURE 1–1   Income Statement—Typical Layout

Income Statement
Red Woodpecker Grill
For the Year Ending December 31, 1995

Sales			
Food Sales	$		%
Beverage Sales	$		%
Total		$	%
Cost of Sales			
Cost of Food Sold	$		%
Cost of Beverages Sold	$		%
Total		$	%
Gross Profit on Sales		$	%
Controllable Expenses			
Payroll	$		%
Payroll Taxes and Employee Benefits	$		%
Other Controllable Expenses	$		%
Total		$	%
Profit before Occupation Costs		$	%
Occupation Costs		$	%
Profit before Depreciation		$	%
Depreciation		$	%
Profit before Income Taxes		$	%

Past Costs Percent

This formula is used to express costs as a percentage of sales:

$$\text{Cost \%} = \frac{\text{Cost}}{\text{Sales}}$$

The resulting percentage represents historical information, or the past, because the percentage realized is based on results that have already taken place.

Present Costs

The second formula, used for computations of present costs, is shown as:

$$\text{Cost} = \text{Sales} \times \text{Cost percent}$$

This formula is used to compute a particular cost, based on current sales figures and current operating percentages. The formula is often used when working with "what ifs." For example, you may desire to change a certain sale price for a sandwich, but you know the restaurant management wants to maintain a desired gross profit level. The cost of the sandwich is computed by multiplying the sale price by the food cost percentage. This cost figure is the desired cost that the operator must use as a target when developing the recipe and purchasing the ingredients for the sandwich.

Future Sales

The third formula is used to determine future sales based on costs and desired cost percentages. This formula is expressed as:

$$\text{Sales} = \frac{\text{Cost}}{\text{Cost percent}}$$

Another name for this formula is *precosting*. Precosting is the process by which a menu item is priced. To precost a menu item, it is first necessary to determine the cost of all the ingredients used to produce the item. The cost is based on actual cost(s) paid today for the ingredient(s). Once you determine the actual cost, divide the total cost by the desired cost percentage you desire. The result will be the sale price that you should sell the item for, or the sale price you would put on your menu.

If the price is too expensive, customers will decide on something that meets their spending limit, or they'll choose another establishment for their next restaurant meal.

COST

To help you better understand the income statement, you need to understand some terminology that further describes costs. The general definition of cost is the price paid by the foodservice operator for goods or services. Cost can be divided into several different categories and you should know the differences among them.

Fixed Costs

The first category of costs is ***fixed costs***—those costs that have no direct relationship to an establishment's volume of sales. As sales volume increases or decreases, fixed costs remain the same. Examples of fixed costs are rent, insurance, real estate taxes, and depreciation.

Variable Costs

The second category is ***variable costs***, which are different from fixed costs in that as sales volume increases, variable costs will increase, and as sales volume decreases, variable costs decrease. The best examples of this type of cost are food cost, beverage cost, and labor cost. There is, however, a difference between how food and beverage costs vary as compared to how labor costs vary with changes in sales volume. Food and beverage costs are considered to be ***directly variable costs***, which means that every increase or decrease in sales volume brings a corresponding increase or decrease in cost.

Semivariable Costs

The third category of costs, ***semivariable costs***, is actually an extension of variable costs. This category includes labor costs because certain fixed costs related to management salaries do not vary. Also, a minimum number of personnel is needed just to open the doors of the facility. Employees who are paid hourly vary directly, as a group, with increases or decreases in sales volume. The total effect of the combination of fixed and variable labor puts labor cost into the semivariable category.

Controllable Costs

Based on this discussion of costs, it must be said that some costs are controllable and some costs are noncontrollable. ***Controllable costs*** are those costs that can be changed in the short term. Variable costs or food and beverage costs are the best examples of controllable costs. Among the fixed costs, those that are controllable include utilities, repairs and maintenance, advertising and promotion, administration, and general expenses.

Noncontrollable Costs

Noncontrollable costs are costs that cannot be changed in the short term. These costs include rent, interest on mortgages, real estate taxes, and depreciation on equipment.

Prime Cost

Another key term necessary for understanding the income statement is *prime cost*—the combined total cost of food, beverages, payroll, payroll taxes, and employee benefits. Most food service establishments concentrate on prime cost. The operator is always trying to figure ways to meet forecasted or budgeted food, beverage, and labor costs. This is one of the most challenging tasks in the business because there is a delicate balance between being able to offer customers perceived value and still generating a profit.

The ideal prime cost is in the 60–70% range. It has been said that 60% is possible and some establishments can accomplish this, but not for very long because someone else inevitably figures out how profitable the business is and then copies the concept. Therefore, 60–65% is considered excellent and 70% is generally still profitable.

With all of these concepts in mind, you should make sure that you understand the relationship among sales, costs, and profit and how they relate to the income statement. This is easily accomplished by playing the *arrow game*.

THE ARROW GAME

This is a simple game of "what if." As shown in Figure 1–2, the categories of sales, costs, and profits are listed vertically with five numbers along the top corresponding to five different scenarios. On the line labeled Sales, under the different scenario columns, one of three arrow symbols has been entered: (1) a "^" sign indicating an increase in sales, (2) a "v" sign indicating a decrease in sales, or (3) a "<>" sign indicating no change in sales. On the next line, labeled Costs, the same has been done with a "^" sign indicating an increase in costs, and so on. The next line is labeled Profit and this is where the expected resultant effect on profit is shown. The same convention for "^," "v," and "<>" is used.

FIGURE 1–2   The Arrow Game

Scenario	1	2	3	4	5
Sales	<>	^	v	<>	^
Costs	<>	^	<>	v	<>
Profit	<>	<>	v	^	^

Legend: "^" = increase; "v" = decrease; "<>" = no change.

First look at the change in sales. Then look at how it affects costs. Do you agree? Do you understand the relationship between sales and costs?

Some managers say the second scenario in Figure 1–2 is the reason business should not be increased. It means more work and more wear and tear on the facility and equipment, yet there is no major increase in profit.

In the fourth scenario, sales remain the same but better control of costs yields a savings, or a reduction in costs, that has been converted to increased profit.

GENERATING PROFIT

It has been said previously that a prime cost of 60–70% is good, but you need to realize that different sectors of the foodservice industry have different sales and costs percentages, hence the resultant prime cost difference. The ultimate goal for all operations, however, is to generate a profit. Figure 1–3 shows the generally accepted industry standards for various foodservice markets in the United States. The percentages shown are averages, and the specific results obtained for a given operation may vary.

An individual operation's sales volume may vary greatly and is a function of many factors, including type of food served, menu prices, operating hours, advertising budget, and location, *location*, LOCATION.

FIGURE 1–3   Costs as a Percentage of Total Sales by Market Segment

	Fast Food	Family Style	Fine Dining
Food and beverage (combined)	25	35	40
Labor	25	25	30
Overhead	35	30	25
Profit	15	10	5

Developing a Budget

You can now go back to the income statement and, as noted previously, convert the dollar amounts to percentages using the three basic formulas. Next, compare the actual operating percentages against the published industry standard percentages and your own desired percentages if you have them. If the operating percentages don't meet your needs, you must create an action plan to change various aspects of the operation in such a way as to improve actual results for future operations. This process is known as ***developing a budget***. Once developed, a budget is then closely compared on a regular basis against actual operating results, using the basic three cost control formulas.

■ Spreadsheet Objectives

The purpose of the following exercises is to help you:

- Recall a stored spreadsheet template;
- Enter data into the spreadsheet template;
- Automatically print and save the updated spreadsheet.

EXERCISES

Figure 1–4 is an example of the Microsoft Excel spreadsheet that will appear on your computer screen. You will enter the data given below into the spreadsheet. You must first load and start Microsoft Excel (refer to the Introduction (p. 3) for information on how to do this). The file name to retrieve is: EX–IA.XLS for Exercise 1–1A or EX–1B.XLS for Exercise 1–1B.

EXERCISE 1–1A

The purpose of this exercise is to familiarize you with the calculation of the financial results for a restaurant.

Task: Enter the following data on the appropriate lines of the spreadsheet shown in Figure 1–4.

Income Statement
Red Woodpecker Grill
For the Year Ending December 31, 1993

Food Sales	$723,556
Payroll Cost	228,456
Beverage Sales	224,945
Other Controllable Expenses	145,532
Beverage Cost	57,534
Payroll Taxes	21,790
Employee Benefits	14,667
Food Cost	265,998
Occupancy Costs	44,860
Depreciation Expense	74,856

When entering these data into the first column of the spreadsheet, keep in mind that the numbers you enter will be automatically added and put into the subtotal column (second column). This is why an income statement is typically printed on a two-column accounting form. When two amounts appear in the subtotal column, a line is drawn. Below this line a new amount is entered that is equal to the difference of the upper figure above the line minus the lower figure above the line. This process continues to the bottom of the statement.

In the percent column, you are to calculate the percentages. The food sales percentage is the dollar amount for food sales divided by the dollar amount for total sales multiplied by one hundred (100). The same holds true for all other line items on the spreadsheet, The exception to this rule is for food and beverage cost percentages, as discussed previously in this lesson. (NOTE: All percentages are calculated to four places to the right of the decimal point. For example, to enter 80% you would enter .800000, which will show up as 80.0000%.)

The percentage for total cost of sales is total cost divided by total sales, (This figure is a composite percentage based on the two costs.)

FIGURE 1–4 Sample Spreadsheet

```
FOODSERVICE COST CONTROL USING MICROSOFT EXCEL                    PG 1 OF 1
STUDENT NAME:              {NAME}            RESTAURANT NAME:
DATE:                      {DATE}            {RESTAURANT NAME}
===================================================================
```

INCOME STATEMENT
{RESTAURANT NAME}
FOR THE YEAR ENDING DECEMBER 31, 1994

SALES		
FOOD SALES	0	0.0000%
BEVERAGE SALES	0	0.0000%
TOTAL SALES	0	0.0000%
COST OF SALES		
FOOD COST	0	0.0000%
BEVERAGE COST	0	0.0000%
TOTAL COST OF SALES	0	ERR
GROSS PROFIT ON SALES	0	0.0000%
CONTROLLABLE EXPENSES		
PAYROLL COST	0	0.0000%
PAYROLL TAXES	0	0.0000%
EMPLOYEE BENEFITS	0	0.0000%
OTHER CONTROLLABLE EXPENSES	0	0.0000%
TOTAL CONTROLLABLE EXPENSES	0	0.0000%
PROFIT BEFORE OCCUPANCY COSTS	0	0.0000%
OCCUPANCY COSTS	0	0.0000%
PROFIT BEFORE DEPRECIATION	0	0.0000%
DEPRECIATION EXPENSE	0	0.0000%
NET PROFIT BEFORE INCOME TAX	0	0.0000%

EXERCISE 1–1B

Task: Enter the following data on the appropriate lines of the spreadsheet shown in Figure 1–4. Then calculate the percentages for the third column of the spreadsheet.

Income Statement
Terrace Garden Restaurant

Food Sales	$896,442
Payroll Costs	202,862
Beverage Sales	324,707
Other Controllable Expenses	163,584
Beverage Cost	75,534
Payroll Taxes	25,654
Employee Benefits	16,235
Food Cost	435,750
Occupancy Costs	39,977
Depreciation Expense	82,001

CHECK YOUR UNDERSTANDING

Answer all of these questions based on either Exercise 1–1A or Exercise 1–1B. (Circle the Exercise number you have chosen.)

1. Food cost percentage = _____% _____

2. Beverage cost percentage = _____%

3. Combined food and beverage cost percentage = _____%

4. Labor cost percentage (payroll + payroll taxes + employee benefits) = _____%

5. Prime cost percentage = _____%

6. Net profit percentage before income tax = _____%

7. What is the formula for finding food Cost percentage?

   _____

   What is different about the method for finding food sales percentage as compared to that for finding food cost percentage?

   _____

8. Are the percentages for food cost and beverage cost in line with industry averages?

   _____

9. Is the net profit percentage considered good? _____

   Would you keep this operation open? _____

   Why? _____

10. The income statement provides information to the cost controller. List four points of information the income statement provides:

1. _____

2. _____

3. _____

4. _____

CRITICAL THINKING QUESTIONS

To answer these questions, you will be comparing Exercise 1–1A to Exercise 1–1B.

1. What type of operation is the Red Woodpecker Grill?

_____

_____

What type of operation is the Terrace Garden Restaurant?

_____

_____

2. Which operation has the better bottom-line income statement?

_____

_____

3. Which operation has the better food cost percentage?

_____

_____

Which operation has the better beverage cost percentage?

_____

_____

Explain why one operation has better percentages. How were the percentages calculated? _____

_____

_____

4. Apply the theory of prime cost to both operations. Which one will excel in bottom-line profit? Why?

_____

_____

CASHIER CONTROL AND SALES HISTORY

■ **OBJECTIVES**

After completing Lesson 2, you should be able to:

1. Define the following terms:

   Tic sheet

   Forecast

   Bank

   Cashier's report

2. Determine the popularity percent of each item on a menu.

3. Forecast the number of daily portions needed for each menu item.

4. Produce a cashier's report and proof the register tape.

■ **KEY TERMS**

Cashier	Charges
Guest check	Point of sale
Tic sheet	Tips
Popularity	Compiled report for management
Bank	Revenue center percent
Cashier's report	Media percent
Proof the register tape	

■ **CONCEPT REVIEW**

When discussing control for a restaurant, most people will say that control should begin with the "back of the house" or "back door." However, management must collect information ("data") to zero in on the type and area of the needed controls. The source of much of these data is the *cashier* (the person who accepts the customer's payment and gives change, if a cash transaction, or who charges the cost of the meal against the customer's credit card) and/or the **guest check** (the written listing of menu items and beverages served, their costs, and the applicable tax) prepared by the foodserver.

RECORDING DATA

Whoever acts as the cashier can easily record data that management needs. The simplest format is to use a menu as a **tic sheet**. Another name for this is a **record of entrees sold**. Each time a "sale" is made (a customer's meal is paid for), it is marked on the menu next to the item selected. At the end of the serving period, the tic marks are counted up and a total number is placed next to the item. By totaling the entrees ("mains"), the total number [#] of guests can be determined. This allows management to find out what items are selling well and how much of each item is in demand. From this information, management can determine the **popularity** of any item.

The formula to calculate popularity is:

$$\frac{\text{Number of each item}}{\substack{\text{Total number of guests} \\ \text{(or main entrees served)}}} = \text{Popularity percent for that item}$$

Popularity percent will allow management to collect "history" and, based on that history, to forecast the need for product in the future. To predict the future from the newly obtained history, use the following formula:

$$\begin{aligned} &\text{Popularity percent} \\ \times\ &\underline{\text{Mains expected}} \\ =\ &\text{Number of portions needed} \end{aligned}$$

It is very important, that, as a cost controller, you collect the above information and record it as written or computer-stored history. With this history, you have some basis to try to predict the future. Aim for that target. As a cost controller, you must budget and then calculate numbers to meet future needs.

Cash Control

Another role of the cashier is to function as a "cash control" or "sales control" individual. It is management's responsibility to establish a **bank**—a predetermined amount of money, decided on by management, to be used to make change and sometimes for petty cash payments. The amount of money may change daily, depending on expected business, but it is best to keep the bank at a constant dollar amount. The cashier will need less time to count the bank, thus saving on labor. Average business volume will determine the daily amount maintained in the bank. Having a bank allows management to know at any time how much money has been produced by a certain hour, during a mealtime, or within a shift or any other period.

Cashier's Report

At the end of a normal period, the cashier should produce a **cashier's report**. Basically, the cashier's report recaps the period involved and is used to **proof the register tape**. To accomplish this, the cashier follows this formula:

Opening cash drawer (bank)
+ Cash taken in
= Total cash on hand
− Bank
= Cash on hand (actual sales
 based on cash)

Once the above formula is completed, someone in management should close out the register to get a total for the register tape. When this is done, the register tape is cleared (totaled) and dated.

The register tape should show cash sales in all areas as well as **charges**. Another formula, used after closing the register tape, computes the final register:

Actual register tape
− Charges
= Drawer balance
− Cash on hand
= ± Difference

When the difference is known, management can calculate percentages of charges, cash sales, beverages, food, dining room; lounge, and so on. These percentages can then be compared to industry averages and to the forecasted numbers. (This information was discussed in Lesson 1.) All of these calculations can be done using electronic cash registers (ECRs) and/or computers used as **point of sale** (POS) terminals.

SALES TAX AND TIP PERCENTAGES

It is necessary to know how to figure sales tax and *tip* (gratuity for the foodserver) percentages on the guest checks. This section presents the formulas for calculating the sales tax and tip percentages when they are included in the total of the check.

Adding Sales Tax to Guest Checks

To compute the sales tax and add it to the guest check, follow these steps:

1. Check total $8.00
    × Sales tax 7%   × .07
    = Amount of sales tax   = $ .5600

2. Original check $8.00
    + Calculated sales tax   + .5600
    = Total of guest check   = $8.5600

Separating Sales Tax from Guest Checks

To separate sales tax from guest checks when the tax has been included in the selling price, follow this formula:

1. Sales tax 7%, shown as decimal   .07
    + 1.00   + 1.00
    = Total tax percent   = 1.07%

2. Total of guest check $8.56
    ÷ Total tax percent   1.07%
    = Net guest check   =$8.00

3. Total of guest check $8.56
    − Net guest check   −8.00
    = Amount of tax for guest check   =$.56

Adding Tips to Guest Checks

To figure the tip on a guest check, follow this formula:

1. Check total $18.00
    × Tip 15%   ×   .15
    = Amount of tip   =$ 2.70

2.   Check total $18.00

      + Amount of tip   +   2.70

      = Total of guest check   = $20.70

Separating Tips from Guest Checks

To separate the tip from the guest check when it has been included in the selling price, use the following formula:

1.   Tip 15%, shown as decimal   .15

      + 1.00   +   1.00

      = Total tip percent   =   1.15%

2.   Total of guest check $20.70

      ÷ Total tip percent   1.15%

      = New guest check   = $18.00

3.   Total of guest check $20.70

      − Net guest check   −   18.00

      = Amount of tip for guest check = $ 2.70

Compiled Report for Management

The last discussion in this lesson deals with what is called the ***compiled report for management***. In the restaurant industry, this might also be referred to as a ***flash report***. Management might not look at each report individually but would like to know the summary of all the reports.

We begin by recording the receipts and charges from the restaurant's profit centers, as shown in Figure 2–1.

FIGURE 2–1 Compiled Report for Management (Flash Report)

	Receipts ($)
Enter total recorded bar charges	
+ Enter total recorded dining room charges	
+ Enter bar cash receipts	
+ Enter dining room cash receipts	
= Total receipts (calculated automatically)	

An actual flash report rnight look like this:

Dining room cash receipts	$100.00
Bar charges	-0-
Dining room charges	$ 50.00
Bar cash receipts	$150.00
Dining room cash receipts	$100.00
	$300.00

Calculating Revenue Center Percent. The next area is called the *revenue center percent.* You will want to know how much business you have done in the bar compared to the dining room.

■ **Hint** _____

The total must equal 100.0000%. The calculation involves the sales—cash or charges—for an area, divided by the total receipts. You will calculate this information for both areas, and the total percent for the revenue center has to equal 100.0000% (see Figure 2–2).

_____

Calculating Media Percent. The next area is the *media percent,* which is a calculation of the percent of receipts from charges and in cash.

■ **Hint**_____

The total media percent must equal 100.0000%. In the calculation, the total for one medium, cash or charges, is divided by the total receipts.

_____

FIGURE 2–2   Calculation of the Revenue Center Percent

Percent of Revenue Center from Bar Receipts

Bar charges	-0-
+ Bar cash receipts	+ $150.00
= Total bar receipts	= $150.00
Total bar receipts	$150.00
÷ Total of all receipts (bar & dining room)	$300.00
= Percent of bar receipts to total	= 50.0000%

Percent of Revenue Center from Dining Receipts

Dining room charges	$ 50.00
+ Diring room cash receipts	+ 100.00
= Total dining room receipts	= $ 150.00
Total dining room receipts	$ 150.00
÷ Total of all receipts (bar & dining room)	$ 300.00
= Percent of dining room receipts to total	= 50.0000%

Bar receipts	50,0000%
+ Dining room receipts	50.0000
= Total receipts	100.0000%

FIGURE 2–3   Management Report Showing Media Percentages and Comparisons

```
FOODSERVICE COST CONTROL USING MICROSOFT EXCEL                      PG 1 OF 1
STUDENT NAME:              {NAME}                    RESTAURANT NAME:
DATE:                      {DATE}                    {RESTAURANT NAME}
====================================================================================
                           BAR CASH PROOF             DINING ROOM CASH PROOF
                           ------------------          ----------------------------

TOTAL CASH IN DRAWER              $0.00                          $0.00
– BANK                            0.00                           0.00
====================================================        ==============================
= CASH ON HAND                    $0.00                          $0.00


ACTUAL REGISTER TAPE READING      $0.00                          $0.00
– RECORDED CHARGES                0.00                           0.00
====================================================        ==============================
= DRAWER BALANCE (TAPE)           0.00                           0.00


CASH ON HAND                      $0.00                          $0.00
– DRAWER BALANCE (TAPE)           0.00                           0.00
====================================================        ==============================
= DIFFERENCE (+=OVER/–=SHORT)     $0.00                          $0.00


***********************************************************************************
COMPILED REPORT FOR MANAGEMENT

RECEIPTS
-----------------------------------------
TOTAL RECORDED BAR CHARGES        $0.00
+ TOTAL RECORDED D.R. CHARGES     0.00
+ TOTAL BAR CASH RECEIPTS         0.00
+ TOTAL D.R. CASH RECEIPTS        0.00
-----------------------------------------
= TOTAL RECEIPTS                  $0.00

REVENUE CENTER %
-----------------------------------------
BAR SALES                         0.0000%
+ DINING ROOM SALES               0.0000%
-----------------------------------------
= TOTAL REVENUE CENTER PERCENT    0.0000%

MEDIA %
-----------------------------------------
CHARGES                           0.0000%
+ CASH                            0.0000%
-----------------------------------------
= TOTAL MEDIA PERCENT             0.0000%

***********************************************************************************
FOR MANAGEMENT USE ONLY           %          %         % THIS DAY
                                  TODAY      TO DATE   LAST MONTH
-----------------------------------------------------------------------------------
BAR                               0.0000%
DINING ROOM                       0.0000%
CHARGES                           0.0000%
CASH                              0.0000%
-----------------------------------------------------------------------------------
```

The formula used for calculating media percent is the same as the one used to calculate revenue center. The only difference is that you are dealing with charges, and cash rather than bar sales and dining room sales.

When you have completed the revenue center percent and media percent calculations, the percentages will automatically be saved and put on a report that says "For Management Use Only." Management will constantly review this report and the final flash report, to know the percent of revenue and the receipts per medium for today. The report can be extended to show percent to date for a particular time period and can compare percent for this day last month or last year. An example of an extended report is shown in Figure 2–3.

■ SPREADSHEET OBJECTIVES

Upon completion of Exercise 2–1, you should be able to:

1. Complete a daily sales history report.
2. Calculate sales tax and tip when already included in the check and when added to the check.

The cover page, or first screen, of the daily sales history report compiles information on the staffing, hours, and environment of the particular restaurant. The format used for entering these facts is shown in Figure 2–4.

FIGURE 2–4   Cover Page for Daily Sales History Report

```
FOODSERVICE COST CONTROL USING MICROSOFT EXCEL                    PG 1 OF 2
STUDENT NAME:          {NAME}          RESTAURANT NAME: {NAME}
DATE:                  {DATE}
==========================================================================

DAILY SALES HISTORY REPORT

SHIFT MANAGER:         {NAME}              MEAL/FUNCTION:    {B/L/D}
DAY:                   {DAY}               SERVING HOURS:    {TIME}
DATE:                  {DATE}              TOTAL TIME:       {HOURS}
MONTH:                 {MONTH}
YEAR:                  {YEAR}              # CAPTAINS        {NUMBER}
                                          # SERVERS         {NUMBER}
WEATHER:               {SNOW, CLEAR, ETC}  # BUSSERS         {NUMBER}
TEMPERATURE:           {DEGREES}
COMMENTS:              {PARADE, HOLIDAY, ETC}  # CHECKS ISSUED   {NUMBER}
                                          # CHECKS RETURN   {NUMBER}
                                          # CHECKS USED          0
==========================================================================
```

EXERCISES

Based on the menus given and the tic marks recorded, you will be entering the figures on the spreadsheet provided to collect data. This spreadsheet, called the menu sales history, will be used later as a management tool. It is broken down into different food classifications: appetizers, soups, entrees, salads, and desserts. Each item name must be put under the proper classification. In Figure 2–5, the item category and name are followed by the number sold. These are the total tics marked for each menu item. The selling price is the menu price for the item. You calculate the total sales by multiplying the number sold by the selling price. For the first item in Figure 2–5, the arithmetic is:

Selling price	$ .95
Tomato juice sold	× 2
Total sales of tomato juice	= $1.90

Two more columns remain in the figure. The percent of each indicates the popularity by classification. When there are only two items in the appetizer classification, only the items sold in that category are used for the calculations.

In Figure 2–5, of the appetizers offered, 2 tomato juice were sold and 6 V-8 juice were sold. The total number of items sold is 8. To calculate the percent of item classification, you must divide the number of items sold by the total sold in that category.

FIGURE 2–5   Menu Sales History, by Food Classifications

MENU SALES HISTORY		STUDENT:	ERR		EX2-1A	PG 2 OF 2
ITEM NUMBER	ITEM NAME	NUMBER SOLD	SELLING PRICE	TOTAL SALES	% OF EACH	% OF TOTAL
*************	APPETIZERS******	*************	*********	*******	*********	**********
	Tomato juice	2	0.95			4.4444%
	V-8 juice	6	0.95			13.3333%
						0.0000%
						0.0000%
						0.0000%
						0.0000%
*************	TOTALS**********	8	*********	$0.00	0.000%	17.7778%
*************	SOUPS***********	*************	*********	*******	*********	**********
	Soup du jour	22	0.95			48.8889%
	Chicken broth	7	0.95			15.5556%
	Potato soup	8	0.95			17.7778%
						0.0000%

■ **Hint** _____

The total percent of each classification will always equal 100.0000%.

	Tomato juice	2
÷	Total number of items sold in appetizer category	÷ 8
=	Popularity percent of tomato juice	= 25.0000%

	V-8 juice	6
÷	Total number of items sold in appetizer category	÷ 8
=	Popularity percent of V-8	= 75.0000%

In the *percent of total* column, all the classifications are listed; therefore, tomato juice is divided by the total of all the classification areas on the spreadsheet.

■ **Hint** _____

The percent will be automatically calculated as you complete the spreadsheet. The key here is that the last number in the percent of total column must be 100.0000%.

This information should prepare you to complete Exercise 2–1A and Exercise 2–1B, and will be of use later when you fill in the Check Your Understanding answers for these Exercises. (You will be asked to record your answers both *with* tax and *without* tax.)

EXERCISE 2–1A   Sales History Popularity Reporting

The items on the luncheon menu for the Red Woodpecker Grill (p. 50) were given tic marks by the cashier to indicate today's luncheon sales.

The Red Woodpecker Grill is a private club; no cash changes hands. The club is located in an area with a 7% sales tax, which management has included in the menu price. Gratuities of 15% are automatically added to each guest check and distributed by management at the end of each shift. Guests are billed weekly. There are 110 seats in the Grill.

As today's shift manager, you are in charge of lunch, which is served from 12:00 P.M. to 2:30 P.M. Two captains, 6 waiters, and 3 buspersons are on duty. Of the 80 guest checks issued, 5 were returned.

Using this information and your computer, complete the daily sales history report begun in Figure 2–6. Use the combined total of the sandwiches and salads to indicate the total number of customers. Usually, the total of the "mains" or "covers" yields an accurate customer count.

RED WOODPECKER GRILL
. . . Luncheon . . .

Appetizers

TOMATO or V-8 JUICE   .95
  || 卌 |

Soups

SOUP du JOUR   .95 卌 卌 卌 卌 || POTATO SOUP   .95

CHICKEN BROTH .95   卌 |||
      卌 ||

Sandwich Selections

TURKEY CLUB SANDWICH (White Meat of Turkey, Crisp Bacon, Lettuce,
Tomato, and Mayonnaise on Toast; Potato Chips, Dill Pickle) 卌 卌 卌 ||| 4.95

WOODPECKER REUBEN (Corned Beef, Swiss Cheese, Sauerkraut,
and Thousand Island Dressing on Grilled Rye Bread; Dill Pickle and
Potato Salad)   卌 卌 || 4.95

THE WOODPECKER BURGER (Ground Beef, Melted Cheese, and Tomato on
Sesame Bun; Cole Slaw, Dill Pickle, and French Fries) 卌 卌 卌 卌 卌 || 4.95

THE WOODPECKER FRANKFURTER (Grilled All-Beef Frankfurter on
Toasted Bun; Cole Slaw, Potato Chips, and Chili) 卌 卌 卌 | 3.25

THE WOODPECKER DIET DELIGHT (Selected Ground Beef Grilled to Order
and Served with Sliced Tomatoes, Hard-Boiled Eggs, Cottage Cheese, and
Crisp Lettuce)   卌 卌 卌 |||| 4.95

Salads

THE BIRDIE (Breast of Chicken on a Bed of Fresh Salad Greens and
Toasted Almonds)   卌 卌 || 4.50

THE FRESH FRUIT SALAD PLATE (Cottage Cheese with Assorted Fresh Fruits
and Honey Dressing)   卌 卌 ||| 4.95

THE CHEF'S SPECIAL SALAD BOWL (A Combination of Deli Meats and Cheese
Served on Fresh Salad Greens; Choice of Dressing) 卌 卌 |||| 4.95

THE WOODPECKER SEAFOOD SALAD (Assorted Seafood Salad Served in a
Lettuce Cup with Avocado, Sliced Tomatoes, and Asparagus)   5.50
                              卌 卌 卌 卌 卌

Desserts

              CAKES and PIES du JOUR   1.50 卌 卌 卌 |||

Ice Cream ∅ 1.25 (one dip)   Sherbet   1.25 (one dip) 卌 卌 卌 |||
                2.00 (two dips)   2.00 (two dips) 卌 ||
                       卌 卌 卌 ||

FIGURE 2–6   Daily Sales History Report—Initial Entries

MENU SALES HISTORY		STUDENT:	ERR		EX2-1A	PG 2 OF 2
ITEM NUMBER	ITEM NAME	NUMBER SOLD	SELLING PRICE	TOTAL SALES	% OF EACH	% OF TOTAL
***************	APPETIZERS******	*********	*********	*******	**********	**********
	Tomato juice	2	0.95	1.90	25.0000%	4.4444%
	V-8 juice	6	0.95	5.70	75.0000%	13.3333%
						0.0000%
						0.0000%
						0.0000%
						0.0000%
***************	TOTALS**********	8	*********	$7.60	100.0000%	17.7778%
***************	SOUPS***********	*********	*********	*******	**********	**********
	Soup du jour	22	0.95	20.90	59.4595%	48.8889%
	Chicken broth	7	0.95	6.65	Not	15.5556%
	Potato soup	8	0.95	7.60	Completed	17.7778%
						0.0000%
***************	TOTALS**********	37	*********	$35.15	59.460%	82.2222%

EXERCISE 2–1B   Sales History: Terrace Garden Restaurant

The luncheon menu for the Terrace Garden Restaurant (p. 52) has been used by the cashier to tic today's luncheon sales.

The restaurant is located in an area with a 7% sales tax, which management has included in the menu price. Gratuities of 15% are automatically added to the guest check and distributed by management at the end of the shift. Guests are billed weekly. There are 70 seats in the dining room.

As today's shift manager, you are in charge of lunch, which is served from 11:30 A.M. to 2:30 P.M. Two captains, 7 servers, and 3 buspersons are on duty. Of the 85 guest checks issued, 11 were returned.

Using this information, prepare a complete daily sales history report, using the format shown in Figure 2–6. Use the combined total of the entrees and salads to indicate the total number of customers. Usually, the total "mains" or "covers" yields an accurate customer count.

■ SPREADSHEET OBJECTIVES

Upon completion of Exercise 2–2, you should be able to:

1. Produce start-of-shift and end-of-shift register reports.

2. Prepare a compiled report for management (flash report) consisting of total receipts, revenue center percents and media (cash and charge) percents.

TERRACE GARDEN RESTAURANT

. . . Appetizers . . .

Fruit Cocktail	┼┼┼ ┼┼┼ ┼┼┼ I	$3.25
Shrimp Cocktail	IIII	$5.95

. . . Soups . . .

Baked French Onion Soup	┼┼┼ ┼┼┼ II		$2.25
Soup du Jour	┼┼┼ ┼┼┼ ┼┼┼ ┼┼┼ ┼┼┼ ┼┼┼ I	cup	$1.25
		bowl	$1.75
		┼┼┼ ┼┼┼ ┼┼┼	

. . . Salad Selections . . .

Chef's Salad ┼┼┼ ┼┼┼ III $5.95
 Julienne strips of ham, turkey, & American cheese served over fresh greens
 and garnished with tomato, egg, and olive.

Cajun Chicken Salad ┼┼┼ ┼┼┼ ┼┼┼ I $4.95
 Julienne strips of Cajun chicken on a bed of greens and vegetables.

Triple Play ┼┼┼ III $5.95
 Chicken salad, tuna salad, and cottage cheese, garnished with fresh fruit
 and served with crackers.

One Half Cantaloupe ┼┼┼ I $4.95
 Served with chicken salad or tuna salad or cottage cheese, vegetable, & fruit
 in season.

. . . Sandwich Selections . . .

Chicken Salad	┼┼┼ III	$4.50
Stacked Ham	IIII	$4.50
Stacked Turkey	┼┼┼ ┼┼┼ I	$4.50
One Half Sandwich and Cup of Soup	┼┼┼ ┼┼┼ ┼┼┼ ┼┼┼ ┼┼┼ I	$3.75
Club Sandwich	┼┼┼ ┼┼┼ ┼┼┼ I	$5.25

 All sandwiches served with a choice of white, rye, or wheat bread, and served
 with chips and a pickle.

. . . Hot Entrees . . .

Chicken Marie ┼┼┼ ┼┼┼ I $6.95
 Boneless, skinless breast of chicken broiled with garlic, lemon, and white wine;
 served with cottage cheese and fruit in season.

Dutch Tuna ┼┼┼ II $4.50
 Tuna on grilled rye bread with Swiss cheese.

Great Divide ┼┼┼ ┼┼┼ III $5.95
 Grilled turkey & ham, with melted cheddar, lettuce, & tomato, served on a hard roll
 with honey mustard.

. . . Desserts . . .

Cakes and Pies du Jour	┼┼┼ II	$2.95
Ice Cream	┼┼┼ ┼┼┼ II	$1.95
Frozen Yogurt	┼┼┼ ┼┼┼ ┼┼┼ III	$1.95

EXERCISE 2–2A and B   Start-of-Shift Cashier's Reports

Two registers are used in your restaurant: one for the bar and the other for the dining room. You are working with the start-of-shift reports for both registers.

You are to enter the dollar value of the denominations. As shown in Figure 2–7, one roll of pennies has 50 coins; therefore, you multiply $.01 × 50 and enter the dollar value: $.50. After listing all the values for the money on hand this spreadsheet will automatically add up the total value.

Using Figure 2–8, complete the spreadsheet for the start of shift for the Red Woodpecker Grill's bar and dining room registers. Repeal the procedure for the Terrace Garden Rest., using Figure 2–9. (You will be using these numbers to complete other exercises in this lesson.)

EXERCISE 2–3A and B   End-of-Shift Cashier's Reports

Your spreadsheet here will look similar to those in Exercise 2–2A, but is adapted for end-of-shift use for both registers. Using the amounts in Figure 2–10, multiply the quantity of each denomination by its dollar value to determine the value of each denomination. The total value will then be automatically calculated for you. In the space for recording charges, enter the amount if it is available, if it is not, enter a zero amount for charges. When this figure is available and is entered, the total cash and recorded charges is the total sales.

Figure 2–11 lists the end-of-shift amounts for the Red Woodpecker Grill's bar and dining room registers. Complete the spreadsheet, filling in all missing dollar amounts. Using Figure 2–12, repeat the procedure for the Terrace Garden Restaurant.

FIGURE 2–7   Start-of-Shift Report

FOODSERVICE COST CONTROL USING MICROSOFT EXCEL   PG 1 OF 1
STUDENT NAME: {NAME}   RESTAURANT NAME:
DATE: {DATE}   {RESTAURANT NAME}
==

BAR REGISTER
OPENING CASH DRAWER (START OF SHIFT)

DENOMINATION	QUANTITY	$ VALUE
PENNIES	1 ROLL(S)	0.50
NICKLES	1 ROLL(S)	0.00
DIMES	1 ROLL(S)	0.00
QUARTERS	1 ROLL(S)	0.00
HALVES	1 ROLL(S)	0.00
SINGLES	10 EACH	0.00
FIVES	5 EACH	0.00
TENS	0 EACH	0.00
TWENTYS	0 EACH	0.00

| TOTAL VALUE | | $0.50 |

FIGURE 2–8   Start-of-Shift Reports—Red Woodpecker Grill

```
FOODSERVICE COST CONTROL USING MICROSOFT EXCEL        PG 1 OF 1
STUDENT NAME:   {NAME}               RESTAURANT NAME:
DATE:           {DATE}               RED WOODPECKER GRILL
==================================================================

BAR REGISTER
OPENING CASH DRAWER (START OF SHIFT)
------------------------------------------------------------------

DENOMINATION            QUANTITY   $ VALUE
------------------------------------------------------------------

PENNIES                 1 ROLL(S)    0.00
NICKLES                 1 ROLL(S)    0.00
DIMES                   1 ROLL(S)    0.00
QUARTERS                1 ROLL(S)    0.00
HALVES                  1 ROLL(S)    0.00
SINGLES                 10 EACH      0.00
FIVES                   5 EACH       0.00
TENS                    0 EACH       0.00
TWENTYS                 0 EACH       0.00
------------------------------------------------------------------

TOTAL VALUE                         $0.00



==============================================

DINING ROOM REGISTER
OPENING CASH DRAWER (START OF SHIFT)
------------------------------------------------------------------

DENOMINATION            QUANTITY   $ VALUE
------------------------------------------------------------------

PENNIES                 2 ROLL(S)    0.00
NICKLES                 1 ROLL(S)    0.00
DIMES                   1 ROLL(S)    0.00
QUARTERS                1 ROLL(S)    0.00
HALVES                  0 ROLL(S)    0.00
SINGLES                 10 EACH      0.00
FIVES                   5 EACH       0.00
TENS                    5 EACH       0.00
TWENTYS                 0 EACH       0.00
------------------------------------------------------------------

TOTAL VALUE                         $0.00
```

FIGURE 2–9   Start-of-Shift Report—Terrace Garden Restaurant

```
FOODSERVICE COST CONTROL USING MICROSOFT EXCEL          PG 1 OF 1
STUDENT NAME:   {NAME}              RESTAURANT NAME:
DATE:           {DATE}             TERRACE GARDEN RESTAURANT

===================================================================
BAR REGISTER
OPENING CASH DRAWER (START OF SHIFT)
-------------------------------------------------------------------
DENOMINATION           QUANTITY  $ VALUE

PENNIES                2 ROLL(S)   0.00
NICKLES                2 ROLL(S)   0.00
DIMES                  2 ROLL(S)   0.00
QUARTERS               2 ROLL(S)   0.00
HALVES                 1 ROLL(S)   0.00
SINGLES               75 EACH      0.00
FIVES                 16 EACH      0.00
TENS                   6 EACH      0.00
TWENTYS                2 EACH      0.00
-------------------------------------------------------------------
TOTAL VALUE                       $0.00
```

```
===================================================================
DINING ROOM REGISTER
OPENING CASH DRAWER (START OF SHIFT)
-------------------------------------------------------------------
DENOMINATION           QUANTITY  $ VALUE

PENNIES                1 ROLL(S)   0.00
NICKLES                1 ROLL(S)   0.00
DIMES                  1 ROLL(S)   0.00
QUARTERS               1 ROLL(S)   0.00
HALVES                 0 ROLL(S)   0.00
SINGLES               50 EACH      0.00
FIVES                 12 EACH      0.00
TENS                   2 EACH      0.00
TWENTYS                0 EACH      0.00
-------------------------------------------------------------------
TOTAL VALUE                       $0.00
```

FIGURE 2–10   End-of-Shift Report

```
FOODSERVICE COST CONTROL USING MICROSOFT EXCEL          PG 1 OF 1
STUDENT NAME:   {NAME}              RESTAURANT NAME:
DATE:           {DATE}             {RESTAURANT NAME}

===================================================================
BAR REGISTER
CLOSING CASH DRAWER (END OF SHIFT)
-------------------------------------------------------------------
DENOMINATION       QUANTITY     $ VALUE
-------------------------------------------------------------------
PENNIES            86 EACH        0.86
NICKLES            75 EACH        3.75
DIMES              45 EACH        0.00
QUARTERS           48 EACH        0.00
HALVES             13 EACH        0.00
SINGLES            88 EACH        0.00
FIVES              29 EACH        0.00
TENS               18 EACH        0.00
TWENTYS             7 EACH        0.00
-------------------------------------------------------------------
TOTAL CASH                        4.61
RECORDED BAR CHARGES              0.00
TOTAL BAR SALES                   4.61
```

FIGURE 2–11   End-of-Shift Report—Red Woodpecker Grill

```
FOODSERVICE COST CONTROL USING MICROSOFT EXCEL           PG 1 OF 1
STUDENT NAME:   {NAME}              RESTAURANT NAME:
DATE:           {DATE}             RED WOODPECKER GRILL
===============================================================================
BAR REGISTER
CLOSING CASH DRAWER (END OF SHIFT)
-------------------------------------------------
DENOMINATION            QUANTITY  $ VALUE
-------------------------------------------------
PENNIES                  86 EACH    0.00
NICKLES                  75 EACH    0.00
DIMES                    45 EACH    0.00
QUARTERS                 48 EACH    0.00
HALVES                   13 EACH    0.00
SINGLES                  88 EACH    0.00
FIVES                    29 EACH    0.00
TENS                     18 EACH    0.00
TWENTYS                   7 EACH    0.00
-------------------------------------------------
TOTAL CASH                          0.00
RECORDED BAR CHARGES                ZERO
TOTAL BAR SALES                     0.00
```

```
=============================================
DINING ROOM REGISTER
CLOSING CASH DRAWER (END OF SHIFT)
-------------------------------------------------
DENOMINATION            QUANTITY  $ VALUE
-------------------------------------------------
PENNIES                  96 EACH    0.00
NICKLES                  45 EACH    0.00
DIMES                    60 EACH    0.00
QUARTERS                 29 EACH    0.00
HALVES                    9 EACH    0.00
SINGLES                  98 EACH    0.00
FIVES                    36 EACH    0.00
TENS                     34 EACH    0.00
TWENTYS                  42 EACH    0.00
-------------------------------------------------
TOTAL CASH                          0.00
RECORDED DINING ROOM CHARGES      645.60
TOTAL DINING ROOM SALES           645.60
```

FIGURE 2–12   End-of-Shift Report—Terrace Garden Restaurant

```
FOODSERVICE COST CONTROL USING MICROSOFT EXCEL          PG 1 OF 1
STUDENT NAME:   {NAME}               RESTAURANT NAME:
DATE:           {DATE}               TERRACE GARDEN RESTAURANT
=================================================================

BAR REGISTER
CLOSING CASH DRAWER (END OF SHIFT)
-----------------------------------------------------------------

DENOMINATION          QUANTITY  $ VALUE
-----------------------------------------------------------------

PENNIES               22 EACH      0.00
NICKLES               86 EACH      0.00
DIMES                 32 EACH      0.00
QUARTERS              48 EACH      0.00
HALVES                 4 EACH      0.00
SINGLES               86 EACH      0.00
FIVES                 25 EACH      0.00
TENS                  57 EACH      0.00
TWENTYS               36 EACH      0.00
-----------------------------------------------------------------

TOTAL CASH                         0.00
RECORDED BAR CHARGES             245.32
TOTAL BAR SALES                  245.32
```

```
=========================================

DINING ROOM REGISTER
CLOSING CASH DRAWER (END OF SHIFT)
-----------------------------------------------------------------

DENOMINATION          QUANTITY  $ VALUE
-----------------------------------------------------------------

PENNIES               71 EACH      0.00
NICKLES               24 EACH      0.00
DIMES                 21 EACH      0.00
QUARTERS               7 EACH      0.00
HALVES                 0 EACH      0.00
SINGLES               13 EACH      0.00
FIVES                 13 EACH      0.00
TENS                  17 EACH      0.00
TWENTYS                9 EACH      0.00
-----------------------------------------------------------------

TOTAL CASH                         0.00
RECORDED DINING ROOM CHARGES       ZERO
TOTAL DINING ROOM SALES            0.00
```

■ **Hint** _____

Because the end-of-shift dollar amount includes the bank in the total, subtract the bank amount from the results of these registers at the end of the shift. (You will use this information to complete other exercises.)

EXERCISE 2–4A and B   Cash Proofs

Your next assignment is to do the cash proofs of both the bar and dining room registers. Using the top portion of Figure 2–13, enter the Red Woodpecker Grill's appropriate amounts for:

Total cash in drawer	Insert this figure from end-of-shift total sales
– Bank	Insert this figure from the start-of-shift report
= Cash on hand	Automatically calculated.
Actual register tape reading	This number is given to you and you must insert it.
– Recorded charges	Insert this figure from the end-of-shift recorded charges.
= Drawer balance (tape)	Automatically calculated.
Cash on hand	This figure is automatically calculated from the preceding entries. It represents actual sales because it shows the cash you have in the cash register at the end of the shift.
– Drawer balance (tape)	This figure is also derived from preceding entries. It should indicate sales but might be different from the actual cash on hand.
= Difference (+ = over/ – = short)	Automatically calculates the amount you are over or short, comparing the cash and drawer balance (tape).

■ **Hint** _____

The difference should, in most cases, be very small. It won't always be zero; there could be a minor overage or shortage because of changes made in the course of the shifts. Large amounts need to be given serious consideration by management. Therefore, this figure should not exceed ±$2.00.

Using the top portion of Figure 2–14, repeat the cash proof procedure for the Terrace Garden Restaurant.

Figures 2–13 and 2–14 represent the complete report delivered to management: the cash proofs, cash and charges receipts, revenue center and media percentages, current and to date totals, and comparison with an earlier date.

FIGURE 2–13   Cash Proofs—Red Woodpecker Grill

FOODSERVICE COST CONTROL USING MICROSOFT EXCEL		PG 1 OF 1
STUDENT NAME:	{NAME}	RESTAURANT NAME:
DATE:	{DATE}	RED WOODPECKER GRILL

	BAR CASH PROOF	DINING ROOM CASH PROOF
TOTAL CASH IN DRAWER	$0.00	$0.00
– BANK	0.00	0.00
= CASH ON HAND	$0.00	$0.00
ACTUAL REGISTER TAPE READING	$518.00	$2,020.06
– RECORDED CHARGES	0.00	0.00
= DRAWER BALANCE (TAPE)	518.00	2,020.06
CASH ON HAND	$0.00	$0.00
– DRAWER BALANCE (TAPE)	0.00	0.00
= DIFFERENCE (+=OVER/–=SHORT)	$0.00	$0.00

COMPILED REPORT FOR MANAGEMENT

RECEIPTS

TOTAL RECORDED BAR CHARGES	$0.00
+ TOTAL RECORDED D.R. CHARGES	0.00
+ TOTAL BAR CASH RECEIPTS	0.00
+ TOTAL D.R. CASH RECEIPTS	0.00
= TOTAL RECEIPTS	$0.00

REVENUE CENTER %

BAR SALES	0.0000%
+ DINING ROOM SALES	0.0000%
= TOTAL REVENUE CENTER PERCENT	0.0000%

MEDIA %

CHARGES	0.0000%
+ CASH	0.0000%
= TOTAL MEDIA PERCENT	0.0000%

FOR MANAGEMENT USE ONLY	% TODAY	% TO DATE	% THIS DAY LAST MONTH
BAR	0.0000%		
DINING ROOM	0.0000%		
CHARGES	0.0000%		
CASH	0.0000%		

FIGURE 2–14 Cash Proofs—Terrace Garden Restaurant

FOODSERVICE COST CONTROL USING MICROSOFT EXCEL		PG 1 OF 1
STUDENT NAME:	{NAME}	RESTAURANT NAME:
DATE:	{DATE}	TERRACE GARDEN RESTAURANT

	BAR CASH PROOF	DINING ROOM CASH PROOF
TOTAL CASH IN DRAWER	$0.00	$0.00
– BANK	0.00	0.00
= CASH ON HAND	$0.00	$0.00
ACTUAL REGISTER TAPE READING	$1,468.93	$286.02
– RECORDED CHARGES	0.00	0.00
= DRAWER BALANCE (TAPE)	1,468.93	286.02
CASH ON HAND	$0.00	$0.00
– DRAWER BALANCE (TAPE)	0.00	0.00
= DIFFERENCE (+=OVER/–=SHORT)	$0.00	$0.00

****

COMPILED REPORT FOR MANAGEMENT

RECEIPTS

TOTAL RECORDED BAR CHARGES	$0.00
+ TOTAL RECORDED D.R. CHARGES	0.00
+ TOTAL BAR CASH RECEIPTS	0.00
+ TOTAL D.R. CASH RECEIPTS	0.00
= TOTAL RECEIPTS	$0.00

REVENUE CENTER %

BAR SALES	0.0000%
+ DINING ROOM SALES	0.0000%
= TOTAL REVENUE CENTER PERCENT	0.0000%

MEDIA %

CHARGES	0.0000%
+ CASH	0.0000%
= TOTAL MEDIA PERCENT	0.0000%

****

FOR MANAGEMENT USE ONLY	% TODAY	% TO DATE	% THIS DAY LAST MONTH
BAR	0.0000%		
DINING ROOM	0.0000%		
CHARGES	0.0000%		
CASH	0.0000%		

CHECK YOUR UNDERSTANDING

Questions 1-10 are based on Exercise 2–1A or 2–1B. Choose the Red Woodpecker Grill or the Terrace Garden Restaurant for your replies to all questions.

Restaurant name: _____ *With Tax*   *Without Tax*

1. What were the total sales for the period? _____ _____
2. What was the average check sales value? _____ _____
3. How many people were served by each waiter, on average? _____
4. What was the average sale per person? _____ _____
5. What items were very popular (salads)? _____
6. What items were slow movers (sandwiches)? _____
7. Compute the average sales tax per check. _____
8. Compute the average tip per waiter. _____ _____
9. What was the average sale per seat for lunch? _____ _____
10. What was the turnover rate for the room? _____

Questions 11–20 are based on Exercises 2–2 and 2–3.

	Bar	*Dining Room*
11. What is the value of the bank?	_____	_____
12. How much money would you deposit in the bank in cash (excluding the charges)?	_____	_____
13. What is the split in percentages for the revenue center percent?	_____	_____
14. Based on question 13, is this a good split according to industry standards? Give your opinion.	_____	_____
15. What is the split in percentages for media percent?		

	Cash	Charges
16. Based on question 15, is this a good split? If not, what are the implications?	_____	_____
17. What was the difference (plus or minus), if any?	_____	
18. If there was a difference, what could have occurred and what you would do?	_____	
19. List the type of charges that can occur in a restaurant. How can charges be treated by the restaurant?	_____	

20. Based on all your answers to the above questions, would you say the operation is running smoothly? _____

CRITICAL THINKING QUESTIONS

A. Sales Histories

1. Compare the number of sandwiches/entrees sold and the number of salads sold at the Red Woodpecker Grill and the Terrace Garden Restaurant. What is the average cover for each restaurant? Which restaurant has the highest amount per cover?

   _____
   _____
   _____
   _____
   _____
   _____
   _____

2. Why would you want to calculate the average cover? Which restaurant would you prefer to operate? Why?

   _____
   _____
   _____
   _____
   _____
   _____
   _____

3. For *each* operation, calculate the average sale per person and the turnover rate for the room. After completing both calculations, determine the average sale per seat for each restaurant.

■ **Hint** _____

This mathematical calculation should be done by multiplication rather than division. The calculation will appear similar, but multiplication is more accurate because of rounding errors.

Using this comparison, which operation would you prefer to operate? Why?

_____
_____
_____
_____
_____

B. Cashier's Reports

1. Why is there such a difference in the start-of-shift banks of the two restaurants?

_____
_____
_____
_____

2. Judging from the sales produced from both operations, what can you conclude?

_____
_____
_____
_____

3. What would you do at the Terrace Garden Restaurant when there is a shortage at the bar register? How would you handle a small overage in the dining room?

_____
_____
_____
_____

4. Why is it necessary to figure out the percentage of revenue for a restaurant? Which restaurant would you prefer to operate?

_____
_____
_____
_____

5. Why is it necessary to figure out the percentage of media for a restaurant?

_____
_____
_____
_____

PURCHASING AND RECEIVING

■ OBJECTIVES

After completing Lesson 3, you should be able to:

1. Define the following terms:
   Informal versus formal purchasing
   Specifications
2. Explain the three control areas involved in the receiving process.
3. Recognize the components of a good invoice.
4. Distinguish between direct purchases and storeroom purchases.

■ KEY TERMS

Receiving report	Receiving
Informal purchasing	Invoice
Formal purchasing	Direct purchases
Specifications	Storeroom purchases
Groceries	Requisition form

■ CONCEPT REVIEW

This lesson covers the control aspect of the receiving department. Prior to studying controls, a true understanding of the purchasing function and of the controls that can be used to assist in the receiving process is necessary.

RECEIVING REPORT

The *receiving report* is used to summarize delivery activities transpiring during a set period of time—in this case, one day. The receiving report is a total of the goods that have been delivered for the day. The deliveries may include food items, nonfood items, and liquor, which are then ready for immediate use or placed in storage.

Purchasing

Purchasing is the process of ordering all food items, nonfood items, and liquor. Purchasing often involves the simple process of ordering from a purveyor over the telephone and having the items delivered the same day. This is called ***informal purchasing***. Another method involves receiving quotes first; this is called ***formal purchasing***. The formal quote process, which can take several months, is done by advertising and allowing anyone in the business to give a quote. The lowest quote usually getting the business. One might use the informal system for the following reasons:

1. Time is restricted;
2. Sellers are limited in number;
3. The amount of purchase is small;
4. The product is perishable;
5. It is not practical to have a formal bid process;
6. Action must be fast.

Formal purchasing is advertised to vendors. The vendors must submit sealed bids or closed quotes to the purchaser, based on definite purchasing specifications.

Specifications

Specifications are exact descriptions of the item or items to be purchased. Requirements of a product must be very specific and the buyer must be allowed to return the product to the vendor/purveyor if the product is not up to the requested specifications. Requirements may include such details as a particular type of container, the temperature of the item, the number of items per case, and so forth. Specifications should be logical. To prepare a proper specification, research the product thoroughly, using several sources. Listed below are some sources that will prove useful when you write specifications:

1. Major meat purveyors—can assist with meat *specification sheets*.
2. *Meat Buyer's Guide* (The National Association of Meat Purveyors Manual)—used in all 50 states.

3. Major grocery dealers—can provide price lists for many items such as canned goods, sugar, dried beans, and so on. *Groceries* are food items that are normally not perishable.

4. Food operations at hotels, motels, and restaurants—facilitate networking with other professionals at national or local meetings.

5. *Wenzel's Menu Maker*—a book that comes with predesigned menus and specifications.

6. U.S. Department of Agriculture—specifications for agricultural products available through its publications. Another option is to review textbooks on purchasing, such as *Quantity Food Purchasing* by Lendal Kotchevar (MacMillan, 1988).

The standard information needed for a typical product specification (in this example, apples) follows:

1. Name of product: Apples—Red Delicious;

2. Additional descriptive information appropriate for each item: Eating apple, for a box lunch;

3. Quantity: 5 cases;

4. Size/Type of unit or container (descriptive): 60s in wax box, separated and wrapped in foam, delivered at temperature of 38°F;

5. Federal grade or brand: U.S. extra fancy;

6. Unit for which price will be quoted: $15.00/case.

Receiving

Receiving is the actual arrival of the ordered (purchased) items from the vendor. Deliveries are normally brought to the back door of the establishment. The Receiving manager should be a responsible, ethical individual who can be trusted with the value of a typical delivery. The responsibility for receiving includes taking delivery of the goods and dispersing them throughout the establishment.

The Receiving Process

The receiving process involves much attention to detail and awareness of control procedures. The focus is on three key concerns:

1. The physical condition of the receiving area: the loading dock's sanitation quality; the security of access to the loading dock and the visibility afforded by its lighting; and a clear line of sight from the

kitchen to the delivery vehicle, which enables various employees to observe activities. Tools used for receiving, such as scales, tables, and devices to open boxes to view the contents, are also important. Establishing set receiving hours allows exclusive personnel access to back-door keys.

2. The procedures and paperwork (forms) needed for documenting proper receipt. The following sequence will simplify paperwork:

   a. Locate the purchase list for a particular purveyor, and check it against the invoice accompanying the order.

   b. If the invoice is correct, open the cartons while the delivery person is present. Weigh, count, and inspect random products for quality.

   c. If the order is short, issue a credit memo in triplicate. Credit memo forms should be numbered so they can be easily traced for control purposes. If the product is short or rejected, the item, the unit ordered, the price, and the extension of prices should be listed on the credit memo. Upon completion of the credit memo, distribute the original memo to the delivery person, attach one copy to the invoice, to be given to the accounting department, and attach the third copy to a copy of the invoice that will be kept in the receiving office file.

3. The control activities involved in receiving, from the actual arrival of the delivery truck to the signing of the invoice. Make it a policy that the delivery person must announce his or her arrival at the back door. Prior to removing any items from the truck, the receiving clerk should review the presenting invoice to be sure the proper order is being delivered at the correct time. If the order is correct and the invoice is approved, the products should be unloaded from the truck and set in an open space within the receiving area. The cartons should then be counted and opened to inspect the product for adherence to specifications and quality. If the product is being purchased by weight, it should be removed from the box or carton and weighed. If there is a discrepancy in the quantity or quality, issue a credit memo noting the discrepancy, the unit price, and the extension price. If the delivery is correct, simply sign the invoice and keep copies for the receiving and accounting offices.

A good rule of thumb or motto to summarize the receiving process and to verify the purchasing process follows:

If buying by weight—weigh it!

If buying by count—count it!

If buying by quality—look at it!

Invoice

The *invoice* is the summary of all the products being delivered in fulfillment of an order. Listed on the invoice are the contents of the order, the quantities, and the prices. The invoice facilitates the receiving clerk's performance of the remainder of the control process related to receiving. The components of a good invoice are:

1. Name, address, and phone number of the purveyor;
2. Name and address of the purchaser (account);
3. Date of delivery;
4. Invoice number or code;
5. Quantity of product, its packaging, and the size of the unit;
6. Description of the product;
7. Unit price;
8. Extension of product price;
9. Total invoice price;
10. Additional notations—back ordered, out of stock, computer number, reorder number;
11. Total number of pieces;
12. Total number of cartons and/or shipping weight;
13. Place for signature;
14. Pages numbered;
15. Payment terms.

The previous explanation of the receiving process should help you understand the control purposes of the invoice components; they are listed here for easy reference. The controls allow you to review or recreate what took place on a certain day with a particular vendor and specific products. The receiving controls relate to the ledger used for accounting purposes. Finally, control of the product from delivery to use is achieved through a proper receiving process.

The Spreadsheet Format

The form used in Figure 3–1A and throughout this lesson can vary from foodservice operation to foodservice operation. The reason for these variations is that the form's design is based on the restaurant's design. The form represents the "flow of costs." (Ideally, you can look at the loading dock, and next to the loading dock see the receiving office, storage and refrigerator areas, and so forth.)

FIGURE 3–1A   Suggested Spreadsheet Format for Daily Receiving Report (First Page)

FOODSERVICE COST CONTROL USING MICROSOFT EXCEL   PG 1 OF 6
                                                      LEFT PG 1

STUDENT NAME: {NAME}   RESTAURANT NAME:
DATE: {DATE}   {RESTAURANT NAME}

DAILY RECEIVING REPORT

A	B	C	D	E	F
ITEM NAME	UNIT SIZE	QUAN PUR	UNIT PRICE	EXTENSION	INVOICE TOTAL
SUPPLIER NAME					
NAME	SIZE	0.00	0.00	0.00	
NAME	SIZE	0.00	0.00	0.00	
NAME	SIZE	0.00	0.00	0.00	
NAME	SIZE	0.00	0.00	0.00	
NAME	SIZE	0.00	0.00	0.00	
NAME	SIZE	0.00	0.00	0.00	
NAME	SIZE	0.00	0.00	0.00	
NAME	SIZE	0.00	0.00	0.00	
NAME	SIZE	0.00	0.00	0.00	
NAME	SIZE	0.00	0.00	0.00	
NAME	SIZE	0.00	0.00	0.00	
INVOICE TOTALS:					0.00
SUPPLIER NAME					
NAME	SIZE	0.00	0.00	0.00	
NAME	SIZE	0.00	0.00	0.00	
NAME	SIZE	0.00	0.00	0.00	
NAME	SIZE	0.00	0.00	0.00	
NAME	SIZE	0.00	0.00	0.00	
NAME	SIZE	0.00	0.00	0.00	
NAME	SIZE	0.00	0.00	0.00	
NAME	SIZE	0.00	0.00	0.00	
NAME	SIZE	0.00	0.00	0.00	
NAME	SIZE	0.00	0.00	0.00	
NAME	SIZE	0.00	0.00	0.00	
INVOICE TOTALS:					0.00
SUPPLIER NAME					
NAME	SIZE	0.00	0.00	0.00	
NAME	SIZE	0.00	0.00	0.00	
NAME	SIZE	0.00	0.00	0.00	
NAME	SIZE	0.00	0.00	0.00	
NAME	SIZE	0.00	0.00	0.00	
NAME	SIZE	0.00	0.00	0.00	
NAME	SIZE	0.00	0.00	0.00	
NAME	SIZE	0.00	0.00	0.00	
NAME	SIZE	0.00	0.00	0.00	
NAME	SIZE	0.00	0.00	0.00	
NAME	SIZE	0.00	0.00	0.00	
INVOICE TOTALS:					0.00
PAGE TOTALS:					0.00

Writing a Daily Receiving Report

The column headings in Figure 3–1A are explained as follows:

Item name—insert the specific name of the product. Give as much information as possible, so the controller knows what products have been received.

Unit size—the most frequently used unit size abbreviations are:

CS.	case
BX.	box
LB.	pound
OZ.	ounce
Bag	bag
Crate	crate

Quantity purchased—number of items; for example, (10) lbs. = enter 10.

Unit price—should be based on unit size. If you buy a product by the case, it should be priced per case.

■ **Hint** _____

Later on, for individual ingredient pricing, you may need to know there are 12 items to a case. This information should be reflected in the item name description.

Extension—determined by multiplying the quantity by the unit price.
Invoice total—the total of all items from the entire vendor's order.

■ **Hint** _____

The invoice total must be the correct total for the order. If there is a mistake on the invoice, you must record the proper dollar amount. The invoice reflects the cost to the operation and is presented to accounting for payment, by the foodservice operation, for the goods received.

When you understand this section, you can begin to distribute the items ordered based on the controls you establish.

Direct Purchases

This is the first of two definitions that are critical to remember. ***Direct purchases*** are purchases made for immediate use. Direct purchases normally go directly to the consuming department (the kitchen) and are used immediately. Therefore, those items have an automatic food cost for the operation, for that day only. Usually, but *not* always, the direct purchase items are perishable in nature.

Storeroom Purchases

The second definition you need to remember is ***storeroom purchases***. Storeroom purchases are made to increase or maintain the storeroom inventory and are usually items that have a long shelf life. Examples of storeroom purchases are sugar, canned goods, and bottled items. These purchases are kept in the storeroom and are requisitioned by a unit when needed. When storeroom items are used, the cost of the item(s) must be identified as a food cost for the day the item is issued. Once an item leaves the storeroom, it carries an immediate food cost ' whether the item is totally used or not. A ***requisition form*** must be filled out to obtain any item from the storeroom. The requisition lists the name and quantity of the food item, and is signed by someone with authority to make the request. The item is then issued by the storeroom to the unit.

Figure 3–1B shows the page of the spreadsheet on which storeroom purchases are costed.

Keeping in mind the above definitions, look at the page (screen) shown in Figure 3–1B and see how the form is divided. Direct purchases have three areas listed:

1. Dairy—all dairy products (milk, cheese, whipped topping, etc.);
2. Produce—all fresh vegetables and fruit;
3. Meat/Poultry/Seafood—all food items properly categorized as meat, poultry, and seafood.

These are the three areas to which direct purchases can be distributed.

The areas under storeroom purchases are:

1. Freezer—food items that can be stored in the freezer;
2. Groceries—all food items that have long shelf life and won't perish if kept in the storeroom;
3. Sundries—nonfood items (supplies, linens, and so on).

The undistributed amount column is used specifically with this spreadsheet. It is designed to help you "proof" your work. If any dollar amount shows up in this column, this is a sign that you have made an error in

FIGURE 3–1B   Suggested Spreadsheet Format for Daily Receiving Report (Storeroom Purchases Page)

FOODSERVICE COST CONTROL USING MICROSOFT EXCEL   PG 4 OF 6
                                                                               RGHT PG 1
STUDENT: {NAME}   RESTAURANT NAME:
DATE: {DATE}   {RESTAURANT NAME}
==

DAILY RECEIVING REPORT

G	H	L	P	R	S	T
DIRECT PURCHASES			STOREROOM PURCHASES			UNDIST
DAIRY	PRODUCE	MEAT/POUL	FREEZER	GROCERIES	SUNDRIES	AMOUNT
0.00	0.00	0.00	0.00	0.00	0.00	0.00
0.00	0.00	0.00	0.00	0.00	0.00	0.00
0.00	0.00	0.00	0.00	0.00	0.00	0.00
0.00	0.00	0.00	0.00	0.00	0.00	0.00
0.00	0.00	0.00	0.00	0.00	0.00	0.00
0.00	0.00	0.00	0.00	0.00	0.00	0.00
0.00	0.00	0.00	0.00	0.00	0.00	0.00
0.00	0.00	0.00	0.00	0.00	0.00	0.00
0.00	0.00	0.00	0.00	0.00	0.00	0.00
0.00	0.00	0.00	0.00	0.00	0.00	0.00
0.00	0.00	0.00	0.00	0.00	0.00	0.00
0.00	0.00	0.00	0.00	0.00	0.00	0.00
0.00	0.00	0.00	0.00	0.00	0.00	0.00
0.00	0.00	0.00	0.00	0.00	0.00	0.00
0.00	0.00	0.00	0.00	0.00	0.00	0.00
0.00	0.00	0.00	0.00	0.00	0.00	0.00
0.00	0.00	0.00	0.00	0.00	0.00	0.00
0.00	0.00	0.00	0.00	0.00	0.00	0.00
0.00	0.00	0.00	0.00	0.00	0.00	0.00
0.00	0.00	0.00	0.00	0.00	0.00	0.00
0.00	0.00	0.00	0.00	0.00	0.00	0.00
0.00	0.00	0.00	0.00	0.00	0.00	0.00
0.00	0.00	0.00	0.00	0.00	0.00	0.00
0.00	0.00	0.00	0.00	0.00	0.00	0.00
0.00	0.00	0.00	0.00	0.00	0.00	0.00
0.00	0.00	0.00	0.00	0.00	0.00	0.00
0.00	0.00	0.00	0.00	0.00	0.00	0.00
0.00	0.00	0.00	0.00	0.00	0.00	0.00
0.00	0.00	0.00	0.00	0.00	0.00	0.00
0.00	0.00	0.00	0.00	0.00	0.00	0.00
0.00	0.00	0.00	0.00	0.00	0.00	0.00
0.00	0.00	0.00	0.00	0.00	0.00	0.00
0.00	0.00	0.00	0.00	0.00	0.00	0.00
0.00	0.00	0.00	0.00	0.00	0.00	0.00
0.00	0.00	0.00	0.00	0.00	0.00	0.00
0.00	0.00	0.00	0.00	0.00	0.00	0.00
0.00	0.00	0.00	0.00	0.00	0.00	0.00
0.00	0.00	0.00	0.00	0.00	0.00	0.00
0.00	0.00	0.00	0.00	0.00	0.00	0.00

your distribution. The amount that shows up must be redistributed to another category. *No dollar amount should remain in the undistributed amount column.*

■ SPREADSHEET OBJECTIVES

Upon completion of the exercises in lesson 3, you should be able to:

1. Analyze an invoice for necessary data and accuracy;
2. Draft a daily receiving report;
3. Examine the receiving report to better understand overall operational management.

FIGURE 3–1C Sample Pages of Completed Spreadsheet

FOODSERVICE COST CONTROL USING MICROSOFT EXCEL					PG 1 OF 6
					LEFT PG 1

STUDENT NAME: {NAME}   RESTAURANT NAME:
DATE: {DATE}   {RESTAURANT NAME}

===

DAILY RECEIVING REPORT

A	B	C	D	E	F
ITEM NAME	UNIT SIZE	QUAN PUR	UNIT PRICE	EXTENSION	INVOICE TOTAL
Lil Sprouts					
Broccoli	cs	2.00	11.25	22.50	
Carrots 5# bags	bg	3.00	1.46	4.38	
Lettuce	cs	2.00	10.00	20.00	
Pineapples	ea	4.00	0.85	3.40	
Strawberries	pts	8.00	1.89	15.12	
INVOICE TOTALS:					65.40

FIGURE 3–1D Sample Pages of Completed Spreadsheet

FOODSERVICE COST CONTROL USING MICROSOFT EXCEL					PG 1 OF 6
					LEFT PG 1

STUDENT NAME: {NAME}   RESTAURANT NAME:
DATE: {DATE}   {RESTAURANT NAME}

===

DAILY RECEIVING REPORT

A	B	C	D	E	F
ITEM NAME	UNIT SIZE	QUAN PUR	UNIT PRICE	EXTENSION	INVOICE TOTAL
Lil Sprouts					
Broccoli	cs	2.00	11.25	22.50	
Carrots 5# bags	bg	3.00	1.46	4.38	
Lettuce	cs	2.00	10.00	20.00	
Pineapples	ea	4.00	0.85	3.40	
Strawberries	pts	8.00	1.89	15.12	
INVOICE TOTALS:					65.40

FIGURE 3–1C (Continued)

FOODSERVICE COST CONTROL USING MICROSOFT EXCEL

STUDENT NAME: {NAME}   RESTAURANT NAME:
DATE: {DATE}   {RESTAURANT NAME}

==

DAILY RECEIVING REPORT

G	H	L	P	R	S	T
DIRECT PURCHASES			STOREROOM PURCHASES			UNDIST
DAIRY	PRODUCE	MEAT/POUL	FREEZER	GROCERIES	SUNDRIES	AMOUNT
	22.00					0.50
	4.38					0.00
	20.00					0.00
	3.50					(0.10)
	15.12					0.00
						0.00
						0.00
						0.00
						0.00
						0.00
						0.00
						0.00
0.00	65.00	0.00	0.00	0.00	0.00	0.40

FIGURE 3–1D (Continued)

FOODSERVICE COST CONTROL USING MICROSOFT EXCEL

STUDENT NAME: {NAME}   RESTAURANT NAME:
DATE: {DATE}   {RESTAURANT NAME}

==

DAILY RECEIVING REPORT

G	H	L	P	R	S	T
DIRECT PURCHASES			STOREROOM PURCHASES			UNDIST
DAIRY	PRODUCE	MEAT/POUL	FREEZER	GROCERIES	SUNDRIES	AMOUNT
	22.50					0.00
	4.38					0.00
	20.00					0.00
	3.40					0.00
	15.12					0.00
						0.00
						0.00
						0.00
						0.00
						0.00
						0.00
0.00	65.40	0.00	0.00	0.00	0.00	0.00

EXERCISES

The exercises in this lesson deal with the topic of food purchasing and food receiving. You are given groups of food invoices for orders that have been checked in by the receiving department. The invoices are typical of those that an operation receives each day. The invoices could be handwritten, typed, or computerized.

You will have to decipher the information, but do not assume that it is correct. Mistakes do occur. Be especially aware of the following:

1. Multiplication of prices;
2. Invoice totals;
3. Returns (credits);
4. Totals, without individual pricing.

The invoice total of the supplier must equal the combined distribution of products in both classifications: direct purchases (directs) and storeroom purchases (stores).

After you complete the spreadsheet, you will total the final calculations to answer the exercise questions. You will add up all the page totals to get a grand total of all invoices, and have the subtotals for directs and stores. The invoice total must match the combined directs and stores totals.

At the end of the lesson are questions that you will answer from the information you have. These questions will help you understand pricing, purchasing information, and terminology, and will enable you to understand management needs and the purposes for completing these forms.

The daily receiving report spreadsheet covers more than one page (screen) horizontally. You must move your cursor over to the right to complete each line by filling in numbers until column AA or the Sundries subheading appears. Take each invoice from the purveyor's statement and enter it on the spreadsheet. First enter the name of the supplier, then list all the food items from that supplier. After completing that information, go to the next supplier's name.

At this point, it is up to you to input item information so that it is understandable. Abbreviations are allowed, but you should supply enough information for the reader to have some visual conception of what was received.

Supply the unit size, quantity purchased, unit price, and extension. This information can be obtained from the invoice but requires careful attention to detail. After entering all the items from one supplier, total the invoice.

When you have finished entering the information, distribute the item under the classifications of direct purchases and storeroom purchases. Each of these classifications has several subcategories. You may select many subheadings to distribute the dollar amount from each extension total, based on your knowledge of the purchasing and receiving functions.

The undistributed amount column will double-check the correct distribution of the entire dollar amount. This column should always have a $0.00 (zero) balance. If, for example, the undistributed amount column has a balance of $1.00, it means the dollar amount in all columns of directs and stores is high by $1.00. Compare that number to the total from the extension column for the line. A mathematical error may have occurred in splitting the amount, or you may have entered the wrong dollar amount.

At the end of each page, the spreadsheet will automatically total all invoices for that page. Keep in mind that the invoice total for the page must equal that of the directs and stores; there should not be a number in the undistributed amount column. (See Figures 3–1C and 3–1D.)

EXERCISE 3–1A   Receiving Report—Red Woodpecker Grill

Enter the following invoice information into the computer. Total each entry and each page, then total the report for the period.

Soapbox Laundry Company

ITEM	COST PER	EXTENSION	TOTAL INVOICE
75 Tabletops 54"	$ .28 each		
150 Napkins 18"	.15 each		
5 Chef Coats	.40 each		
5 Aprons	.20 each		
5 Chef Pants	.60 each		$ 49.50

Penguin Frozen Foods

ITEM	COST PER	EXTENSION	TOTAL INVOICE
1 case Frozen spinach (2 lb. box)	$15.60 case		
2 cases Horseradish (5½ oz.) frozen	26.90 case		
1 case Frozen French Cut Green Beans (2½)	16.90 case		
1 case Frozen Cut Corn (2½)	14. 10 case		
1 lb. Paprika	2.60 lb.		
2 qts. Maggi	1.60 qt		
			$102.50

R.U. Dunn Meats

ITEM	COST PER	EXTENSION	TOTAL INVOICE
20# Boneless Lamb Chuck	$1.45 lb.		
1 Rack Lamb (7 lbs. 1 oz.)	2.21 lb.		
9 Lamb Loins (80 lbs. 6 oz.)	1.47 lb.		
10# Ground Beef Bulk	.84 lb.		
45 Head 2½# Chix (142 lbs.)	.50 lb.		
12 each Steer Filets (72 lb. 3 oz.)	2.75 lb.		
2 ea. Legs Veal canceled * #10 head 5–6 lb. (65 lbs.) Roaster Chix	.79 lb.		$491.53

* You are instructed to return the Roaster Chickens. Make the corrections.

Farmer Bob's

ITEM	COST PER	EXTENSION	TOTAL INVOICE
1 box Lemons #115	$12.00 case		
6 pts. Strawberries	1.75 pt.		
12 bunches Leeks	1.00 each		
2 cases Lettuce	10.00 each		
6 heads Chicory	.40 each		
6 heads Romaine	.40 each		
10 lbs. Green Grapes	1.00 each		
1 box Pears # 120	14.00 case		
9 each Pineapples	.85 each		

Sticky Buns Bakery

ITEM	COST PER	EXTENSION	TOTAL INVOICE
16 medium Bread		$11.20	
2 dozen Rolls	$1.20/doz.		
5 sliced Pullman		6.75	
2 dozen Torpedo Rolls	1.32/doz.		$ 22.49

Morgans Supplies

ITEM	COST PER	EXTENSION	TOTAL INVOICE
3 (1M) Bake Pan Liners	$39.75 per M		
4 Rose's Lime Juice	2.87 each		$130.73

Moore Dairy

ITEM	COST PER	EXTENSION	TOTAL INVOICE
5/24 Cont. Milk Qts.	$.42 qt.		
3/30 Eggs	.69 doz.		
1 lb. Cottage Cheese	.73 lb.		

B.A. Fische Co.

ITEM	COST PER	EXTENSION	TOTAL INVOICE
15 lbs. Haddock Fillet	$1.50 lb.		
8 lbs. Sole		$ 28.00	
20 lbs. Brook Trout	2.75 lb.		
40 lbs. Red Snapper Fillet		150.00	
			$255.50

Flowers for All

ITEM	COST PER	EXTENSION	TOTAL INVOICE
1 Centerpiece	$12.00 each		
2 bunches Loose Flowers	7.50 each		
1 bunch Greens	2.75		
			$ 29.75

CHECK YOUR UNDERSTANDING

1. What items do you have listed under sundries?

   _____

   _____

   _____

2. The flowers are considered perishables. Where did you put them?

   _____

   _____

3. Answer the following:

   What is the cost of one box of frozen cut green beans? _____

   What is the average cost of a loin of lamb? _____

   What is the average weight of a chicken? _____

   What is the cost of 1 pound of cut corn? _____

4. What is the dollar breakdown for perishables? _____

   Nonperishables? _____

5. What were the total purchases for the period? _____

6. Which invoices should be brought to the attention of the management? List each and explain why.

_____

_____

_____

_____

_____

EXERCISE 3–1B   Receiving Report—Terrace Garden Restaurant

Enter the following invoice information into the computer. Total each entry and each page, then total the report for the period.

Frosty Foods, Inc.

ITEM	COST PER	EXTENSION	TOTAL INVOICE
10 cases Light Rye Bread Dough	$12.65 cs.		
2 cases Raisin Bread Dough (24 pcs/cs)	22.55 cs.		
5 cases Wheat Bread Dough	12.92 cs.		
5 cases White Bread Dough	11.79 cs.		
			$295.15

La Tissue Co.

ITEM	COST PER	EXTENSION	TOTAL INVOICE
1 case Bleach	$ 6.62 cs.		
1 roll Aluminum Foil Hvy Dty 18" × 500'	19.94 cs.		
1 roll Film Cutter Box 18" × 2000'	10.55 cs.		
1 case Rose's Lime Juice	23.89 cs.		
			$ 61.00

Purple Cow

ITEM	COST PER	EXTENSION	TOTAL INVOICE
20 ST. Homo. gal. pl.	$1.88 gal.		
1/24 ST. Skim	.37 qt.		
4/24 ST. Hvy Cream	1.57 qt.		
4 Sour Cream	7.99 tub		
4 Natural Yogurt		$31.96	
2 UL Half & Half Cream (pcs.)	7.16 box		
3/24 ST. Half & Half (qts)	.76 qt.		
			$306.40

T-Bone Meats

ITEM	COST PER	EXTENSION	TOTAL INVOICE
2 cases Chix Breast 24/8 oz. (24 lbs. 0 oz.)	$2.69 lb.		
9 cases Chix Breast 24/6 oz. (81 lbs. 0 oz.)	2.69 lb.		
3 pcs CH Tenderloin w/silver (26 lbs. 3 oz.)	5.49 lb.		
1 cs. Bacon Slice 15 lbs. LO	1.49 lb.		
1 Oven Roasted Turkey Breast (10 lbs. 2 oz.)	2.69 lb.		
1 Proscuitto (8 lbs. 9 oz.)	6.48 lb.		
1 Pulled Chix Meat canceled (10 lbs.)			
1 CH #173 Shortloin (26 lbs. 8 oz.)	3.19 lb.		
*1 CH Top Round (26 lbs. 4 oz.)	1.98 lb.		

* You are instructed to return the Top Round. Make the corrections.

Mom & Pop's

ITEM	COST PER	EXTENSION	TOTAL INVOICE
1 Cracker Medley	$19.83 cs.		
1 Cranberry Juice 48/6 oz	14.89 cs.		
1 Orange Juice 48/6 oz	13.04 cs.		
1 Pineapple Juice 48/6 oz	12.20 cs.		
2 bags Shredded 50/50 Mozzarella	7.25/per bag		
1 Apple Juice 48/6 oz	12.06 cs.		
2 Whole Tomatoes 6/#10	15.88 cs.		
3 Chunk Light Tuna	cs.	$81.69	
2/30 Eggs	doz.	42.00	
			$228.63

Carrot Patch

ITEM	COST PER	EXTENSION	TOTAL INVOICE
2 Broccoli F.S.	$11.20 cs.		
1 Carrots (25 lb. bag)	4.99 bg.		
5 each Cauliflower	.99 ea.		
5 lbs. Bananas	.41 lb.		
10 lbs. Grapes, Red Seedless	.98 lb.		
1 Grapes, White Seedless	16.52 cs.		
1 flat Kiwi fruit	10.36 cs.		
6 each Pineapples	2.04 ea		
3 flats Strawberries	14.56 cs.		

Romaine Co.

ITEM	COST PER	EXTENSION	TOTAL INVOICE
1 Mushrooms (10 lbs)	$12.04 cs.		
5 bunches Green Onions	.40 ea.		
1 Onion	23.13 bag		
2 Parsley	.40 bunch		
1 Romaine	19.04 cs.		
1 Spinach	11.88 box		
			$ 57.81

Garden Spot

ITEM	COST PER	EXTENSION	TOTAL INVOICE
1 case Asparagus	$34.16 cs.		
5 lbs. Red Onions	lb.	$ 5.30	
4 bunch Leeks	1.50 bunch		
5 lbs. Dry Garlic	1.75 lb.		
5 lbs. Dry Shallots	3.00 lb.		
1 bag Chives	4.50 bag		
3 bags Tarragon	bag	13.50	
4 bags Basil	6.00 bag		
2 bags Mint	4.00 bag		
2 bags Thyme	4.50 bag		
			$136.21

C. Bass Co.

ITEM	COST PER	EXTENSION	TOTAL INVOICE
10 lbs. Seaflake	$ 2.68 lb.		
6 bags Alatex (3 lb. bags)	4.99 lb.		
3 lbs. 16/20 P.D.	11.99 lb.		
9 lbs. 40/50 P.D.	6.59 lb.		
10 lbs. W.W. Tail (9 oz.)	15.95 lb.		
2 Fresh Salmon Fillets (5 lb. 8 oz.)	6.99 lb.		
1 lb. Crab	7.25 lb.		
10 lb. Haddock	3.59 lb.		
1 can Lobster Meat (2 lbs.)	17.50 lb.		
3 dozen Oyster Shells	4.79 doz.		

CHECK YOUR UNDERSTANDING

1. What items do you have listed under sundries?

_____

_____

2. The raisin bread are considered perishables. Where did you put it?

   _____

   _____

3. Answer the following:

   What is the cost of one loaf of raisin bread? $ _____

   What is the cost of a case of heavy cream? $ _____

   What is the cost of 1 can of orange juice? $ _____

4. What is the dollar breakdown for perishables? $ _____

   Nonperishables? $ _____

5. What were the total purchases for the period? $ _____

6. Which invoices should be brought to the attention of the management? List each and explain why.

   _____

   _____

   _____

   _____

   _____

   _____

   _____

   _____

   _____

   _____

   _____

CRITICAL THINKING QUESTIONS

1. Because direct purchases are considered immediate costs, they have a daily impact on food cost percentage. For example, if cost for dairy is $100.00 daily and sales are $1,000.00, dairy's food cost percentage is 10%. Calculate the food cost percentage for the Red Woodpecker Grill's and Terrace Garden Restaurant's direct purchases.

Sales at Red Woodpecker Grill for the day	$ 6,266.12
Sales at Terrace Garden Restaurant for the day	$15,584.92

	Red Woodpecker	Terrace Garden
Dairy	_____	_____
Produce	_____	_____
Meat/Poultry/Fish	_____	_____

2. Compare food cost percentage between the Red Woodpecker and Terrace Garden in the direct purchase areas: dairy, produce, and meat/poultry/fish. What recommendations could you make to management, based on this comparison?

   _____

   _____

   _____

3. How do purchases from Sticky Buns Bakery for the Red Woodpecker Grill differ from purchases from Frosty Foods, Inc., for the Terrace Garden Restaurant?

   _____

   _____

   _____

   _____

4. If different types of purchases and a difference in refrigeration or storeroom layout led you to change the format of the receiving report, which items would be added or deleted if you were in charge of the Red Woodpecker Grill? Which items would be added or deleted if you were in charge of the Terrace Garden Restaurant?

   _____

   _____

   _____

   _____

   _____

5. What are the most critical points of information in the receiving report? What does the receiving report tell management?

   _____

   _____

   _____

   _____

   _____

   _____

   _____

   _____

STOREROOM CONTROL REPORT

■ OBJECTIVES

After completing Lesson 4, you should be able to:

1. Define the following terms:
    Direct purchase versus storeroom issue
    Daily gross food cost
    Gross food cost percent (today and to date)
    Storeroom purchases
2. Draft a storeroom control report.
3. Calculate the rate of inventory turnover.
4. Explain various methods for pricing inventory and their optimal application.

■ KEY TERMS

Direct purchases	To date
Storeroom issues	Storeroom purchases
Daily gross food cost	Storeroom control
Daily sales	Storeroom requisition form
Gross food cost percent today	

■ CONCEPT REVIEW

This lesson discusses controlling the storeroom. After completing the lesson, you will be able to report to management from information supplied on the storeroom control report. You must know the terms in order to understand where the reported numbers come from. Each of the terms explained here is a column heading in Figure 4–1.

OVERVIEW

Direct Purchases

Direct purchases are perishable items that go immediately to the department that will use or consume them. Because the items are perishable, they receive an immediate food cost for the operation of a particular day.

> ■ **Hint**
>
> This dollar amount comes from the direct purchases, for the day as listed in the receiving report (see Lesson 3).

Storeroom Issues

Storeroom issues are items that are requisitioned (ordered) by a department for a particular day. The items are issued from the storeroom only after a proper storeroom requisition has been completed. Once the items are priced out by the storeroom manager, that total is a food cost for the day.

Daily Gross Food Cost

The *daily gross food cost* is the cost of all food for the day (direct purchases + storeroom issues = daily gross food cost).

Daily Sales

Daily sales are the total sales of food, liquor, or both, for the day, depending on what information is needed. In this lesson, you will be looking for food sales. This information comes from the cashier's report for food sales for the day—the type of form you created and used in Lesson 2. Remember, this figure *must* be verified by the accountant in the event that there was a shortage in the deposit for the day, or a mistake in charges, or a check that was not good.

Gross Food Cost Percent Today

Gross food cost percent today is determined by dividing the cost of food for the day by the food sales for the day. The formula for calculating this information is:

$$\frac{\text{Food cost for the day}}{\text{Food sales for the day}} = \text{Gross food cost percent for the day}$$

The gross food cost percent for the day can be very low or very high, and it fluctuates every single day. The percent is expressed in decimals and is carried out to four places. This is done in order to be as accurate as possible without rounding numbers.

To Date

To date refers to the cumulative cost total from day 1 to the current day. The costs expressed as "to dates" are:

Gross food cost to date—the cost of all food purchased or requisitioned from the storeroom to date;

Food sales to date—the dollar value of all food sold to date;

Gross food cost percent to date—the relation of costs to sales to date, expressed as a percentage. The formula is:

$$\frac{\text{All food cost to date}}{\text{All food sales to date}} = \text{Gross food cost percent to date}$$

■ Hint

It is very important to understand the gross food cost percent to date. This is a cumulative percentage, and it may fluctuate from very low to very high for up to 10–15 days. After that time, the figure will not change much unless there are large jumps in the day-to-day figures. If you are aiming for a certain food cost percent to date, you should look for a trend toward the middle of the month. Otherwise, some management decisions will have to be made from the standpoint of daily food cost or daily food sales.

The method above was established by Holiday Inns when the chain primarily dealt with daily cash payments. When this running percentage was calculated, if the food cost percent to date was running high because of lack of sales to date, the foodservice management at Holiday Inns was instructed to make the daily specials using food in storage rather than purchasing more. The practice was a forced way of selling menu items and making a designed profit on the food already purchased. The solution makes good financial sense but limits the selections on the menu of the cost-cutting establishment.

FIGURE 4–1 Format for Storeroom Control Report

STUDENT NAME: {NAME}   RESTAURANT NAME:
DATE: {DATE}   {RESTAURANT NAME}

STOREROOM CONTROL

A	B	C	D	E	F
DATE	DIRECT PURCHASES	STOREROOM ISSUES	DAILY GROSS FOOD COST	DAILY SALES	GROSS F.C. % TODAY
MONTH					
1	0.00	0.00	0.00	0.00	ERR
2	0.00	0.00	0.00	0.00	ERR
3	0.00	0.00	0.00	0.00	ERR
4	0.00	0.00	0.00	0.00	ERR
5	0.00	0.00	0.00	0.00	ERR
6	0.00	0.00	0.00	0.00	ERR
7	0.00	0.00	0.00	0.00	ERR
SUB	0.00	0.00	0.00	0.00	ERR
8	0.00	0.00	0.00	0.00	ERR
9	0.00	0.00	0.00	0.00	ERR
10	0.00	0.00	0.00	0.00	ERR
11	0.00	0.00	0.00	0.00	ERR
12	0.00	0.00	0.00	0.00	ERR
13	0.00	0.00	0.00	0.00	ERR
14	0.00	0.00	0.00	0.00	ERR
SUB	0.00	0.00	0.00	0.00	ERR
15	0.00	0.00	0.00	0.00	ERR
16	0.00	0.00	0.00	0.00	ERR
17	0.00	0.00	0.00	0.00	ERR
18	0.00	0.00	0.00	0.00	ERR
19	0.00	0.00	0.00	0.00	ERR
20	0.00	0.00	0.00	0.00	ERR
21	0.00	0.00	0.00	0.00	ERR
SUB	0.00	0.00	0.00	0.00	ERR
22	0.00	0.00	0.00	0.00	ERR
23	0.00	0.00	0.00	0.00	ERR
24	0.00	0.00	0.00	0.00	ERR
25	0.00	0.00	0.00	0.00	ERR
26	0.00	0.00	0.00	0.00	ERR
27	0.00	0.00	0.00	0.00	ERR
28	0.00	0.00	0.00	0.00	ERR
29	0.00	0.00	0.00	0.00	ERR
30	0.00	0.00	0.00	0.00	ERR
31	0.00	0.00	0.00	0.00	ERR
SUB	0.00	0.00	0.00	0.00	ERR
TOTAL	0.00	0.00	0.00	0.00	ERR

FIGURE 4–1   (Continued)

STUDENT NAME: {NAME}   RESTAURANT NAME:
DATE: {DATE}   {RESTAURANT NAME}

STOREROOM CONTROL

G	H	L	P	R
GROSS F.C. TO DATE	FOOD SALES TO DATE	GROSS F.C. % TO DATE	STOREROOM PURCHASES	STOREROOM CONTROL
		OPENING INVENTORY =		0.00
0.00	0.00	ERR	0.00	0.00
0.00	0.00	ERR	0.00	0.00
0.00	0.00	ERR	0.00	0.00
0.00	0.00	ERR	0.00	0.00
0.00	0.00	ERR	0.00	0.00
0.00	0.00	ERR	0.00	0.00
0.00	0.00	ERR	0.00	0.00
0.00	0.00	ERR	0.00	0.00
0.00	0.00	ERR	0.00	0.00
0.00	0.00	ERR	0.00	0.00
0.00	0.00	ERR	0.00	0.00
0.00	0.00	ERR	0.00	0.00
0.00	0.00	ERR	0.00	0.00
0.00	0.00	ERR	0.00	0.00
0.00	0.00	ERR	0.00	0.00
0.00	0.00	ERR	0.00	0.00
0.00	0.00	ERR	0.00	0.00
0.00	0.00	ERR	0.00	0.00
0.00	0.00	ERR	0.00	0.00
0.00	0.00	ERR	0.00	0.00
0.00	0.00	ERR	0.00	0.00
0.00	0.00	ERR	0.00	0.00
0.00	0.00	ERR	0.00	0.00
0.00	0.00	ERR	0.00	0.00
0.00	0.00	ERR	0.00	0.00
0.00	0.00	ERR	0.00	0.00
0.00	0.00	ERR	0.00	0.00
0.00	0.00	ERR	0.00	0.00
0.00	0.00	ERR	0.00	0.00
0.00	0.00	ERR	0.00	0.00
0.00	0.00	ERR	0.00	0.00
0.00	0.00	ERR	0.00	0.00
0.00	0.00	ERR	0.00	0.00
0.00	0.00	ERR	0.00	0.00
0.00	0.00	ERR	0.00	0.00
0.00	0.00	ERR	0.00	0.00
0.00	0.00	ERR	0.00	0.00

STOREROOM PURCHASES

The next column on your screen is ***storeroom purchases***—items purchased for placement in the storeroom. Storeroom purchases have a cost to the restaurant, but the cost is not immediate. The cost is applied *after* the food is requested and issued. When items leave the storeroom, the cost for the operation for that day must include an amount recorded as storeroom issues. The storeroom purchases dollar amount comes from the daily receiving report (see Lesson 3) and refers to items that are sent to the storeroom to be issued at a later date.

The last column in Figure 4–1 is ***storeroom control***, the method for tracking the inventory actually on hand in the storeroom.

The formula for arriving at the dollar amount for inventory is illustrated in this example:

Opening inventory	$4,000.00
+ Storeroom purchases	+ 800.00
= Total inventory available	$4,800.00
− Storeroom issues	−1,600.00
= Storeroom control	$3,200.00

Explanation of Formula

Opening inventory is the closing inventory from the previous period. On the first day of the month, the figure duplicates last months closing figure. It states the actual physical-count dollar amount.

Storeroom purchases—food items bought specifically to be put in the storeroom—are entered in the Storeroom Purchases column on your spreadsheet.

The *total inventory available* figure now represents all the food available for use by the restaurant.

Storeroom issues are food items released from the storeroom in response to a properly filled out storeroom requisition form for that day. A ***storeroom requisition form*** lists food items by description and count, and requests that they be transferred from the storeroom to the kitchen(s) for use that day. The pricing of the storeroom requisition form can be done several ways and is, therefore, considered to be only an estimate.

Storeroom control is the amount of inventory in the storeroom at the end of the day. This amount, which could be considered closing inventory, is an estimate because of the estimated number used in storeroom issues.

INTERPRETING STOREROOM CONTROL FIGURES

At the completion of a storeroom control report, there are certain segments that you can examine to determine management decisions, based on how you interpret the numbers. The first set of numbers for you to focus on is the entries and subtotals for the first week, shown in Figure 4–2.

Subtotals for Week One

As you study the 7 days' activity of storeroom control shown in Figure 4–2, note that you have a target food cost percent of 40.0000%. You would check this at the completion of the first week or at the end of any specific day you want to focus on. If the cost percent is low, then it is safe to say that either you increased your sales or reduced the cost overall. As mentioned earlier, the percent to date should not fluctuate at high rates after the middle of the month. This allows management to make drastic price reductions or to try to increase sales with less cost.

The second set of numbers that you will want to examine is the totals for the entire month, for the purpose of calculating the rate of inventory. (See Figure 4–3.)

Calculating the Rate of Inventory Turnover

The formula for finding the rate of inventory turnover is a true formula based on actual figures, not estimated numbers. Here, the totals for storeroom purchases and storeroom control are in the last two columns of Figure 4–3. The formula is composed of three steps.

1.

Opening inventory		$ 5,698.00
+ Storeroom purchases		+ 4,333.00
= Total inventory available for use (consumption)		$10,031.00
– Closing inventory		– 3,458.00
= Consumption (amount of food used or consumed)		$ 6,573.00

The number that will make this formula true is the closing inventory figure. That number is arrived at through an actual counting of the inventory by the manager and the cost controller of the property. The number of items is counted, multiplied by the cost per item, and then totaled.

FIGURE 4–2 Storeroom Control Report—Week One

FOODSERVICE COST CONTROL USING MICROSOFT EXCEL   PG 1 OF 2
STUDENT NAME: {NAME}   RESTAURANT NAME:
DATE: {DATE}   {RESTAURANT NAME}

STOREROOM CONTROL

A	B	C	D	E	F
DATE	DIRECT PURCHASES	STOREROOM ISSUES	DAILY GROSS FOOD COST	DAILY SALES	GROSS F.C. % TODAY
Aug.					
1	100.00	223.00	323.00	869.00	37.1692%
2	50.00	150.00	200.00	550.00	36.3636%
3	100.00	500.00	600.00	1,501.00	39.9734%
4	25.00	275.00	300.00	700.00	42.8571%
5	0.00	380.00	380.00	1,141.00	33.3041%
6	0.00	370.00	370.00	1,002.00	36.9261%
7	185.00	380.00	565.00	1,628.00	34.7052%
SUB	460.00	2,278.00	2,738.00	7,391.00	37.0451%

FIGURE 4–3 Storeroom Control Report—Totals for Month

FOODSERVICE COST CONTROL USING MICROSOFT EXCEL   PG 1 OF 2
STUDENT NAME: {NAME}   RESTAURANT NAME:
DATE: {DATE}   {RESTAURANT NAME}

STOREROOM CONTROL

A	B	C	D	E	F
DATE	DIRECT PURCHASES	STOREROOM ISSUES	DAILY GROSS FOOD COST	DAILY SALES	GROSS F.C. % TODAY
Aug.					
1	100.00	223.00	323.00	869.00	37.1692%
2	50.00	150.00	200.00	550.00	36.3636%
3	100.00	500.00	600.00	1,501.00	39.9734%
4	25.00	275.00	300.00	700.00	42.8571%
5	0.00	380.00	380.00	1,141.00	33.3041%
6	0.00	370.00	370.00	1,002.00	36.9261%
7	185.00	380.00	565.00	1,628.00	34.7052%
SUB	460.00	2,278.00	2,738.00	7,391.00	37.0451%
SUB	701.00	2,573.00	3,274.00	8,731.00	37.4986%
TOTAL	2,145.00	6,573.00	8,718.00	26,077.00	33.4318%

FIGURE 4–2   (Continued)

FOODSERVICE COST CONTROL USING MICROSOFT EXCEL   PG 2 OF 2
STUDENT: {NAME}   RESTAURANT NAME:
DATE: {DATE}   {RESTAURANT NAME}

STOREROOM CONTROL

G	H	L	P	R
GROSS F.C. TO DATE	FOOD SALES TO DATE	GROSS F.C. % TO DATE	STOREROOM PURCHASES	STOREROOM CONTROL
		OPENING INVENTORY =		5,698.00
323.00	869.00	37.1692%	150.00	5,625.00
523.00	1,419.00	36.8569%	500.00	5,975.00
1,123.00	2,920.00	38.4589%	684.00	6,159.00
1,423.00	3,620.00	39.3094%	631.00	6,515.00
1,803.00	4,761.00	37.8702%	0.00	6,135.00
2,173.00	5,763.00	37.7061%	0.00	5,765.00
2,738.00	7,391.00	37.0451%	1,265.00	6,650.00
2,738.00	7,391.00	37.0451%	3,230.00	6,650.00

FIGURE 4–3   (Continued)

FOODSERVICE COST CONTROL USING MICROSOFT EXCEL   PG 2 OF 2
STUDENT: {NAME}   RESTAURANT NAME:
DATE: {DATE}   {RESTAURANT NAME}

STOREROOM CONTROL

G	H	L	P	R
GROSS F.C. TO DATE	FOOD SALES TO DATE	GROSS F.C. % TO DATE	STOREROOM PURCHASES	STOREROOM CONTROL
		OPENING INVENTORY =		5,698.00
323.00	869.00	37.1692%	150.00	5,625.00
523.00	1,419.00	36.8569%	500.00	5,975.00
1,123.00	2,920.00	38.4589%	684.00	6,159.00
1,423.00	3,620.00	39.3094%	631.00	6,515.00
1,803.00	4,761.00	37.8702%	0.00	6,135.00
2,173.00	5,763.00	37.7061%	0.00	5,765.00
2,738.00	7,391.00	37.0451%	1,265.00	6,650.00
2,738.00	7,391.00	37.0451%	3,230.00	6,650.00
8,718.00	26,077.00	33.4318%	1,103.00	3,458.00
8,718.00	26,077.00	33.4318%	4,333.00	3,458.00

2.   Opening inventory $ 5,698.00
    + Closing inventory   + 3,458.00
    = Total of inventories $ 9,156.00

$$\frac{\text{Total of inventories}}{2} = \text{Average inventory}$$

$$\frac{\$9,156.00}{2} = \$4,578.00$$

3. $$\frac{\text{Consumption}}{\text{Average inventory}} = \text{Rate of inventory turnover}$$

$$\frac{\$6,573.00}{\$4,578.00} = 1.4357$$

When you complete the third step, the resulting figure is the rate of inventory turnover.

Interpreting the Rate of Inventory Turnover

The rate of inventory turnover can be expressed in numbers—for example, 1, 2, 3, 4, and so on. These figures are expressed as a factor number.

For example, one would represent the inventory turnover calculated once a month, or every 30 days, as 1×30. An inventory calculated twice a month, or every 15 days, is represented as $2 \times 15 = 30$. Calculations done every 10 days would be $3 \times 10 = 30$; every 4 days or approximately once a week would be $4 \times 7 = 28$. If the rate is expressed as 15, it represents 30 days divided by 15, or calculations done every 2 days. This number might be very good for a high-volume fast-food restaurant with little storage space on the premises. The rate-of-inventory-turnover number will depend on the purchasing philosophy of the company or owners. In some cases, to economize, a company will buy large amounts of supplies for a good savings. The number for inventory turnover would then be low. On the other hand, a company that has very limited funds would buy only small amounts of food as needed. This would possibly result in a large number for inventory turnover.

For a good "table cloth restaurant" with a fairly good sales income, a good number for inventory turnover would be 4. The food will turn over once a week, which indicates that the food flow in and out of the storeroom has some quality control of rotation.

What would you expect the number to be for the inventory turnover rate of a bar? If you said 1, you are correct. Certain cordials ordered for a bar have a high cost. If you buy a full case of Green Crème de Menthe, for example, it might take you a long time to sell 12 bottles. On that item, you would keep a high dollar amount of inventory in stock. However, a case of vodka comes in and gets used quickly. You must be careful not to order and store large quantities of high-cost items that are not used quickly.

■ Hint

When you do a storeroom control report, you are working with estimated numbers. The storeroom control number is the number that you would *like* to come up with, but it is strictly a guesstimate number that you work with daily for a period of a month. The only time you verify the number is when you actually perform your inventory. The actual value of storeroom inventory is derived by counting the inventory in the storeroom, pricing it by the method you have chosen, and completing the extension.

Because you work with an estimated number for the storeroom control report, the issued items need not always be 100% correctly priced. A good estimate should help to give you a sense of the value of your inventory on a daily basis.

METHODS FOR PRICING INVENTORY

The concept of pricing physical inventory is important, and you should learn the methods involved. The methods described here are standard accounting procedures that are acceptable for pricing physical inventory.

Actual Purchase Price Method

Every time you buy a product, tag it with the price you paid for it. Then, when it leaves the storeroom, take the price on the tag and record it on the requisition form to reflect the cost.

First-in, First-Out (FIFO) Method

With this method, the stock is rotated and the items that arrived first on the shelf are the first ones consumed. The items remaining on the shelf should be those that were more recently purchased.

Weighted Average Purchase Price Method

This method would be used when large quantities are stored and no rotation takes place. Multiply the items in the opening inventory, and in each subsequent purchase, by individual purchase prices. Add these items to determine a total value for the inventory, and divide by the number of items. For this method to work, you need an accurate account of purchases made for the month.

Latest Purchase Price Method (Most Recent Price)

This very easy method is often used in foodservice establishments. The last price paid for an item is divided by the number of items on hand. This practice does have an effect on inventory, if prices fluctuate from the last time the product was purchased. The method devalues cost or inflates cost as opposed to using actual cost.

Last-in, First-Out (LIFO) Method

This method uses the original price as opposed to the last price. Using this method could have the same effect as the latest purchase price method, but it is usually used to devalue cost, making the assumption that prices are higher on later purchases.

FIGURE 4-4   Storeroom Control Report—Weekly Totals

FOODSERVICE COST CONTROL USING MICROSOFT EXCEL   PG I OF 2
STUDENT NAME: {NAME}   RESTAURANT NAME:
DATE: {DATE}   {RESTAURANT NAME}

STOREROOM CONTROL

A	B	C	D	E	F
DATE	DIRECT PURCHASES	STOREROOM ISSUES	DAILY GROSS FOOD COST	DAILY SALES	GROSS F.C. % TODAY
Aug.					
1	100.00	223.00	323.00	869.00	37.1692%
2	50.00	150.00	200.00	550.00	36.3636%
3	100.00	500.00	600.00	1,501.00	39.9734%
4	25.00	275.00	300.00	700.00	42.8571%
5	0.00	380.00	380.00	1,141.00	33.3041%
6	0.00	370.00	370.00	1,002.00	36.9261%
7	185.00	380.00	565.00	1,628.00	34.7052%
SUB	460.00	2,278.00	2,738.00	7,391.00	37.0451%

All these methods are acceptable. It is normally up to the accountants of a particular foodservice establishment to choose and abide by *one* of these methods. These methods are identified tax purposes when reporting to the Internal Revenue Service.

Double-Checking Weekly Totals

Use the screen shown in Figure 4–4 for this task. This section explains the columns you will work with.

Direct Purchases—add down this column for 7 days and get the subtotal.

Storeroom Issues—add down this column for 7 days and get the subtotal.

Daily Gross Food Cost—add down this column for 7 days and get the subtotal.

Daily Sales—add down this column for 7 days and get the subtotal.

Now divide the subtotal for Daily Gross Food Cost by the subtotal for Daily Sales, to find the Gross Food Cost Percent Today. Put this figure in column F in Figure 4–4.

Look at the subtotals. They should be duplicated for a double-check. Column G, Gross Food Cost to Date, should equal the subtotal of column D, Daily Gross Food Cost. Column H, Food Sales to Date, should equal the subtotal of column E, Daily Sales. Column L, Gross Food Cost Percent to Date, should equal the subtotal of column F.

FIGURE 4–4 (Continued)

FOODSERVICE COST CONTROL USING MICROSOFT EXCEL   PG 2 OF 2
STUDENT: {NAME}   RESTAURANT NAME:
DATE: {DATE}   {RESTAURANT NAME}

STOREROOM CONTROL

G	H	L	P	R
GROSS F.C. TO DATE	FOOD SALES TO DATE	GROSS F.C. % TO DATE	STOREROOM PURCHASES	STOREROOM CONTROL
		OPENING INVENTORY =		5,698.00
323.00	869.00	37.1692%	150.00	5,625.00
523.00	1,419.00	36.8569%	500.00	5,975.00
1,123.00	2,920.00	38.4589%	684.00	6,159.00
1,423.00	3,620.00	39.3094%	631.00	6,515.00
1,803.00	4,761.00	37.8702%	0.00	6,135.00
2,173.00	5,763.00	37.7061%	0.00	5,765.00
2,738.00	7,391.00	37.0451%	1,265.00	6,650.00
2,738.00	7,391.00	37.0451%	3,230.00	6,650.00

The subtotal of daily figures, added together for the 7-day subtotals, should equal the to-date figure. To-date figures are subtotals acquired by adding one day to the next day.

Now go to column P, Storeroom Purchases; add down this column for 7 days and get the subtotal.

Look at column R, Storeroom Control. This is a total that you need to check from all the other columns, using this formula:

Opening inventory (first day of new period, or figure from last day of previous period)

+ Storeroom purchases (column P subtotal)

= Amount available (subtotal)

− Storeroom issues (column C subtotal)

= Storeroom control = should equal figure in column R

The numbers are done for you in Figure 4–4, but you should know how to double-check them, to know when your own numbers are correct. Otherwise, for the first week, you could have made 70 number errors and these errors would continue down to the last day of the month. Always double-check your numbers.

■ SPREADSHEET OBJECTIVES

Upon completion of Lesson 4, you should be able to:

1. Use the storeroom control report to analyze daily and weekly sales performances.

2. Make recommendations to management concerning the viability of the restaurant.

EXERCISES

The numbers for direct purchases, storeroom issues, daily sales, storeroom purchases, and the opening inventory are given. All subtotal spaces (blocks) will add automatically.

Direct purchases plus storeroom issues equal the amount shown as daily gross food cost.

Daily gross food cost divided by daily sales will yield the gross food cost percent today.

Gross food cost to date is a running total of the daily gross food cost.

Gross food sales to date is a running total of daily food sales.

Storeroom control is figured automatically by adding storeroom control to storeroom purchases and subtracting storeroom issues.

EXERCISE 4–1A   Perpetual Inventory Control, Red Woodpecker Grill

Using the storeroom control report format shown in the figures in Lesson 4, set up the inventory control.

The information shown in Figure 4–5 was obtained from the receiving sheet, stewards report, and cashiers report. Using the numbers in the figure, complete the columns. (Where there are no numbers, nothing has been purchased; therefore, the number is 0.)

EXERCISE 4–1B   Perpetual Inventory Control, Terrace Garden Restaurant

Using the storeroom control report format shown in the figures in Lesson 4, set up the inventory control.

The information shown in Figure 4–6 was obtained from the receiving sheet, steward's report, and cashier's report. Using the numbers given in the figure, complete the columns. (Where there are no numbers, nothing has been purchased, therefore, the number is 0.)

FIGURE 4–5   Inventory Data–Red Woodpecker Grill

Date	Sales	Storeroom Purchases	Direct Purchases	Storeroom Issues
Oct. 1	$ 550	$100	$ 50	$150
2	375	250	25	75
3	400	200	40	110
4	625	200	100	200
5	650			100
6	525			120
7	575	100	50	150
8	869	115	100	223
9	1,186	115	127	498
10	703	215	83	275
11	981	156	98	323
12	1,141			379
13	1,496			582
14	1,207	283	182	481
15	1,121	128	155	210
16	1,092	250	142	215
17	975	375	149	190
18	1,226	362	147	275
19	1,086			205
20	782			270
21	628	295	115	180
22	1,201			200
23	1,234	225	100	195
24	1,159	660		230
25	1,362		101	285
26	1,220			247
27	1,201			313
28	927	575		212
29	936		72	200
30	1,223			215
31	1,132		40	75

Closing Inventory, September 30 = $6,250.00

FIGURE 4–6 Inventory Data—Terrace Garden Restaurant

Date	Sales	Storeroom Purchases	Direct Purchases	Storeroom Issues
Oct. 1	$ 650	$ 500	$ 50	$150
2	675	650	25	275
3	1,000	800	40	110
4	1,500	800	100	200
5	650			200
6	1,525			420
7	1,575	500	150	295
8	1,800	1,215	200	323
9	1,286	415	327	498
10	1,303	800	283	375
11	1,981	356	198	323
12	1,141			379
13	996			582
14	1,507	183	195	681
15	1,621	1,500	155	610
16	1,692	450	152	415
17	1,775	375	249	390
18	2,226	400	157	675
19	3,086			805
20	1,002			370
21	1,628	795	185	380
22	1,501	900	100	500
23	1,634	800	200	395
24	1,757	160		330
25	2,362		501	285
26	3,220			647
27	1,501			613
28	927	75		312
29	1,936		172	500
30	2,223		200	515
31	3,132		340	275

Closing Inventory, September 30 = $1,500.00

CHECK YOUR UNDERSTANDING

1. Close out all columns and prove the report weekly and at the end of the month.
2. What is the rate of inventory turnover?

3. What days are Sundays?

4. What day of the week, on average, has the highest sales?

5. Analyze each week. What do you see happening?

Week 1 _____

_____

_____

_____

Week 2 _____

_____

_____

_____

Week 3 _____

_____

_____

Week 4 _____

_____

_____

_____

6. Write a short evaluation of this operation. Should the owners keep it open?

_____

_____

_____

_____

_____

_____

CRITICAL THINKING QUESTIONS

1. Compare the inventory turnover rates of the Red Woodpecker Grill and the Terrace Garden Restaurant. Explain each operation's numbers and indicate which number you would prefer.

_____

_____

_____

_____

2. Why is there such a difference in beginning inventory between the Red Woodpecker Grill and the Terrace Garden Restaurant?

_____

_____

_____

_____

3. Why is there such a difference in ending inventory between the Red Woodpecker Grill and the Terrace Garden Restaurant?

_____

_____

_____

_____

4. If you owned the Red Woodpecker Grill or the Terrace Garden Restaurant, which beginning inventory and ending inventory numbers would you prefer?

_____

_____

_____

_____

5. Describe how the Red Woodpecker Grill and the Terrace Garden Restaurant manipulate their purchases and issues. Would you be content with running either operation?

_____

_____

_____

_____

_____

_____

MULTIUNIT OPERATIONS AND CUMULATIVE CONTROL FORMS

■ OBJECTIVES

After completing Lesson 5, you should be able to:

1. Define the term *multiunit* and give examples.

2. Explain the concept of adjustments, including transfers, credits, and general adjustments.

3. Work with various formulas involved in calculating the daily cumulative report.

4. Distinguish between actual/reported and estimated costs.

5. Calculate estimated cost of the main unit.

6. Calculate true cost of the main unit.

■ KEY TERMS

Multiunit	Employee meals
Commissary operations	Officers (managers) meals
Satellite operations	Steward sales
Hotel and restaurant operations	Transfer from restaurant to bar
Restaurant operation	Transfer from bar to restaurant
Adjustments	Credits—spoilage
Plus and minus adjustments	Daily cumulative reports
Sales of grease	

■ CONCEPT REVIEW

The term ***multiunit*** is used to refer to any operation that has *more than one* income-generating facility and *more than one* cost-generating facility. Keep in mind that it must have an income unit and a cost unit.

MULTIUNIT OPERATIONS

There are several examples of typical multiunit operations. In ***commissary operations*** the product is made at one location and distributed to different outlets. An example of a commissary operation would be a toll road operation. The food is purchased and prepared at one location and distributed to several other sites on the toll road.

 Satellite operations, a variation of commissary operations, are often used in school or industrial foodservice situations. Purchasing is centralized for different sales/preparation locations. Figure 5–1 is a diagram of a satellite operation. Keep in mind that, in a satellite operation, the costs are incurred at the production unit. Costs are then appropriated to each school, which generates sales at its own location.

 Hotel and restaurant operations are microcosms of commissary or satellite operations. In a hotel, all of the food is usually delivered to one major location and is then prepared in a central kitchen and distributed to smaller warming kitchens or other facilities that can produce revenues (banquet sales, dining sales, cocktail lounge sales). Restaurant operations function in the same manner as a hotel, offering dining room sales, take-out sales, catering sales, and banquet sales.

CONTROLLING MULTIUNIT OPERATIONS

To control (gather information) in multiunit operations, the controller needs data on the following:

Sale income of distribution, by unit;

Total income or sales;

Gross food cost (direct purchases + storeroom issues);

Adjustment to the total operation;

Net food cost (actual cost to the units);

Cost percentages;

Unit percentages.

■ **Hint** _____

Notice that the main categories are the same as in the income statement in Lesson 1–1.

FIGURE 5–1 Satellite Operation

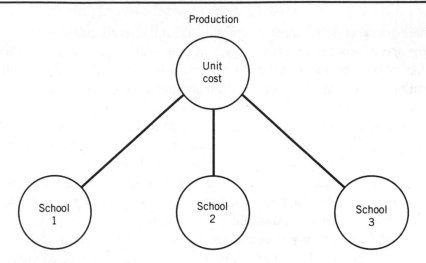

Adjustments

A new concept that needs to be discussed is *adjustments*—changes in the income or expense originally recorded. Many adjustments can take place in a foodservice establishment. An example of an adjustment would be employee meals. The goal of multiunit control is finding the *net* food cost. This is done by month-end adjustments. In general, anything that adds to cost is a positive (+) adjustment; anything that subtracts from cost is a negative (–) adjustment. In an accounting sense, for every addition there must be a subtraction, and for every subtraction there must be an addition.

There are three basic types of adjustments:

1. Transfers from unit to unit; examples of direct transfers would be bar 1 to bar 2 or restaurant to bar.
2. *Credits:*
   Returns to steward of unused items;
   Returns to inventory;
   Credits given by steward;
   Spoilage.
3. *General* (an adjustment to the entire operation):
   Sales of grease;
   Employee meals;
   Officers' (managers') meals
   Steward sales

These adjustments can be made on a daily basis for all items except inventory averages or shortages, which will be discovered when monthly inventories are taken. (Gross food cost plus or minus the adjustments listed will equal the net food cost or cost of food sold.)

The items in the General category of adjustments are explained as follows:

- Plus and minus adjustments. You add or subtract an adjustment from the food cost because you are not selling this food to customers for a profit. Therefore, you only want to calculate the *true* cost of the food in order to come up with the true food cost percent, based on the sales or markup you have decided to make on the menu.

- Sale of grease. This refers to the sale, to rending companies, of animal fat and grease from frying. You are allowed to store the grease outside in drums, which are normally picked up once a month. The grease will be converted to soap or perfumes. Rending companies pay you by the pound, which reduces the cost to you for the fat or grease you buy. Rending cost is deducted from the food cost.

- Employee meals. The meals you provide to your employees are deducted from the food cost.

- Officers' (managers') meals. This amount reflects the costs managers accrue when they entertain guests and pick up the meal check as a cost of promoting the business. Because you are not making a profit from these meals, you deduct this amount from the food cost to find the true food cost percent. This category is sometimes treated in another way. It is recorded and, at the end of the month, the business writes a check to itself for a certain percentage of the overall cost; in effect, it is writing a check for just the raw cost of entertaining. This allows the business to deduct this amount on its tax return as a cost of doing business. For example, if the total value is $1,000.00, then a check is written for a desired food cost percent—say, 40%. The check is made out for $400.00, which would be the true cost without making a profit.

- Steward sales. This entry refers to the sale of food to staff or friends at cost, without any profit. To illustrate, imagine that a quart of milk in a restaurant sells for $4.00: $1.00 for each 8 ounces, and therefore a price of $4.00 per quart. This is really expensive; a gallon of milk in the grocery store is $2.50. Someone had an emergency and you didn't want to take advantage of the situation, so you sold the quart of milk for $1.09. This did not yield a profit; therefore, it is deducted from the food cost because no profit was made on this item.

Transfers

- Transfer from restaurant to bar. This term refers to transferring food such as oranges, limes, or cherries from the retaurant to the bar. The cost is deducted from the restaurant's food cost and added to the bar's beverage costs (which raises the cost of the beverages' ingredients used in preparing the drinks).

- Transfer from bar to restaurant. This refers to the transfer of liquor to the kitchen, for sauces, flambé presentation, and so on, which adds to the cost of preparing the food and reduces the cost of liquor at the bar.

Credits—Spoilage

This term reflects a deduction from the food cost in the event that a refrigerator was accidentally turned off, or the area suffered a prolonged power failure or flood, and all the food had to be discarded. This food cannot be sold; therefore, no profit can be derived, so the amount is deducted from the food cost.

DAILY CUMULATIVE REPORT

Spreadsheet Information

The spreadsheet used here is different from those in past lessons, in that you are given the first column of numbers. The first column reflects the to-date figures from the previous day, October 26th. You are to enter the numbers for the daily cumulative report for October 27th. This assignment should help you understand the formulas used for the daily cumulative report. Sometimes, when you enter the numbers, the calculation is straightforward and it adds down or subtracts, to get a subtotal. Sometimes, you can be working backward, which will indicate that you know the makeup of the formulas. For example, Figure 5–2 gives you information in four sales areas:

Banquet sales	$ 9,782
Dining room sales	10,453
Cocktail lounge sales	4,620
Coffee shop sales	?
Total sales	$26,212

FIGURE 5–2   Sample Incomplete Daily Cumulative Report

```
FOODSFRVICE COST CONTROL USING MICROSOFT EXCEL                    PG 1 OF 1
STUDENT NAME:          {NAME}              RESTAURANT NAME:
DATE:                  {DATE}              {RESTAURANT NAME}
================================================================================
                        DAILY CUMULATIVE REPORT
--------------------------------------  ----------------  ----------------  ----------------  ----------------  ----------------
                                              A
--------------------------------------  ----------------
        DEPARTMENT                        TO DATE

--------------------------------------  ----------------
BANQUET SALES                            9,782.00
DINING ROOM SALES                       10,453.00      24,855.00    Subtotal of given sales
COCKTAIL LOUNGE SALES                    4,620.00
COFFEE SHOP SALES                            0.00
TOTAL SALES                             26,212.00      26,212.00    Total Sales
DIRECT PURCHASES                             0.00     –24,855.00    Subtotal of given sales
STOREROOM ISSUES                             0.00     -----------
GROSS COST                                   0.00     $ 1,375.00    Coffee Shop Sales
```

Given all but one figure, how would you find the dollar amount of the missing unit (coffee shop sales)? Add all the sales figures that are given, and subtract this subtotal from the total sales. The result is the dollar figure for the unit that is missing.

When you add direct purchases and storeroom issues, the total will equal the gross cost. If the gross cost and direct purchases are given, you would subtract the direct purchases from the gross cost to determine the storeroom issues. The formula of gross cost minus direct purchases equals storeroom issues is shown in Figure 5–3.

To determine net cost, subtract *all* your adjustment(s) from gross cost. (The example shows only *one* adjustment. In a true working situation, you may have several.) The formula of gross cost minus adjustments equals net cost is shown in Figure 5–4.

When you are working in the area of net cost, remember that net cost equals the net cost proof. On your computer, the net cost proof line has been added to serve as a double-check. If you have entered the costs and the net cost proof is *less than* the net cost, the difference will be the missing cost of the unit cost. You need to insert that difference in the proper unit cost. Figure 5–5 shows the computation of the net cost proof. Keep these rules in mind:

■ Net cost equals all unit costs.
■ Net cost equals net cost proof.

FIGURE 5–3   Daily Cumulative Report—Determining Storeroom Issues

FOODSERVICE COST CONTROL USING MICROSOFT EXCEL   PG 1 OF 1
STUDENT NAME: {NAME}   RESTAURANT NAME:
DATE: {DATE}   {RESTAURANT NAME}

==

DAILY CUMULATIVE REPORT

------------------------------------ --------------- --------------- --------------- --------------- ---------------

                                             A

------------------------------------ ---------------

               DEPARTMENT   TO DATE

------------------------------------ ---------------

DEPARTMENT	TO DATE		
BANQUET SALES	0.00		
DINING ROOM SALES	0.00		
COCKTAIL LOUNGE SALES	0.00		
COFFEE SHOP SALES	0.00		
TOTAL SALES	0.00		
DIRECT PURCHASES	786.00		
STOREROOM ISSUES	0.00		
GROSS COST	7,373.00	7,373.00	Gross Cost
EMPLOYEE'S MEALS	0.00	– 786.00	Direct Purchases
NET COST	0.00	-----------	
BANQUET COST	0.00	$ 6,587.00	Storeroom Issues
DINING ROOM COST	0.00		

FIGURE 5–4   Daily Cumulative Report-Determining Net Cost

FOODSERVICE COST CONTROL USING MICROSOFT EXCEL   PG 1 OF 1
STUDENT NAME: {NAME}   RESTAURANT NAME:
DATE: {DATE}   {RESTAURANT NAME}

==

DAILY CUMULATIVE REPORT

------------------------------------ --------------- --------------- --------------- --------------- ---------------

                                             A

------------------------------------ ---------------

               DEPARTMENT   TO DATE

------------------------------------ ---------------

DEPARTMENT	TO DATE		
BANQUET SALES	0.00		
DINING ROOM SALES	0.00		
COCKTAIL LOUNGE SALES	0.00		
COFFEE SHOP SALES	0.00		
TOTAL SALES	0.00		
DIRECT PURCHASES	0.00		
STOREROOM ISSUES	0.00		
GROSS COST	7,373.00	7,373.00	Gross Cost
EMPLOYEE'S MEALS	233.00	– 233.00	Adjustments
NET COST	0.00	-----------	
BANQUET COST	0.00	$ 7,140.00	Net Cost
DINING ROOM COST	0.00		

Calculating Percentage

At the end of the Daily Cumulative Report there are blank spaces for percentages. You will use the appropriate cost divided by sales to come up with the correct percentages.

FIGURE 5–5   Daily Cumulative Report Net Cost Proof Feature

```
FOODSERVICE COST CONTROL USING MICROSOFT EXCEL                    PG 1 OF 1
STUDENT NAME:   {NAME}                RESTAURANT NAME:
DATE:           {DATE}                {RESTAURANT NAME}
===============================================================================
                          DAILY CUMULATIVE REPORT
----------------------------------  --------------  --------------  --------------  --------------  --------------
                                           A

----------------------------------  ---------------
            DEPARTMENT                 TO DATE

----------------------------------  ---------------
BANQUET SALES                           0.00
DINING ROOM SALES                       0.00
COCKTAIL LOUNGE SALES                   0.00
COFFEE SHOP SALES                       0.00
TOTAL SALES                             0.00
DIRECT PURCHASES                        0.00
STOREROOM ISSUES                        0.00
GROSS COST                              0.00
EMPLOYEE'S MEALS                        0.00
NET COST                             7,140.00       2,807.00      Banquet Cost
BANQUET COST                         2,807.00       3,086.00      Dining Room Cost
DINING ROOM COST                     3,086.00       1,043.00      Cocktail Lounge Cost
COCKTAIL LOUNGE COST                 1,043.00       + 204.00      Coffee Shop Cost
COFFEE SHOP COST                       204.00       -----------
NET COST PROOF                          0.00        7,140.00      Net Cost Proof = Net Cost
```

■ Hint

Keep in mind that when you calculate these percentages, they should reflect, to some degree, (1) some average industry numbers related to the units or (2) the percentages found in the income statement (see Lesson 1). The formulas you need are:

$$\text{Gross cost percent} = \frac{\text{Gross cost}}{\text{Total sales}}$$

$$\text{Net cost percent} = \frac{\text{Net cost}}{\text{Total sales}}$$

$$\text{Unit cost percent} = \frac{\text{Unit cost}}{\text{Unit sales}}$$

MULTIUNIT END-OF-MONTH ADJUSTMENT

The Multiunit end-of-month adjustment form and worksheet is shown in Figure 5–6. This section will help you determine the true cost of the main unit when there are many units within the operation.

FIGURE 5–6 Multiunit End-of-Month Adjustment Form and Worksheet

FOODSERVICE COST CONTROL USING MICROSOFT EXCEL   PG 1 OF 1
STUDENT NAME: {NAME}   RESTAURANT NAME:
DATE: {DATE}   {RESTAURANT NAME}

MONTH END ADJUSTMENT COSTS

	A	B	C	D	E
	School A	School B	School C	School D	School E
STOREROOM ISSUES	1,258.00	0.00	9,543.00	8,541.00	2,555.00
DIRECT PURCHASES	302.00	127.00	356.00	478.00	132.00
TOTALS	1,560.00	127.00	9,899.00	9,019.00	2,687.00
SALES $	5,650.00	23,460.00	0.00	28,016.00	9,111.00
FOOD COST PERCENT %	27.6106%	0.5413%	0.0000%	32.1923%	29.4918%

FORMULAS & WORK		TRUE KNOWN UNIT(S):	ESTIMATED UNIT(S):
STOREROOM PURCHASES	20,892.00	1,560.00	9,899.00
+ DIRECT PURCHASES	1,395.00	9,019.00	127.00
= TOTAL REPORTED AVAIL	22,287.00	2,687.00	0.00
+ OPENING INVENTORY	17,414.00	0.00	0.00
= AVAILABLE INVENTORY	39,701.00	0.00	0.00
– CLOSING INVENTORY	13,073.00		
= GROSS FOOD COST	26,628.00	13,266.00	10,026.00
– FOOD TO BAR	167.00		
+ BEVERAGE TO KITCHEN	86.00		
– SALE OF GREASE	206.00		
– OFFICER MEALS	244.00		
– STEWARD SALES	979.00		
– EMPLOYEE MEALS	2,379.00		
= ADJUSTED NET COST	22,739.00	ESTIMATED FOOD COST % 42.7365%	
– KNOWN UNITS (TRUE)	13,266.00	TRUE FOOD COST % 40.3793%	
= TRUE COST OF MAIN UNIT	9,473.00	DIFFERENCE BETWEEN ESTIMATED & TRUE 553.00	

You are given a fact sheet on the operation, which allows you to enter the necessary numbers in the appropriate categories on the spreadsheet. The fact sheet gives you amounts for categories that you should be familiar with after completing the daily cumulative report, learning how to determine gross food cost by making plus or minus adjustments to food cost, and learning what makes up the true cost of the main unit.

It is very important to be sure that you are entering the proper amounts in the proper places on the spreadsheets. Your figures are for *specific dates* that are appropriate for the calculation for the month-end figures. You will deal with inventory figures and storeroom purchases. For example, if you are calculating for the month ending February 19XX, you may be given the following numbers (see Figure 5–6):

Ending inventory January 31, 19XX $17,414.00

Storeroom purchases for the month of February 19XX $20,892.00

Actual figures, sometimes indicated with (*), and reported figures, sometimes indicated with (**), *cannot be doubted.* In all instances, the actual and reported figures are *true* figures. The only number that can be questionable is a number that is reported as *estimated* (Est).

■ **Hint** _____

The top part of the form shows the costs for all the units of a multiunit foodservice establishment. Storeroom issues and direct purchases, added together, make up the total cost of the unit. (You could deduct adjustments, but this example has no individual adjustments that affect a unit. However, keep in mind that there could be individual adjustments to individual units.)

After completing the cost of a unit, it would be wise to apply sales to cost and to calculate the food cost percent for the unit. Remember that when you are dealing with multiunits, all units must have a cost and all units must have sales. If a unit does not have one of these elements, you may have to merge two or more units. To determine whether a merger might work, you would have to add cost or sales, recalculate the food cost percent, and see whether the percent is within industry standards. Also, remember to look for the actual, reported, and estimated amounts. All actual numbers would make a unit true. Any number with an estimated amount would be only an estimate and would probably indicate that the unit is not a true unit. This would affect how you would determine the actual calculation of the true main unit. (See Figure 5–6.)

Calculating the True Cost of the Main Unit

In this section, you will learn to use the formulas needed to calculate the true cost of the main unit. For actual operational figures, all numbers are actual and must be true numbers. This is the formula (see Figure 5–6):

Storeroom purchases

    + Direct purchases

    = Total purchases for the period(total reported available)

+ Opening inventory (inventory from the closing day of the previous period, or inventory for the first day of the new period)

= Total available (available inventory)

– Closing inventory (actual counting of physical inventory: Price × Quantity = Total)

= Gross food cost (cost of product consumed)

+ General Adjustments

= Net cost (cost of product sold)

   or Adjusted net cost

   or True net cost of the entire multiunit

– Known unit cost (cost of true known units)

= True cost of the main unit

■ **Hint** _____

Plus or minus adjustments are specific to the entire operation. There cannot be a direct plus or minus adjustment to an individual unit of a multiunit organization.

The figure you arrive at is the true cost of the main unit and includes the food that leaves the main unit for the purpose of receiving, storing, and issuing to other units that don't have a control person receiving, storing, or issuing food from a central location.

Calculating the Estimated Cost of the Main Unit

When looking at the multiunit month-end adjustment cost worksheet (Figure 5–6), keep in mind that each unit must have cost *and* sales. If a unit has true costs and sales, it is then a true known unit. A unit can stand by itself if it has cost and sales. If you apply the standard basic food cost percent formula (cost divided by sales equals percent) and the percentage is realistic for a typical food operation, then the unit can be determined as a true known unit. If a unit has an estimated figure, you should be alerted that this is probably the known unit for which you are trying to find the true cost. In a real example, the storeroom issuing all the food to other units is always a number that you *estimate* until you actually count the storeroom at the end of the month.

You have to know which unit has the estimated amount. It is also possible that several units could be merged. If you merge two units to get a realistic cost and realistic sales resulting in a good food cost percent, the unit remains true as long as all the amounts are true cost. On the other hand, a unit that has an estimated storeroom issue and a true direct purchase would be estimated and, therefore, not a true unit. If another unit has all true costs but is not in line with an industry food cost percentage, it is possible that this unit could be merged with the estimated unit. Together, the two units, one true and the other estimated, would be the estimated main unit that you are trying to determine. If you then apply sales to this estimated unit, and the food cost percentage is in line for a main unit, you can feel confident that you have a match between the estimated unit and the cost of the true main unit.

When you deduct the true cost of each unit from the adjusted net cost, this total will equal, or should be close to, the cost of the estimated unit. (See Figure 5–6.)

When there is a difference between the true cost of the main unit and the estimated unit, this will show the problems associated with issuing from a storeroom. It will point to either a difference in pricing inventory in the main storeroom or a deficiency in the issuing and storeroom aspect of cost control. (See Figure 5–6.)

The true cost of the main unit can be associated with the final number of the storeroom control report in Exercise 4–1. Remember, however, that this number is an *estimated* number and you have basically found out the true cost. There may be a difference between the estimated number and the true cost, and you can determine whether there is a major problem when you calculate the cost percent of the units. If the unit(s) cost percentages are not in accordance with industry percentages, you might have incorrectly calculated the cost of the main unit. From month to month, compare whether all the units have the same basic cost and cost percent.

Again, the top management of a foodservice establishment will look at the overall food cost percent for the entire operation to see whether the organization is profitable.

■ SPREADSHEET OBJECTIVES

Upon completion of Lesson 5, you should be able to:

1. Understand all formulas involved in calculating the daily cumulative report and related percentages.
2. Accurately compile a monthly adjustments form.
3. Calculate and compare the true cost and estimated cost of a main unit.

EXERCISES

Figure 5–7 lists the given figures from the daily cumulative report for October 27 and 28, and Figure 5–8 shows the end-of-month adjustments for the Red Woodpecker Grill. Figures 5–9 and 5–10 give the same information for the Terrace Garden Restaurant. Use these figures to complete the question sections at the end of the chapter. Work with either the Red Woodpecker Grill or the Terrace Garden Restaurant information.

FIGURE 5–7   Daily Cumulative Report, Input Figures—Red Woodpecker Grill

Red Woodpecker Grill
Daily Cumulative Report
(Input figures from the daily report)

OCT 27	
Total Receipts	$3,349.00
Dining Room—Cash and Charges	1,288.00
Coffee Shop Cash	996.00
Cocktail Lounge Cash	475.00
Storeroom Requisitions	872.00
Direct Purchases	33.00
Employees' Meals @ $.50 ea. (32)	16.00
Dining Room Cost	396.00
Bar Cost	187.00
Coffee Shop Cost	146.00
Banquet Cost	160.00
OCT 28	
SALES REPORT	
Banquet	$900.00
Dining Room	1,385.00
Cocktail Lounge	560.00
Coffee Shop	823.00
COST REPORT	
Dining Room	402.00
Cocktail Lounge	188.00
Coffee Shop	232.00
EMPLOYEES' MEALS @ $.50 ea. (28)	14.00
DIRECT PURCHASES	48.00
GROSS COST	1,016.00

FIGURE 5–8 End-of-Month Adjustments—Red Woodpecker Grill

Red Woodpecker Grill
End-of-Month Adjustments

The following figures have been compiled for the month of April.

Sales:	Banquet Sales	$10,200*
	Dining Room Sales	27,600*
	Coffee Shop Sales	6,750*
	Cocktail Lounge Sales	8,740*
Direct Purchases to:		
	Banquet Room	185.00*
	Dining Room	245.00*
	Kitchen	376.00*
	Coffee Shop	50.00*
	Bar	100.00*
Storeroom Issues for:		
	Banquet Kitchen	3,282.00**
	Main Kitchen	(Estimated) 10,453.00
	Coffee Shop	2,010.00**
	Bar	2,500.00**
Employees' Meals		2,070.00**
Food to Bar		1,054.00**
Officers' Meals		127.00**
Beverage to Kitchen		427.00**
Sale of Grease		204.00**
Steward's Sales		112.00**
Inventory, April 1		10,345.00*
Inventory, April 30		11,011.00*
Storeroom Purchases for the Month		21,607.00*

  * Actual figures.
** Report figures.

CHECK YOUR UNDERSTANDING

1. A. Answer only if you worked on the Red Woodpecker Grill information. How do you calculate the Banquet Sales for October 27?

   _____

   _____

   B. Answer only if you worked on the Terrace Garden Restaurant information. How do you calculate the Coffee Shop Sales for October 27?

   _____

   _____

FIGURE 5–9   Daily Cumulative Report, Input Figures—Terrace Garden Restaurant

Terrace Garden Restaurant
Daily Cumulative Report
(Input figures from the daily report)

OCT 27

Total Receipts	$4,367.00
Dining Room—Cash and Charges	1,401.00
Banquet Room Cash	1,219.00
Cocktail Lounge Cash	982.00
Storeroom Requisitions	971.00
Direct Purchases	96.00
Employees' Meals @ $.50 ea. (34)	17.00
Dining Room Cost	434.00
Bar Cost	390.00
Coffee Shop Cost	98.00
Banquet Cost	128.00

OCT 28

SALES REPORT	
Banquet	$ 962.00
Dining Room	1,538.00
Cocktail Lounge	610.00
Coffee Shop	901.00
COST REPORT	
Dining Room	446.00
Cocktail Lounge	201.00
Banquet Room	202.00
EMPLOYEES' MEALS @ $.50 ea. (30)	15.00
STOREROOM ISSUES	1,021.00
GROSS COST	1,097.00

2. For the restaurant you worked on, how do you calculate gross cost for October 27?

_____

_____

_____

_____

_____

What costs make up the net cost for October 27?

_____

_____

_____

_____

_____

FIGURE 5–10   End-of-Month Adjustments—Terrace Garden Restaurant

Terrace Garden Restaurant
End-of-Month Adjustments

The following figures have been compiled for the month of April.

Sales:	Banquet Sales	$25,100.00*
	Dining Room Sales	28,760.00*
	Coffee Shop Sales	7,650 00*
	Cocktail Lounge Sales	9,120.00*
Direct Purchases to:		
	Banquet Room	108.00*
	Dining Room	485 00*
	Kitchen	387.00*
	Coffee Shop	299.00*
	Cocktail Lounge	125.00*
Storeroom Issues for:		
	Dining Room	9,193.00**
	Main Kitchen	(Estimated) 10,543.00
	Coffee Shop	2,065.00**
	Cocktail Lounge	2,519.00**
Employees' Meals		2,191.00**
Food to Bar		872.00**
Officers' Meals		145.00**
Beverage to Kitchen		396.00**
Sale of Grease		201.00**
Steward's Sales		127.00**
Inventory, April 1		16,423.00*
Inventory, April 30		12,211.00*
Storeroom Purchases for the Month		22,746.00*

  * Actual figures.
** Reported figures.

3. What are the guidelines for calculating food cost percentages in a multiunit operation for the following categories?

Banquet _____

Dining Room _____

Cocktail Lounge _____

Coffee Shop _____

The following questions involve end-of-month adjustments for the restaurant you worked on.

4. Prepare the complete month-end worksheet and then fill in the blanks below. **Carry all decimals to four places.**

    A. Total Purchases for the Month $ _____

    B. Inventory on Hand $ _____

    C. True Gross Cost $ _____

    D. True Net Cost $ _____

       True Net Cost Percent   _____ %

    E. True Net Banquet Cost $ _____

       True Net Banquet Percent   _____ %

    F. True Net Dining Room Cost $ _____

       True Net Dining Room Percent   _____ %

    G. True Net Coffee Shop Cost $ _____

       True Net Coffee Shop Percent   _____ %

    H. True Net Cocktail Lounge Cost $ _____

       True Net Cocktail Lounge Percent   _____ %

    I. Answer only if you worked on the Red Woodpecker Grill: What is the **difference** between the estimated dining room cost and the actual dining room cost?
       $ _____

    J. Answer only if you worked on the Terrace Garden Restaurant: What is the **difference** between the estimated banquet room cost and the actual banquet room cost?
       $ _____

    K. What is the rate of inventory turnover?   _____ %

CRITICAL THINKING QUESTIONS

1. What comprises a multiunit operation?

    _____

    _____

    _____

2. Why is gross cost expressed as an estimate?

    _____

    _____

    _____

3. Why must the net cost and net cost proof be equal?

_____

_____

_____

4. For the Red Woodpecker Grill (R.W.G.) or Terrace Garden Restaurant (T.G.R.), indicate whether the following percentages are acceptable.

	R.W.G.	T.G.R.		R.W.G.	T.G.R.
Gross Cost	_____%	_____%	Coffee Shop	_____%	_____%
Net Cost	_____%	_____%	Dining Room	_____%	_____%
Banquet	_____%	_____%	Cocktail Lounge	_____%	_____%

5. What adjustments can be made to a daily cumulative report? Are these plus changes or minus changes?

_____

_____

_____

_____

6. What two items make up a cost for a unit?

_____

_____

_____

_____

7. Can adjustments be made to individual units? If yes, list two examples, indicating whether they are plus or minus adjustments.

_____

_____

_____

_____

8. What comprises a "true" unit?

_____

_____

_____

_____

9. What comprises a unit that is not "true"?

   _____

   _____

   _____

   _____

10. What is the formula for finding the true cost of the main unit?

    _____

    _____

    _____

11. Compare the cost percentages for all of the following units between the Red Wood-pecker Grill and the Terrace Garden Restaurant. Which units are in line with your understanding of industry percentages?

	R.W.G.	T.G.R.		R.W.G.	T.G.R.
Gross Cost	_____%	_____%	Coffee Shop	_____%	_____%
Net Cost	_____%	_____%	Dining Room	_____%	_____%

    Circle any percentages that should be brought to management's attention.

12. How would you initially address inventory on hand for the Red Woodpecker Grill and the Terrace Garden Restaurant? Which operation has a dollar figure of inventory on hand that is justifiable to management?

    _____

    _____

    _____

    _____

    _____

    _____

    _____

13. Defend the rates of inventory for the Red Woodpecker Grill and the Terrace Garden Restaurant. Can either one be justified for a better effect?

    _____

    _____

    _____

    _____

    _____

    _____

    _____

    _____

BUTCHER'S YIELD TEST/COOKING LOSS TEST

■ **OBJECTIVES**

Upon completing Lesson 6, you should be able to:

1. Define the following terms:
   Butcher's yield test
      A.R (as purchased)
      E.R (edible portion)
      O.P. (oven prepared)
2. Perform butcher's yield tests for raw portion cost and cooked portion cost.
3. Calculate the cost implications of purchasing meat, fish, or poultry already cut to specification versus cutting after arrival at the restaurant.

■ **KEY TERMS**

Butchers Yield Test $_____ per _____
   A. P. (as purchased)   Purveyor
   E. P. (edible portion)   Weight of each item
Butcher's Yield Test Card Terms   Ratio of total weight
   Item   Value per pound
   Grade   Total value
   Date   Cost of each pound (lb) and
   Pieces   ounce (oz)
   Weight   Portion part
   Average weight   Cost factor per pound (lb)
   Total cost in $ Oven prepared

■ **CONCEPT REVIEW**

It is important to know that when you discuss the butcher's yield test, you are dealing primarily with food products in the categories of meat, fish, and poultry. A ***butcher's yield test*** determines prices for items that are purchased in bulk and then sold in portions. Most portions of food sold to consumers are not in excess of 14 ounces. There are exceptions in specialty meat, fish, or poultry theme restaurants that try to capture the customer by serving giant-size portions as a gimmick. The terms A.P. (as purchased) and E.P. (edible portion) must be understood. A piece of meat as purchased (A.P.) is trimmed and cut into serving pieces and by-products, for stock and sausages, for example. The end result is the edible portion (E.P.) of the amount purchased.

BUTCHER'S YIELD TEST

The underlying purpose of the butcher's yield test is to determine the cost per portion sold. Foodservice establishments pay the same price for each and every pound, even though, after butchering, the resulting parts may have entirely different values. For example, a side of beef, a standard bulk order item, contains fat, bone, and meat. These parts have different uses and different values, but the purchase price per pound is the same. More details regarding dollars and formulas will be given later in this lesson.

When doing a butcher's yield test, approach and timing must be considered; arithmetical efficiency alone is not enough. The actual test work must be done with care, and the accuracy of the employees who help perform the test is crucial. It is not advisable to barge in on people performing the butcher's yield test and demand instant compliance to a formula associated with the test. Arranging a suitable time to do a butcher's yield test is more likely to ensure cooperation and reduce the likelihood of employee hostility. With this approach, there is a better chance that a successful and accurate butcher's yield test will be performed.

The butcher's yield test also helps in deciding whether to buy a bulk piece that includes the salable item or only a quantity of the salable item. The goal of the test is to determine the cost per pound of the salable pieces for which you might buy and cut up a bulk piece. Which would result in greater savings: purchasing from a purveyor a quantity of an item cut to your specifications *or* a bulk piece from which you cut the item yourself?

There are two types of butcher's yield tests: one results in the raw portion cost, and one results in the cooked portion cost. Both of these tests will be examined in this lesson.

Formulas for Butcher's Yield Test

Before beginning, study the following formulas for the butcher's yield test:

1. Total weight of original piece
   − Secondary weight of trimmed pieces
   = Weight of the primary piece

2. $\dfrac{\text{Individual weight of secondary pieces}}{\text{Total weight of bulk pieces}}$ = Ratio to total weight

3. Total cost of bulk piece
   − Value of secondary pieces
   = Value of primary piece

4. $\dfrac{\text{Value of primary piece}}{\text{Total weight of primary piece}}$ = Cost per salable pound of primary piece

5. $\dfrac{\text{Value of primary piece}}{\text{Total number of portions}}$ = Cost per portion

6. $\dfrac{\text{Cost per salable pound}}{\text{Dealers' price per pound}}$ = Cost factor per pound of original wholesale piece

7. Cost factor per pound
   × (New) Dealers' price of a whole piece
   = Cost per salable pound

8. Cost per salable pound
   × Decimal equivalent per portion
   = Cost per portion

9. Cost factor per pound
   × Decimal equivalent per portion
   = Cost factor per portion

10. Cost factor per portion
    × (New) Dealers' price of a whole piece
    = New portion cost

Butcher's Yield Test Card Terms

By looking at the format of the butcher's yield test card (Figure 6–1), you can begin to learn how to enter the heading information. Reading horizontally on each line, this is what you need to know:

■ Item refers to the name of the article being purchased in bulk form. Example: New York Sirloin #173; or Red Snapper (whole).

■ Grade is established according to U. S. Government standards. Some of the food categories will have certain grade levels. Example: Meat = prime or choice.

■ Date refers to the day the item was purchased.

FIGURE 6-1 Butcher's Yield Test—Sample Form

YIELD TEST CARD

ITEM _____ GRADE _____ DATE _____

PIECES _____ WEIGHT _____ LBS _____ OZ. AVERAGE WT. _____ LBS. _____ OZ.

TOTAL COST $ _____ AT $ _____ PER _____ PURVEYOR _____

BREAKDOWN	NO.	WEIGHT		RATIO TO TOTAL WEIGHT	VALUE PER POUND	TOTAL VALUE	COST OF EACH		PORTION		COST FACTOR PER	
		LB.	OZ.				LB.	OZ.	SIZE	VALUE	LB.	PORTION
				%							%	%
TOTAL												

$$\text{COST FACTOR PER LB. OR PORTION} = \frac{\text{READY-TO-EAT VALUE PER LB. OR PORTION}}{\text{PURCHASE PRICE PER LB.}}$$

To find value of item at a new market price, multiply new price by the cost factor.

126

- Pieces refers to number of items. In most cases, the number is 1.
- Weight (lbs., oz.) refers to the total weight of the item in bulk form. In most cases, this item should exceed at least 1 pound.

■ **Hint** _____

The weight should be recorded by pounds and ounces *and* by pounds and decimal equivalent of ounces. Example: 5 lbs. 4 ozs./5.2500 lbs.

- **Average weight (lbs., oz.)** is eventually filled out by the establishment after determining the total weight of the order for this item. Every item received is weighed and recorded, then the total weight is divided by the number of items to calculate the average weight in pounds and ounces. The average weight, when calculated and recorded over a long period of time, will provide a reference as to whether future orders are within the average weight guidelines for that particular bulk item. A reference source for double-checking average weight is the *National Association of Meat Purveyors (NAMP) Guide*. The *Guide* indicates an average weight for a certain cut of meat. You will then know whether the meat you are buying is smaller or larger than average.
- **Total cost** $ is the total cost of the quantity of the item bought from the purveyor.
- **At $_____ per _____** is the individual cost per unit. Example: Meat, fish, and poultry are sold at a dollar amount per pound.
- **Purveyor** refers to the name of the vendor from whom you purchased the food items.

Figure 6–2 shows the heading information for purchase of a bulk piece of meat. Next, continue to the main part of the butcher's yield test card. The first column of the card is called the **breakdown**. The breakdown list starts with items that will be referred to as *secondary pieces*—by-products of the whole piece, excluding the primary pieces for which you bought the bulk item. For example, suppose the bulk item you have bought is a beef short loin, and the item you want is New York Strip Steak (the primary piece). The breakdown column, as shown in Figure 6–3, lists the by-products (fat and bones), then the secondary pieces (stew meat, ground meat, and filet), and, finally, the primary piece—"NY Strip."

The person dividing the whole bulk item separates the pieces into categories and determines what can be used. The weight of the usable items is recorded for the breakdown.

Weight of each item refers to the weight of the separated portions of the secondary and primary pieces. When the weight column is added up,

FIGURE 6-2 Butcher's Yield Test—Heading Information

YIELD TEST CARD

ITEM ___#173 Short Loin___   GRADE ___Choice___   DATE ___4-19-93___

PIECES ___1___   WEIGHT ___18___ LBS ___4___ OZ.   AVERAGE WT. ___19___ LBS. ___0___ OZ.

TOTAL COST $ ___63.6925___ AT $ ___3.49___ PER ___LB___   PURVEYOR ___R.U. DUNN MEATS___

BREAKDOWN	NO.	WEIGHT		RATIO TO TOTAL WEIGHT	VALUE PER POUND	TOTAL VALUE	COST OF EACH		PORTION			COST FACTOR PER	
		LB.	OZ.				LB.	OZ.	SIZE	VALUE		LB.	PORTION
				%								%	%
TOTAL													

COST FACTOR =   READY-TO-EAT VALUE PER LB. OR PORTION
PER LB. OR PORTION   PURCHASE PRICE PER LB.

To find value of item at a new market price, multiply new price by the cost factor.

FIGURE 6-3 Butcher's Yield Test—Breakdown and Weight

YIELD TEST CARD

ITEM _____ #173 Short Loin _____ GRADE _____ Choice _____ DATE _____ 4-19-93 _____

PIECES _____ 1 _____ WEIGHT _____ 18 _____ LBS _____ 4 _____ OZ. AVERAGE WT. _____ 19 _____ LBS. _____ 0 _____ OZ.

TOTAL COST $ _____ 63.6925 _____ AT $ _____ 3.49 _____ PER _____ LB _____ PURVEYOR _____ R.U. DUNN MEATS _____

BREAKDOWN	NO.	WEIGHT		RATIO TO TOTAL WEIGHT	VALUE PER POUND	TOTAL VALUE	COST OF EACH		PORTION			COST FACTOR PER	
		LB.	OZ.	%			LB.	OZ.	SIZE	VALUE		LB.	PORTION
												%	%
Fat		3	4										
Bones		4	2										
Stew Meat		2	3										
Ground Meat 80/20		1	14										
Filet		1	5										
Loss in cutting			5										
Subtotal		13	1										
NY Strip		5	3										
TOTAL		18	4										

COST FACTOR PER LB. OR PORTION $=\dfrac{\text{READY-TO-EAT VALUE PER LB. OR PORTION}}{\text{PURCHASE PRICE PER LB.}}$

To find value of item at a new market price, multiply new price by the cost factor.

129

the total ideally equals the total original weight. There will usually be a small loss in weight after cutting, resulting from fragments left on the cutting board or falling off the table. Therefore, most butcher's yield test cards record a loss in cutting weight between the secondary and the primary weights. Any difference between the secondary and primary weights should be inserted as a loss in cutting. When the secondary weight, primary weight, and difference are added together, they should equal the original total weight.

■ Hint

Weights should be recorded two ways: (1) in pounds and ounces, and (2) also where in pounds decimal weight. Where you can enter both sets of numbers, do so.

Ratio to total weight results from dividing one item's individual weight by the total weight. The end product is the **ratio to total weight percent**. This ratio gives the controller a sense of how the cost of one item compares to the cost of the whole item. The ratio can be used for comparison of other pieces of like items, to see whether the quality is of equal value. This comparison can be good or bad, depending on the overall quality evaluation. Figure 6–4 shows the calculation of ratio to total weight for the item described in Figures 6–2 and 6–3.

Value per pound is an easy column because the values of the secondary pieces are obtained from a purveyor that sells the associated secondary pieces. Another way of stating the value per pound is to give the secondary pieces the current market value—that is, the price they are sold at, by the pound, from a meat distributor. The reason the value per pound is obtained and is crucial to the test is that it gives the price you would have to pay to buy each of the parts separately. The price recorded will ordinarily be its reasonable value. No value per pound for the primary part is entered at this point. The primary part's value is determined after the total values for the secondary parts have been calculated in the next column, the total value column. (See Figure 6–5.) More details will be given in the spreadsheet information portion of this lesson.

Total value is the dollar amount calculated by multiplying the weight times the value per pound of the secondary pieces. The total value of the primary piece is determined by using formula 3 for the butcher's yield test (page 125). More details will be given in the spreadsheet information portion of this lesson.

Cost of each pound (lb) and ounce (oz) is calculated by using the dollar amount in the total value column. (See Figure 6–6.) For finding the

FIGURE 6-4 Butcher's Yield Test—Ratio to Total Weight

YIELD TEST CARD

ITEM ___ #173 Short Loin ___ GRADE ___ Choice ___ DATE ___ 4-19-93

PIECES ___ 1 ___ WEIGHT ___ 18 ___ LBS ___ 4 ___ OZ. AVERAGE WT. ___ 19 ___ LBS. ___ 0 ___ OZ.

TOTAL COST $ ___ 63.6925 ___ AT $ ___ 3.49 ___ PER ___ LB ___ PURVEYOR ___ R.U. DUNN MEATS

BREAKDOWN	NO.	WEIGHT LB.	WEIGHT OZ.	RATIO TO TOTAL WEIGHT	VALUE PER POUND	TOTAL VALUE	COST OF EACH LB.	COST OF EACH OZ.	PORTION SIZE	PORTION VALUE	COST FACTOR PER LB.	COST FACTOR PORTION
Fat		3	4	17.8082%							%	%
Bones		4	2	22.6027								
Stew Meat		2	3	11.9863								
Ground Meat 80/20		1	14	10.2759								
Filet		1	5	7.1917								
Loss in cutting			5	1.7123								
Subtotal		13	1									
NY Strip		5	3	28.4246								
TOTAL		18	4	99.9997								

COST FACTOR = READY-TO-EAT VALUE PER LB. OR PORTION
PER LB. OR PORTION   PURCHASE PRICE PER LB.

To find value of item at a new market price, multiply new price by the cost factor.

131

FIGURE 6–5 Butcher's Yield Test—Value per Pound and Total Value

YIELD TEST CARD

ITEM ____#175 Short Loin____ GRADE ____Choice____ DATE ____4-19-93____

PIECES ___1___ WEIGHT ___18___ LBS ___4___ OZ.   AVERAGE WT. ___19___ LBS. ___0___ OZ.

TOTAL COST $ __63.6925__ AT $ __3.49__ PER __LB__   PURVEYOR ____R.U. DUNN MEATS____

BREAKDOWN	NO.	WEIGHT LB.	OZ.	RATIO TO TOTAL WEIGHT	VALUE PER POUND	TOTAL VALUE		COST OF EACH LB.	OZ.	PORTION SIZE	VALUE	COST FACTOR PER LB. %	PORTION %
Fat		3	4	17.8082%	.83	2	6975						
Bones		4	2	22.6027	.19		7837						
Stew Meat		2	3	11.9863	2.17	4	7468						
Ground Meat 80/20		1	14	10.2739	1.45	2	7187						
Filet		1	5	7.1917	12.94	16	9837						
Loss in cutting			5	1.7123	——	——							
Subtotal		13	1			27	9304						
NY Strip		5	3	28.4246	6.8938	35	7621						
TOTAL		18	4	99.9997	——	63	6925						

COST FACTOR PER LB. OR PORTION = READY-TO-EAT VALUE PER LB. OR PORTION / PURCHASE PRICE PER LB.

To find value of item at a new market price, multiply new price by the cost factor.

FIGURE 6–6 Butcher's Yield Test—Cost of Each Pound and Ounce

YIELD TEST CARD

ITEM **#173 Short Loin**   GRADE **Choice**   DATE **4-19-93**

PIECES **1**   WEIGHT **18** LBS **4** OZ.   AVERAGE WT. **19** LBS. **0** OZ.

TOTAL COST $ **63.6925** AT $ **3.49** PER **LB**   PURVEYOR **R.U. DUNN MEATS**

BREAKDOWN	NO.	WEIGHT LB.	WEIGHT OZ.	RATIO TO TOTAL WEIGHT	VALUE PER POUND	TOTAL VALUE	COST OF EACH LB.	COST OF EACH OZ.	PORTION SIZE	PORTION VALUE	COST FACTOR PER LB. %	PORTION %
Fat		3	4	17.8082 %	.83	2.6975	.83	.0518				
Bones		4	2	22.6027	.19	.7837	.19	.0118				
Stew Meat		2	3	11.9863	2.17	4.7468	2.17	.1356				
Ground Meat 80/20		1	14	10.2739	1.45	2.7187	1.45	.0906				
Filet		1	5	7.1917	12.94	16.9837	12.94	.8087				
Loss in cutting			5	1.7123	—	—	—	—				
Subtotal		13	1		—	27.9340	—	—				
NY Strip		5	3	28.4246	6.8938	35.7621	6.8938	.4308				
TOTAL		18	4	99.9997	—	63.6925						

COST FACTOR = $\dfrac{\text{READY-TO-EAT VALUE PER LB. OR PORTION}}{\text{PURCHASE PRICE PER LB.}}$
PER LB. OR PORTION

To find value of item at a new market price, multiply new price by the cost factor.

cost of a pound, use the dollar amounts already obtained for the secondary pieces or the amount calculated for the primary piece. Once the amounts are entered in the pound column, the ounce column can be calculated. To find the ounce amount, take the total value per pound and divide by 16, which will give you the price per ounce. (Example: $1.39 divided by 16 = $.0868) Another method of calculating the ounce amount will be explained in more detail in the spreadsheet information portion of this lesson.

Portion refers to a serving's size and value. The portion size, determined by the management for the establishment, is stated in ounces. The reason for listing the portion in ounces is that, in most food establishments, bulk items are broken down into smaller portions to be sold to the consumer. In many food establishments, the menu states how many ounces a steak or a serving of fish fillet will weigh. The portion weights of today are more accurate than in the past because of the truth-in-menu guidelines used by restaurateurs.

Also keep in mind that portion sizes do not have to be given for all secondary pieces, and you don't always have to give the portion size for the primary piece. The reason for determining portion size is that it expresses how a bulk item is converted to a number of servings in a particular establishment. For example, a secondary product of a piece of beef is ground beef. It would be sold as hamburgers, and therefore could be expressed as a number of servings, each having a particular portion size. Items like fat or bones are not sold as food items, so there would be no need to have a portion size. The opposite holds true if you had saved a quantity of beef rib bones, one of the by-products of the butcher's test, and eventually sold them as an item on the menu.

Portion value is derived from multiplying the portion size (applied to the secondary or primary items) by the dollar amount of the cost of each ounce. The result is the portion value. An example would be:

Portion size	8 oz.
× Cost of each ounce	× $.10
= Portion value	= $.8000

In Figure 6–7, the portion value has been calculated for the primary item and two secondary items. The by-products had no portion value, and the stew meat portions may vary because of the presence of other ingredients in each serving.

The portion value can be calculated in another way, which will be explained in the spreadsheet information section of this lesson.

The last section of the butcher's yield test indicates the cost factor per pound (lb.) or per portion. These numbers are **factor numbers**.

FIGURE 6-7 Butcher's Yield Test—Cost of Each Pound and Ounce

YIELD TEST CARD

ITEM ___#173 Short Loin___ GRADE ___Choice___ DATE ___4-19-93___

PIECES ___1___ WEIGHT ___18___ LBS ___4___ OZ. AVERAGE WT. ___19___ LBS. ___0___ OZ.

TOTAL COST $ ___63.6925___ AT $ ___3.49___ PER ___LB___ PURVEYOR ___R.U. DUNN MEATS___

BREAKDOWN	NO.	WEIGHT LB.	WEIGHT OZ.	RATIO TO TOTAL WEIGHT	VALUE PER POUND	TOTAL VALUE		COST OF EACH LB.	COST OF EACH OZ.	PORTION SIZE	PORTION VALUE	COST FACTOR PER LB.	COST FACTOR PER PORTION
Fat		3	4	17.8082 %	.83	2	6975	.83	.0518	X	X	X %	X %
Bones		4	2	22.6027	.19		7837	.19	.0118	X	X	X	X
Stew Meat		2	3	11.9863	2.17	4	7468	2.17	.1356	X	X	X	X
Ground Meat 80/20		1	14	10.2739	1.45	2	7187	1.45	.0906	.5000 8 oz	.7250	X	X
Filet		1	5	7.1917	12.94	16	9337	12.94	.8087	.6250 10 oz	8.0875	X	X
Loss in cutting			5	1.7123									
Subtotal		13	1		—	27	9340	—	—	X	X	X	X
NY Strip		5	3	28.4246	6.8938	35	7621	6.8938	.4308	.8125 13 oz	5.6012	X	X
TOTAL		18	4	99.9997	—	63	6925						

COST FACTOR PER LB. OR PORTION = READY-TO-EAT VALUE PER LB. OR PORTION / PURCHASE PRICE PER LB.

To find value of item at a new market price, multiply new price by the cost factor.

135

■ **Hint** _____

A factor number is a number that will eventually be used to calculate another number. We have done this several times in earlier lessons.

_____

In the **cost-factor-per-pound/portion** column, the key numbers to find are those for the primary item. Turn to the formulas for the butcher's yield test (page 125), and apply formula 5 and formula 6. (See the spreadsheet information for more details.)

NOTE: This lesson has several references to the spreadsheet information because many of these calculations can be done two ways. Most calculations have been explained via a straight method that uses pounds and ounces and takes the place of the actual cutting and weighing of an item. A butcher's yield test is most often done with a pen or pencil and a calculator. When using the yield test card for both the butcher's yield test and the cooking loss test, you must use the decimal equivalent for ounces. You will be able to find out the decimal equivalents for various measurements in the appendix.

Because decimal equivalents are used for this exercise on a Lotus spreadsheet, it will look similar but not identical to a butcher's yield test done by pen or pencil. The key column that will *not* look like the version done by hand is ratio to total weight. Most likely, the pen or pencil worksheet will equal $99.999 \times \%$. On the Microsoft Excel spreadsheet, this column must and will always round that number in the division problem; therefore, the final number will equal 100.0000%. Keep in mind the preceding information when reading through the spreadsheet instruction.

Figure 6–8 shows the two-step calculation needed when using decimal equivalents for pounds and ounces.

COOKING LOSS TEST

In the foodservice industry, the cooking loss test can be a continuation of the butcher's yield test or it can stand by itself. Because it can be one or the other, it has been continued through the lesson, and the original weight is set at 100.0000%. If you want, you can start the test with the percent that you have as the ratio to total weight for the primary price. Figure 6–9 shows the basic format for the report on the cooking loss test.

Compared to the butcher's yield test, only one thing changes when doing a cooking test: the item that was butchered and oven prepared (O.P.) gets cooked. For example, suppose you prepare a $30.00, 10-pound top round roast (beef) and put it in a pan in the oven. You turn the oven on to

FIGURE 6-8 Butcher's Yield Test—Calculating Decimal Equivalents

YIELD TEST CARD

ITEM ____#173 Short Loin____

PIECES __1__ WEIGHT __18__ LBS __4__ OZ.   GRADE ____Choice____   DATE __4-19-93__

TOTAL COST $ __63.6925__ AT $ __3.49__ PER __LB__   AVERAGE WT. __19__ LBS. __0__ OZ.

PURVEYOR __R.U. DUNN MEATS__

BREAKDOWN	NO.	WEIGHT LB.	WEIGHT OZ.	RATIO TO TOTAL WEIGHT	VALUE PER POUND	TOTAL VALUE		COST OF EACH LB.	COST OF EACH OZ.	PORTION SIZE	PORTION VALUE	COST FACTOR PER LB.	COST FACTOR PER PORTION
Fat		3	2500 4	17.8082%	.83	2	6975	.83	.0518	X	X	X %	X %
Bones		4	1250 2	22.6027	.19		7837	.19	.0118	X	X	X	X
Stew Meat		2	1275 3	11.9863	2.17	4	7468	2.17	.1356	X	X	X	X
Ground Meat		1	8750 14	10.2739	1.45	2	7187	1.45	.0906	.5000 8 oz	.7250	X	X
Filet		1	3125 5	7.1917	12.94	16	9837	12.94	.8087	.6250 10 oz	8.0875	X	X
Loss in cutting			3125 5	1.7123	—			—	—	X	X	X	X
Subtotal		13	1			27	9340			X	X	X	X
NY Strip		5	1875 3	28.4246	6.8938	35	7621	6.8938	.4308	.8125 13 oz	5.6012	X	X
TOTAL		18	4	99.9997	—	63	6925						

STEP 1 $\dfrac{6.8938}{3.4900}$ = (1.9753)

CF per LB

STEP 2 CF per LB × DECIMAL EQUIV (PORTION)

1.9753 × .8125 = 1.6049 (13 oz)

COST FACTOR PER LB. OR PORTION = $\dfrac{\text{READY-TO-EAT VALUE PER LB. OR PORTION}}{\text{PURCHASE PRICE PER LB.}}$

To find value of item at a new market price, multiply new price by the cost factor.

FIGURE 6-9 Cooking Loss Test—Sample Format

COOKING LOSS

ITEM _____

PORTION SIZE _____

PORTION COST FACTOR _____

COOKED _____ HOURS _____ MINUTES AT _____ DEGREES

_____ HOURS _____ MINUTES AT _____ DEGREES

BREAKDOWN	NO.	WEIGHT		RATIO TO TOTAL WEIGHT	VALUE PER POUND	TOTAL VALUE	READY TO EAT VALUE PER		READY TO EAT PORTION		COST FACTOR PER	
		LB.	OZ.				LB.	OZ.	SIZE	VALUE	LB.	PORTION
ORIGINAL WEIGHT												
LOSS IN TRIMMING												
TRIMMED WEIGHT												
LOSS IN COOKING												
COOKED WEIGHT												
BONES AND TRIM												
LOSS IN SLICING												
SALABLE MEAT												

REMARKS

$$\text{COST FACTOR PER LB. OR PORTION} = \frac{\text{READY-TO-EAT VALUE PER LB. OR PORTION}}{\text{PURCHASE PRICE PER LB.}}$$

To find ready to eat value of cuts at a new market price, multiply new price per lb. by the cost factor.

350 degrees and cook the meat for 4 hours. When you open the oven, you have a $30.00, 8-pound cooked roast. What is the value of the roast when it comes out of the oven? Still $30.00. Because of cooking loss, the 10-pound roast now weighs 8 pounds, but is *still* worth $30.00. If you had started with a $30.00, 10-pound rib roast instead, and, after cooking, trimmed off the fat and bone, you would now have only about 6 pounds of roast beef. Its value is *still* $30.00. The point is: the total value after cooking *always* remains the same as the cost of the primary piece after butchering. The only figure that changes is the value per pound. The formula used is:

$$\frac{\text{Total value}}{\text{Weight in pounds and decimal equivalents of ounces}} = \text{New value per pound}$$

Applying the formula to the two 10-pound roasts would give:

$$\text{Cooked top round or rib roast} \quad \frac{\$30.00}{8.0000 \text{ lbs.}} = \$3.7500 \text{ value per pound}$$

$$\text{Cooked rib roast after being trimmed and boned} \quad \frac{\$30.00}{6.0000 \text{ lbs.}} = \$5.0000 \text{ value per pound}$$

After completing these steps, there are other numbers to be concerned with, but they are calculated exactly as in the butcher's yield test: ready-to-eat value (in pounds + ounces), ready-to-eat portion size/value, and cost factor per pound and per portion. Figure 6–10 shows a completed cooking loss test report, including the steps to calculate the decimal equivalents for pounds and ounces.

■ SPREADSHEET OBJECTIVES

Upon completion of Lesson 6, you sholdd be able to:

1. Perform a butcher's yield test and cooking loss test by hand and by computer.

2. Use cost factor per pound or per portion to make purchasing decisions.

This section contains the spreadsheet information referred to in several discussions earlier in this lesson. Figure 6–11 shows a sample spreadsheet, before entry of any data.

FIGURE 6–10 Cooking Loss Test Report—Calculating Decimal Equivalents

ITEM __O.P. RIB/N.Y. STRIP__

PORTION SIZE _____

PORTION COST FACTOR _____

COOKING LOSS

COOKED __4__ HOURS __15__ MINUTES AT __350__ DEGREES

_____ HOURS _____ MINUTES AT _____ DEGREES

BREAKDOWN	NO.	WEIGHT LB.	WEIGHT OZ.	RATIO TO TOTAL WEIGHT	VALUE PER POUND	TOTAL VALUE		READY TO EAT VALUE PER LB.	READY TO EAT VALUE PER OZ.	READY TO EAT PORTION SIZE	READY TO EAT PORTION VALUE	COST FACTOR PER LB.	COST FACTOR PER PORTION
ORIGINAL WEIGHT		5	1875 / 3	100.0000	6.8938	35	7621	X	X	X	X	X	X
LOSS IN TRIMMING		—	—	—	—	—	—	X	X	X	X	X	X
TRIMMED WEIGHT		—	—	—	—	—	—	X	X	X	X	X	X
LOSS IN COOKING		1	1875 / —	—	—	—	—	X	X	X	X	X	X
COOKED WEIGHT		4	1875 / 3	80.7228	8.5402	35	7621	X	X	X	X	X	X
BONES AND TRIM			3	—	—	—	—	X	X	X	X	X	X
LOSS IN SLICING			5	—	—	—	—	X	X	X	X	X	X
SALABLE MEAT		3	6875 / 11	71.0843	9.6981	35	7621	9.6981	.6061	.8125 / 13oz.	7.8797	X	X
REMARKS													

$$\text{COST FACTOR PER LB. OR PORTION} = \frac{\text{READY-TO-EAT VALUE PER LB. OR PORTION}}{\text{PURCHASE PRICE PER LB.}}$$

To find ready to eat value of cuts at a new market price, multiply new price per lb. by the cost factor.

STEP 1 $\dfrac{9.6981}{3.4900} = 2.7788$ CF per LB

STEP 2 CF per LB x DECIMAL EQUIV (PORTION)

2.7788 x .8125 = 2.2577

13 oz

FIGURE 6–11 Butcher's Yield Test—Sample Spreadsheet Format

FOODSERVICE COST CONTROL USING MICROSOFT EXCEL   PG 1 OF 1
STUDENT NAME: {NAME}
DATE: {DATE}

RESTAURANT NAME:
{RESTAURANT NAME}

YIELD TEST

ITEM: {NAME}   GRADE: {NAME}
SUPPLIER: {NAME}   DATE: {DATE}

WEIGHT: 0 LBS.   0 OZ.

TOTAL COST: $0.0000 AT $0.00 PER LB.

BREAKDOWN:	WEIGHT LBS.	WEIGHT OZ.	RATIO TO TTL. WT.	VALUE/ POUND	TOTAL VALUE	COST OF EACH LBS.	COST OF EACH OZ.	PORTION SIZE	PORTION VALUE	COST FACTOR PER/ LB.	COST FACTOR PER/ PORTION
FAT	0	0	0.0000%	$0.0000	$0.0000	$0.0000	$0.0000	0.0000	$0.0000	0.0000	0.0000
BONES	0	0	0.0000%	$0.0000	$0.0000	$0.0000	$0.0000	0.0000	$0.0000	0.0000	0.0000
SECONDARY PIECES	0	0	0.0000%	$0.0000	$0.0000	$0.0000	$0.0000	0.0000	$0.0000	0.0000	0.0000
SECONDARY PIECES	0	0	0.0000%	$0.0000	$0.0000	$0.0000	$0.0000	0.0000	$0.0000	0.0000	0.0000
SECONDARY PIECES	0	0	0.0000%	$0.0000	$0.0000	$0.0000	$0.0000	0.0000	$0.0000	0.0000	0.0000
SECONDARY PIECES	0	0	0.0000%	$0.0000	$0.0000	$0.0000	$0.0000	0.0000	$0.0000	0.0000	0.0000
SECONDARY PIECES	0	0	0.0000%	$0.0000	$0.0000	$0.0000	$0.0000	0.0000	$0.0000	0.0000	0.0000
SECONDARY PIECES	0	0	0.0000%	$0.0000	$0.0000	$0.0000	$0.0000	0.0000	$0.0000	0.0000	0.0000
TTL. SECONDARIES	0	0	0.0000%	XXXXXXX	$0.000C	XXXXXX	XXXXXX	XXXXXX	XXXXXX	XXXXXX	XXXXXX
PRIMARY PIECE	0	0	0.0000%	$0.0000	$0.0000	$0.0000	$0.0000	0.0000	$0.0000	0.0000	0.0000
TOTALS	0	0	0.0000%	XXXXXX	$0.0000	XXXXXX	XXXXXX	XXXXXX	XXXXXX	XXXXXX	XXXXXX

When you filled out the heading section on the butcher's yield test card, you calculated total cost by multiplying total weight by cost per pound. To calculate total cost on the computer, the formula is: Total weight in decimals × Cost per pound = Total cost. You must have two of these three numbers to find the third number. What would happen if you had total cost and cost per pound? How would you find the total weight?

$$\frac{\text{Total cost}}{\text{Cost per lb.}} = \text{Total weight}$$

Reversed, so you can double-check, the format would be:

$$\frac{\text{Total cost}}{\text{Total weight}} = \text{Cost per pound (lb. and decimals)}$$

The next section is the breakdown. In some areas of the spreadsheet, *the secondary pieces have been inserted*; insert the *other parts of the secondary pieces* where needed. In the breakdown exercises, and only in these exercises, loss in cutting is not used. You will also have to insert the name of the primary piece.

Figure 6–12 shows the spreadsheet with the heading and breakdown column completed.

The next column shows the weight, in pounds and ounces, for secondary and primary pieces. Insert the pounds and the ounces. To find the amount of ounces, use the formula of 16 oz. equals 1. (In the pen or pencil version, make sure you use both the raw pounds and ounces and the raw pounds and decimal equivalent of ounces. This will provide you with a double-check procedure.) Keep in mind that you are instructed, for spreadsheet purposes, to enter *only* the pounds and ounces numbers. Use formula 1 (page 125) to find the weight of the primary piece. To double-check this figure, the totals in the weight column should equal the total pounds and ounces stated in the heading.

Figure 6–13 shows this activity has been completed.

Ratio to total weight is calculated using formula 2 on page 125. This column will differ from the handwritten version because the numbers here are rounded to always equal 100.0000%. Remember, the number you calculated by hand is *not* incorrect if it is 99.999X%. For computer purposes, it has to equal and will equal 100.0000%, and the number that you calculate by hand must equal 99.999X%. If these numbers don't match, it means that a error has been made in the total weight, and the total weight column of pounds and ounces might not match.

Value per pound is the amount you get from the purveyor for the secondary items. The only number to find here is the primary piece, but it

FIGURE 6-12 Butcher's Yield Test Spreadsheet—Heading and Breakdown

FOODSERVICE COST CONTROL USING MICROSOFT EXCEL   PG 1 OF 1
STUDENT NAME: RESTAURANT NAME:
DATE: {RESTAURANT NAME}
        {NAME}
        {DATE}

YIELD TEST

ITEM: #173 SHORT LOIN   GRADE: CHOICE
SUPPLIER: R.U. DUNN MEATS   DATE: 4/19/94

WEIGHT: 18 LBS.   4 OZ.

TOTAL COST: $63.6925 AT $3.49 PER LB.

BREAKDOWN:	WEIGHT LBS.	OZ.	RATIO TO TTL. WT.	VALUE/ POUND	TOTAL VALUE	COST OF EACH LBS.	OZ.	PORTION SIZE	VALUE	COST FACTOR PER/ LB.	PORTION
FAT	0	0	0.0000%	$0.0000	$0.0000	$0.0000	$0.0000	0.0000	$0.0000	0.0000	0.0000
BONES	0	0	0.0000%	$0.0000	$0.0000	$0.0000	$0.0000	0.0000	$0.0000	0.0000	0.0000
STEW MEAT	0	0	0.0000%	$0.0000	$0.0000	$0.0000	$0.0000	0.0000	$0.0000	0.0000	0.0000
GROUND MEAT	0	0	0.0000%	$0.0000	$0.0000	$0.0000	$0.0000	0.0000	$0.0000	0.0000	0.0000
FILET	0	0	0.0000%	$0.0000	$0.0000	$0.0000	$0.0000	0.0000	$0.0000	0.0000	0.0000
LOSS IN CUTTING	0	0	0.0000%	$0.0000	$0.0000	$0.0000	$0.0000	0.0000	$0.0000	0.0000	0.0000
	0	0	0.0000%	$0.0000	$0.0000	$0.0000	$0.0000	0.0000	$0.0000	0.0000	0.0000
	0	0	0.0000%	$0.0000	$0.0000	$0.0000	$0.0000	0.0000	$0.0000	0.0000	0.0000
TTL. SECONDARIES	0	0	0.0000%	XXXXXX	$0.0000	XXXXXX	XXXXXX	XXXXXX	XXXXXX	XXXXXX	XXXXXX
NY STRIP	0	0	0.0000%	$0.0000	$0.0000	$0.0000	$0.0000	0.0000	$0.0000	0.0000	0.0000
TOTALS	0	0	0.0000%	XXXXXX	$0.0000	XXXXXX	XXXXXX	XXXXXX	XXXXXX	XXXXXX	XXXXXX

FIGURE 6–13   Butcher's Yield Test Spreadsheet—Weight in Pounds and Ounces

FOODSERVICE COST CONTROL USING MICROSOFT EXCEL   PG 1 OF 1
STUDENT NAME: RESTAURANT NAME:
DATE: {RESTAURANT NAME}
          {NAME}
          {DATE}

YIELD TEST

ITEM: #173 SHORT LOIN   GRADE: CHOICE
SUPPLIER: R.U. DUNN MEATS   DATE: 4/19/94

WEIGHT: 18 LBS.   4 OZ.

TOTAL COST: $63.6925   AT $3.49 PER LB.

BREAKDOWN:	WEIGHT LBS.	OZ.	RATIO TO TTL. WT.	VALUE/ POUND	TOTAL VALUE	COST OF EACH LBS.	OZ.	PORTION SIZE	VALUE	COST FACTOR PER/ LB.	PORTION
FAT	3	4	17.8082%	$0.0000	$0.0000	$0.0000	$0.0000	0.0000	$0.0000	0.0000	0.0000
BONES	4	2	22.6027%	$0.0000.	$0.0000	$0.0000	$0.0000	0.0000	$0.0000	0.0000	0.0000
STEW MEAT	2	3	11.9863%	$0.0000	$0.0000	$0.0000	$0.0000	0.0000	$0.0000	0.0000	0.0000
GROUND MEAT	1	14	10.2740%	$0.0000	$0.0000	$0.0000	$0.0000	0.0000	$0.0000	0.0000	0.0000
FILET	1	5	7.1918%	$0.0000	$0.0000	$0.0000	$0.0000	0.0000	$0.0000	0.0000	0.0000
LOSS IN CUTTING	0	5	1.7123%	$0.0000	$0.0000	$0.0000	$0.0000	0.0000	$0.0000	0.0000	0.0000
	0	0	0.0000%	$0.0000	$0.0000	$0.0000	$0.0000	0.0000	$0.0000	0.0000	0.0000
	0	0	0.0000%	$0.0000	$0.0000	$0.0000	$0.0000	0.0000	$0.0000	0.0000	0.0000
TTL. SECONDARIES	13	1	71.5753%	XXXXXXX	$0.0000	XXXXXXX	XXXXXXX	XXXXXXX	XXXXXXX	XXXXXXX	XXXXXXX
NY STRIP	5	3	28.4247%	$0.0000	$0.0000	$0.0000	$0.0000	0.0000	$0.0000	0.0000	0.0000
TOTALS	18	4	100.0000%	XXXXXXX	$0.0000	XXXXXXX	XXXXXXX	XXXXXXX	XXXXXXX	XXXXXXX	XXXXXXX

cannot be calculated until you complete the total value column. (See Figure 6–14.)

Total value is calculated by multiplying the weight of the secondary items, in pounds and the decimal equivalent of ounces, times the value per pound. For example:

$$(5 \text{ lbs. } 8 \text{ oz.} = 5.5000 \times .1000 = .5500)$$

This is where you have to convert the ounces into their decimal equivalents to be accurate.

After you have completed the column for the secondary items, you should complete the primary piece total value. Use formula 3 on page 125.

Restated, the formula is:

> Total cost of bulk piece
> − Value of secondary piece
> = Value of primary piece

Now that the amount is calculated for the primary piece, you can go back to the previous column, value per pound. Using formula 4 on page 125, you would calculate in the following manner:

$$\frac{\text{Value of primary piece}}{\text{Total weight of primary piece}} = \text{Value/pound (lb.)}$$

(See Figure 6–15.)

■ **Hint** _____

You must use the decimal equivalent of the weight. Therefore, it will have to read as follows:

$$\frac{\$XXX \text{ value of primary piece}}{\text{Lbs. + decimal of oz.}} = 15.5000$$

You have to divide by the decimal equivalent, otherwise you have miscalculated this number.

The columns that show the cost of each pound and ounce are automatically calculated. In the lbs. column, all the numbers come from the value-per-pound column, which equals the cost of each pound. The cost of each ounce is the number in the cost-of-each-pound column divided by 16.

FIGURE 6-14 Butcher's Yield Test Spreadsheet—Value per Pound and Total Value

STUDENT NAME: {NAME}   RESTAURANT NAME:
DATE: {DATE}   {RESTAURANT NAME}

YIELD TEST

ITEM: #173 SHORT LOIN   GRADE: CHOICE
SUPPLIER: R.U. DUNN MEATS   DATE: 4/19/94

WEIGHT: 18 LBS.   4 OZ.

TOTAL COST: $63.6925   AT $3.49 PER LB.

BREAKDOWN:	WEIGHT LBS.	OZ.	RATIO TO TTL. WT.	VALUE/POUND	TOTAL VALUE	COST OF EACH LBS.	COST OF EACH OZ.	PORTION SIZE	PORTION VALUE	COST FACTOR PER LB.	COST FACTOR PORTION
FAT	3	4	17.80822%	$0.8300	$2.6975	$0.8300	$0.0519	0.0000	$0.0000	0.0000	0.0000
BONES	4	2	22.60227%	$0.1900	$0.7838	$0.1900	$0.0119	0.0000	$0.0000	0.0000	0.0000
STEW MEAT	2	3	11.98630%	$2.1700	$4.7469	$2.1700	$0.1356	0.0000	$0.0000	0.0000	0.0000
GROUND MEAT	1	14	10.27400%	$1.4500	$2.7188	$1.4500	$0.0906	0.0000	$0.0000	0.0000	0.0000
FILET	1	5	7.19180%	$12.9400	$16.9838	$12.9400	$0.8088	0.0000	$0.0000	0.0000	0.0000
LOSS IN CUTTING	0	5	1.71230%	$0.0000	$0.0000	$0.0000	$0.0000	0.0000	$0.0000	0.0000	0.0000
	0	0	0.00000%	$0.0000	$0.0000	$0.0000	$0.0000	0.0000	$0.0000	0.0000	0.0000
	0	0	0.00000%	$0.0000	$0.0000	$0.0000	$0.0000	0.0000	$0.0000	0.0000	0.0000
TTL. SECONDARIES	13	1	71.57530%	XXXXXX	$27.9306	XXXXXX	XXXXXX	XXXXXX	XXXXXX	XXXXXXX	XXXXXXX
NY STRIP	5	3	28.42470%	$0.0000	$0.0000	$0.0000	$0.0000	0.0000	$0.0000	0.0000	0.0000
TOTALS	18	4	100.00000%	XXXXXX	$27.9306	XXXXXX	XXXXXX	XXXXXX	XXXXXX	XXXXXXX	XXXXXXX

146

FIGURE 6–15 Butcher's Yield Test Spreadsheet—Value of Primary

FOODSERVICE COST CONTROL USING MICROSOFT EXCEL   PG 1 OF 1
STUDENT NAME: {NAME}
DATE: {DATE}   RESTAURANT NAME:
                                 {RESTAURANT NAME}

YIELD TEST

ITEM: #173 SHORT LOIN   GRADE: CHOICE
SUPPLIER: R.U. DUNN MEATS   DATE: 4/19/94

WEIGHT: 18 LBS.   4 OZ.

TOTAL COST: $63.6925   AT $3.49 PER LB.

BREAKDOWN:	WEIGHT LBS.	OZ.	RATIO TO TTL. WT.	VALUE/ POUND	TOTAL VALUE	COST OF EACH LBS.	OZ.	PORTION SIZE	VALUE	COST FACTOR PER/ LB.	PORTION
FAT	3	4	17.8082%	$0.8300	$2.6975	$0.8300	$0.0519	0.0000	$0.0000	0.0000	0.0000
BONES	4	2	22.6027%	$0.1900	$0.7838	$0.1900	$0.0119	0.0000	$0.0000	0.0000	0.0000
STEW MEAT	2	3	11.9863%	$2.1700	$4.7469	$2.1700	$0.1356	0.0000	$0.0000	0.0000	0.0000
GROUND MEAT	1	14	10.2740%	$1.4500	$2.7183	$1.4500	$0.0906	0.0000	$0.0000	0.0000	0.0000
FILET	1	5	7.1918%	$12.9400	$16.9833	$12.9400	$0.8088	0.0000	$0.0000	0.0000	0.0000
LOSS IN CUTTING	0	5	1.7123%	$0.0000	$0.0000	$0.0000	$0.0000	0.0000	$0.0000	0.0000	0.0000
	0	0	0.0000%	$0.0000	$0.0000	$0.0000	$0.0000	0.0000	$0.0000	0.0000	0.0000
	0	0	0.0000%	$0.0000	$0.0000	$0.0000	$0.0000	0.0000	$0.0000	0.0000	0.0000
TTL. SECONDARIES	13	1	71.5753%	XXXXXXX	$27.9306	XXXXXXX	XXXXXXX	XXXXXXX	XXXXXXX	XXXXXX	XXXXXX
NY STRIP	5	3	28.4247%	$6.8938	$35.7619	$6.8938	$0.4309	0.0000	$0.0000	0.0000	0.0000
TOTALS	18	4	100.0000%	XXXXXXX	$63.6925	XXXXXXX	XXXXXXX	XXXXXXX	XXXXXXX	XXXXXX	XXXXXX

Portion size and value are sizes or portions of the primary item (or possibly the secondary items) that are sold. In this lesson, you need only be concerned about the primary piece. Once you insert the portion size, which is given to you in ounces, it *must be converted to the decimal equivalent*. As an example, 8 oz. converts to .5000. (See Figure 6–16.)

After you enter the decimal equivalent of the portion size, it will automatically multiply the portion size times the cost per pound, which will give you the value of that portion size of the primary piece.

The following example illustrates the mathematics:

$$\$5.0000 \text{ (cost per pound for primary)}$$
$$\times \quad .5000 \text{ (decimal equivalent of 8-oz. portion)}$$
$$= \$2.5000 \text{ (value of } \tfrac{1}{2} \text{ lb. of a food item)}$$

NOTE: Assume the number entered was .8000 instead of .5000 (which is the decimal equivalent of 8 oz.). Because of the way the formula is set up, the answer would be $4.0000. The formula would have to be changed if ounces were to be entered in this column. If ounces are entered, then the ounces amount multiplied by the per-ounce price will give a cost close to the $2.5000 amount. Because of rounding, the amount will come close but will not be exactly the same. Rounding out numbers, which are actually pennies, could result in a loss of thousands of dollars over a year. For that reason, the decimal equivalent plays an important part in the calculation of the butcher's yield test by hand or via a computer using the Microsoft Excel program.

Cost factor per pound and portion is the next column. The calculation to use for finding this amount is formula 6 on page 125 and is illustrated below:

$$\frac{\text{Cost per salable pound (value per pound of primary)}}{\text{Cost of original dealer's price per pound}} = \frac{\text{Cost factor per pound of}}{\text{original wholesale piece}}$$

Figure 6–17 shows the completed calculations for the primary. The only number to find here is that of the primary piece. This number is then entered into the cost-factor-per-pound column. *This number is a factor*. Once this number is entered, the computer automatically calculates the cost factor per portion, which is the portion size decimal equivalent multiplied by the cost factor per pound. This equals the cost factor per portion. *This number is only a factor number*. Both of these factor numbers—for pound and portion—will be used to calculate other amounts.

Figure 6–18 shows the format for a cooking loss test report, and Figure 6–19 compares the original weight to the cooked weight.

FIGURE 6–16 Butcher's Yield Test Spreadsheet—Decimal Equivalent of Ounces

STUDENT NAME: {NAME}   RESTAURANT NAME
DATE: {RESTAURANT NAME}

YIELD TEST

ITEM: #173 SHORT LOIN   GRADE: CHOICE
SUPPLIER: R.U. DUNN MEATS   DATE: 4/19/94

WEIGHT: 18 LBS.   4 OZ.

TOTAL COST: $63.6925   AT $3.49 PER LB.

BREAKDOWN:	WEIGHT LBS.	WEIGHT OZ.	RATIO TO TTL. WT.	VALUE/ POUND	TOTAL VALUE	COST OF EACH LBS.	COST OF EACH OZ.	PORTION SIZE	PORTION VALUE	COST FACTOR PER LB.	COST FACTOR PER PORTION
FAT	3	4	17.8082%	$0.8300	$2.6975	$0.8300	$0.0519	0.0000	$0.0000	0.0000	0.0000
BONES	4	2	22.6027%	$0.1900	$0.7638	$0.1900	$0.0119	0.0000	$0.0000	0.0000	0.0000
STEW MEAT	2	3	11.9863%	$2.1700	$4.7469	$2.1700	$0.1356	0.0000	$0.0000	0.0000	0.0000
GROUND MEAT	1	14	10.2740%	$1.4500	$2.7188	$1.4500	$0.0906	0.5000	$0.7250	0.0000	0.0000
FILET	1	5	7.1918%	$12.9400	$16.9838	$12.9400	$0.8088	0.6250	$8.0875	0.0000	0.0000
LOSS IN CUTTING	0	5	1.7123%	$0.0000	$0.0000	$0.0000	$0.0000	0.0000	$0.0000	0.0000	0.0000
	0	0	0.0000%	$0.0000	$0.0000	$0.0000	$0.0000	0.0000	$0.0000	0.0000	0.0000
	0	0	0.0000%	$0.0000	$0.0000	$0.0000	$0.0000	0.0000	$0.0000	0.0000	0.0000
TTL. SECONDARIES	13	1	71.5753%	XXXXXX	$27.9306	XXXXXX	XXXXXX	XXXXXX	XXXXXX	XXXXXXX	XXXXXX
NY STRIP	5	3	28.4247%	$6.8938	$35.76.9	$6.8938	$0.4309	0.8125	$5.6012	0.0000	0.0000
TOTALS	18	4	100.0000%	XXXXXX	$63.6925	XXXXXX	XXXXXX	XXXXXX	XXXXXX	XXXXXXX	XXXXXX

FIGURE 6–17 Butcher's Yield Test Spreadsheet—Calculations for Primary

STUDENT NAME: {NAME}   RESTAURANT NAME:
DATE: {DATE}   {RESTAURANT NAME}

YIELD TEST

ITEM: #173 SHORT LOIN   GRADE: CHOICE
SUPPLIER: R.U. DUNN MEATS   DATE: 4/19/94

WEIGHT: 18 LBS.   4 OZ.

TOTAL COST: $63.6925   AT $3.49 PER LB.

BREAKDOWN:	WEIGHT LBS.	WEIGHT OZ.	RATIO TO TTL. WT.	VALUE/ POUND	TOTAL VALUE	COST OF EACH LBS.	COST OF EACH OZ.	PORTION SIZE	PORTION VALUE	COST FACTOR PER LB.	COST FACTOR PER PORTION
FAT	3	4	17.80082%	$0.8300	$2.6975	$0.8300	$0.0519	0.0000	$0.0000	0.0000	0.0000
BONES	4	2	22.6027%	$0.1900	$0.7838	$0.1900	$0.0119	0.0000	$0.0000	0.0000	0.0000
STEW MEAT	2	3	11.9863%	$2.1700	$4.7469	$2.1700	$0.1356	0.0000	$0.0000	0.0000	0.0000
GROUND MEAT	1	14	10.2740%	$1.4500	$2.7188	$1.4500	$0.0906	0.5000	$0.7250	0.0000	0.0000
FILET	1	5	7.1918%	$12.9400	$16.9838	$12.9400	$0.8088	0.6250	$8.0875	0.0000	0.0000
LOSS IN CUTTING	0	5	1.7123%	$0.0000	$0.0000	$0.0000	$0.0000	0.0000	$0.0000	0.0000	0.0000
	0	0	0.0000%	$0.0000	$0.0000	$0.0000	$0.0000	0.0000	$0.0000	0.0000	0.0000
	0	0	0.0000%	$0.0000	$0.0000	$0.0000	$0.0000	0.0000	$0.0000	0.0000	0.0000
TTL. SECONDARIES	13	1	71.5753%	XXXXXXX	$27.9306	XXXXXXX	XXXXXXX	XXXXXXX	XXXXXXX	XXXXXXX	XXXXXXX
NY STRIP	5	3	28.4247%	$6.8938	$35.7619	$6.8938	$0.4309	0.8125	$5.6012	1.9753	1.6049
TOTALS	18	4	100.0000%	XXXXXXX	$63.6925	XXXXXXX	XXXXXXX	XXXXXXX	XXXXXXX	XXXXXXX	XXXXXXX

FIGURE 6-18 Cooking Loss Test Spreadsheet—Sample Format

FOODSERVICE COST CONTROL USING MICROSOFT EXCEL   PC 1 OF
STUDENT NAME: {NAME}   RESTAURANT NAME:
DATE: {DATE}   {RESTAURANT NAME}

COOKING LOSS

ITEM: {NAME}

BREAKDOWN:	WEIGHT LBS.	OZ.	RATIO TO TTL. WT.	VALUE/ POUND	TOTAL VALUE	READY TO EAT VALUE LBS.	OZ.	READY TO EAT PORTION SIZE	VALUE	COST FACTOR PER/ LB.	PORTION
ORIGINAL WEIGHT	0	0	100.0000%	$0.0000	$0.0000						
LOSS IN TRIMMING											
TRIMMED WEIGHT											
LOSS IN COOKING	0	0									
COOKED WEIGHT	0	0	ERR	$0.0000	$0.0000						
BONES & TRIM	0	0									
LOSS IN SLICING	0	0									
SALABLE MEAT	0	0	ERR	$0.0000	$0.0000	$0.0000	$0.0000	0.0000	$0.0000	0.0000	0.0000

FIGURE 6-19 Cooking Loss Test Spreadsheet—Original Weight versus Cooked Weight

FOODSERVICE COST CONTROL USING MICROSOFT EXCEL   PG 1 OF 1
STUDENT NAME: {NAME}   RESTAURANT NAME:
DATE: {DATE}   {RESTAURANT NAME}

COOKING LOSS

ITEM: {NAME}

BREAKDOWN:	WEIGHT LBS.	OZ.	RATIO TO TTL. WT.	VALUE/ POUND	TOTAL VALUE	READY TO EAT VALUE LBS.	OZ.	READY TO EAT PORTION SIZE	VALUE	COST FACTOR PER/ LB.	PORTION
ORIGINAL WEIGHT	5	3	100.0000%	$6.8983	$35.7621						
LOSS IN TRIMMING											
TRIMMED WEIGHT											
LOSS IN COOKING	1	0									
COOKED WEIGHT	4	3	80.7229%	$8.5402	$35.7621						
BONES & TRIM	0	3									
LOSS IN SLICING	0	5									
SALABLE MEAT	3	11	71.0843%	$9.6981	$35.7621	$9.6981	$0.6061	0.8125	$7.8797	2.7788	2.2578

At the conclusion of the butcher's yield test and cooking loss test, the cost factors per pound and portion will allow the calculation of other amounts. For that reason, the butcher's yield test must be done as accurately as possible, especially if you feel a similar item may differ in average weight, or you are purchasing from a different purveyor, or time is short. When appropriate, the cost per portion can be determined as accurately as possible.

Rather than continue with these tests, you should turn your attention to the cost factor per pound or portion. When purveyors sell items and raise or lower the price charged for bulk weight, calculating the price change could affect the final cost per pound of the primary piece. The final cost helps to determine whether the price per pound of the primary piece would be less if you were to cut the piece yourself or would cost less if purchased already cut and prepared for cooking. To calculate these figures, you will be able to apply formulas 7 through 10 on page 125, as appropriate.

EXERCISES

Figures 6–20 and 6–21 show, respectively, a butcher's yield test card and a cooking loss test report for the Red Woodpecker Grill. Figures 6–22 and 6–23 give similar information for the Terrace Garden Restaurant. Study these figures and use them to answer the end-of-lesson questions.

CHECK YOUR UNDERSTANDING

1. What is the cost per salable pound?

   Raw _____

   Cooked _____

2. What is the cost factor per pound?

   Raw _____

   Cooked _____

3. What does the O.P. rib cost?

   Raw _____

   Cooked _____

Using the formulas for the butcher's yield test or the cooking loss test, answer the following questions.

4. What is the cost per portion of the O.P. rib based on 18 cuts?

   Raw _____

   Cooked _____

5. What is the cost per 14-oz. portion of rib, when the dealer's price per pound for the Red Woodpecker Grill is $1.48?

   Raw _____

   Cooked _____

6. What is the cost per 14-oz. portion of rib, when the dealer's price per pound for the Terrace Garden Restaurant is $2.79?

   Raw _____

   Cooked _____

7. What is the cost of a 14-oz. portion of rib, when the dealer's price per pound for the Red Woodpecker Grill is $1.25?

   Raw _____

   Cooked _____

FIGURE 6–20 Butcher's Yield Test Spreadsheet—Red Woodpecker Grill

YIELD TEST CARD

ITEM __Rib of Beef as it Falls__

GRADE __Choice__ DATE __5/6__

PIECES __1__ WEIGHT __38__ LBS __4__ OZ. AVERAGE WT. _____ LBS. _____ OZ.

TOTAL COST $ _____ AT $ __1.38__ PER __lb.__ PURVEYOR __R.I.T.__

BREAKDOWN	NO.	WEIGHT		RATIO TO TOTAL WEIGHT	VALUE PER POUND	TOTAL VALUE	COST OF EACH		PORTION			COST FACTOR PER	
		LB.	OZ.	%			LB.	OZ.	SIZE	VALUE		LB.	PORTION
Short Ribs	1	4	4	%	1.23				10 oz.			X %	X %
Hamburger	2	3	8		.82				8 oz.	8 oz.		X	X
Fat	3	4	0		.10				X	X		X	X
Bones	4	2	4		.08				X	X		X	X
O.P. Ribs	5								8 oz.				
TOTAL													

COST FACTOR = READY-TO-EAT VALUE PER LB. OR PORTION
PER LB. OR PORTION   ─────────────────────────────────
                        PURCHASE PRICE PER LB.

To find value of item at a new market price, multiply new price by the cost factor.

155

FIGURE 6-21 Cooking Loss Test Report—Red Woodpecker Grill

COOKING LOSS

ITEM ___Rib of Beef O.P.___

PORTION SIZE _____

PORTION COST FACTOR _____

COOKED ___3___ HOURS ___45___ MINUTES AT ___325___ DEGREES

_____ HOURS _____ MINUTES AT _____ DEGREES

BREAKDOWN	NO.	WEIGHT LB.	WEIGHT OZ.	RATIO TO TOTAL WEIGHT	VALUE PER POUND	TOTAL VALUE		READY TO EAT VALUE PER LB.	READY TO EAT VALUE PER OZ.	READY TO EAT PORTION SIZE	READY TO EAT PORTION VALUE	COST FACTOR PER LB.	COST FACTOR PER PORTION
ORIGINAL WEIGHT		24	4										
LOSS IN TRIMMING		X	X	X	X	X	X						
TRIMMED WEIGHT		X	X	X	X	X	X						
LOSS IN COOKING		2	4	X	X	X	X						
COOKED WEIGHT													
BONES AND TRIM			12	X	X	X	X						
LOSS IN SLICING			4	X	X	X	X			12 OZ.			
SALABLE MEAT													
REMARKS													

COST FACTOR PER LB. OR PORTION = READY-TO-EAT VALUE PER LB. OR PORTION / PURCHASE PRICE PER LB.

To find ready to eat value of cuts at a new market price, multiply new price per lb. by the cost factor.

FIGURE 6-22 Butcher's Yield Test—Terrace Garden Restaurant

YIELD TEST CARD

ITEM __Rib of Beef as it Falls__

GRADE __Choice__ DATE __5/6__

PIECES __1__ WEIGHT __45__ LBS __14__ OZ. AVERAGE WT. ____ LBS. ____ OZ.

TOTAL COST $ ____ AT $ __2.69__ PER __lb.__ PURVEYOR ____

BREAKDOWN	NO.	WEIGHT LB.	WEIGHT OZ.	RATIO TO TOTAL WEIGHT	VALUE PER POUND	TOTAL VALUE	COST OF EACH LB.	COST OF EACH OZ.	PORTION SIZE	PORTION VALUE	COST FACTOR PER LB.	COST FACTOR PER PORTION
Short Ribs	1	5	12	%	2.36				10 oz.		%	%
Hamburger	2	4	4		1.59				8 oz.			
Fat	3	6	1		.15							
Bones	4	4	2		.29							
O.P. Ribs	5								8 oz			
TOTAL												

COST FACTOR PER LB. OR PORTION = READY TO EAT VALUE PER LB. OR PORTION / PURCHASE PRICE PER LB.

To find value of item at a new market price, multiply new price by the cost factor.

FIGURE 6-23 Cooking Loss Test—Terrace Garden Restaurant

ITEM ___Rib of Beef O.P.___

PORTION SIZE _____

PORTION COST FACTOR _____

COOKING LOSS

COOKED ___4___ HOURS ___15___ MINUTES AT ___375___ DEGREES

_____ HOURS _____ MINUTES AT _____ DEGREES

BREAKDOWN	NO.	WEIGHT LB.	WEIGHT OZ.	RATIO TO TOTAL WEIGHT	VALUE PER POUND	TOTAL VALUE	READY TO EAT VALUE PER LB.	READY TO EAT VALUE PER OZ.	READY TO EAT PORTION SIZE	READY TO EAT PORTION VALUE	COST FACTOR PER LB.	COST FACTOR PER PORTION
ORIGINAL WEIGHT		25	11				X	X	X	X	X	X
LOSS IN TRIMMING		X	X				X	X	X	X	X	X
TRIMMED WEIGHT		X	X				X	X	X	X	X	X
LOSS IN COOKING		5	0				X	X	X	X	X	X
COOKED WEIGHT												
BONES AND TRIM		1	2				X	X	X	X	X	X
LOSS IN SLICING			6				X	X	X	X	X	X
SALABLE MEAT									12 oz.			
REMARKS												

COST FACTOR = READY-TO-EAT VALUE
PER LB. OR PORTION ———————————————
PER LB. OR PORTION PURCHASE PRICE PER LB.

To find ready to eat value of cuts at a new market price, multiply new price per lb. by the cost factor.

158

8. What is the cost of a 14-oz. portion of rib, when the dealer's price per pound for the Terrace Garden Restaurant is $2.45?

   Raw _____

   Cooked _____

9. Based on questions 5 or 6 above, at a 32% forecasted food cost, what would the selling price of a 14-oz. rib dinner be if the menu frame costs $.75?

   Raw _____

   Cooked _____

10. Based on questions 7 or 8 above, how many portions did the O.P. rib yield?

    Raw _____

    Cooked _____

11. If an O.P. rib could be purchased at $2.25 per pound, what would you suggest the operation do?

    Raw _____

    Cooked _____

CRITICAL THINKING

1. A. What are the differences between the butcher's yield test for the Red Woodpecker Grill (Figure 6–20) and the Terrace Garden Restaurant (Figure 6–22)?
   B. Which piece of beef would be the better choice? Elaborate on the reasons for your decision.

   _____

   _____

2. A. What are the differences between the cooking loss test for the Red Woodpecker Grill (Figure 6–21) and with the Terrace Garden Restaurant (Figure 6–23)?
   B. Which piece of beef would be the better choice? Elaborate on the reasons for your decision.

   _____

   _____

3. If you were to buy the same piece of beef, could you get other secondary parts? If yes, what parts? Could you possibly choose, from the existing parts and any new parts you listed, items that could be used as the primary piece?

   _____

   _____

4. How much would a 10-oz. O.P. rib cost, using the existing information on the butcher's yield test for:

    A. The Red Woodpecker Grill $_____

    B. The Terrace Carden Restaurant $_____

5. How much would a 14-oz. O.P. rib cost, using the existing information from the cooking loss test, for:

    A. The Red Woodpecker Grill $_____

    B. The Terrace Garden Restaurant $_____

RECIPE/PORTION COST ANALYSIS

■ OBJECTIVES

Upon completing Lesson 7, you should be able to:

1. Describe the three sections of a standard recipe card.

   This lesson starts with an explanation of the use of a standard recipe card. The information obtained from a standard recipe card is then utilized for the second part of the lesson, which is portion cost analysis.

■ KEY TERMS

Item	Ingredients
Amount produced	Purchase price
Cost per	Unit price
Number of portions	Total cost
Portion size	Procedure
Portion cost	Time
Quantity	Temperature
Unit	Remarks

■ CONCEPT REVIEW

A standard recipe card, which is fairly "standard" throughout the foodservice industry, includes (1) a list of ingredients and the quantities needed to prepare a particular menu item, (2) the unit costs of the ingredients, and (3) a preparation procedure that should be followed closely. By using a standard recipe card, you are assuring the consumer and management that menu items will be made exactly the same way every time, upholding the standard for the establishment.

The information entered on a typical standard recipe card is shown in Figure 7–1.

FIGURE 7–1   Standard Recipe Card—Typical Restaurant Recipe

STUFFED BAKED MEATLOAF VIENNESE STYLE

15 Portions to a Loaf

Onions	3 l bs.	8.00/50 lbs.
Celery	1 lb.	.60/2 lbs.
Butter	8 oz.	1.71/lb.
Flavored Bread Crumbs	1½ lbs.	15 /lb.
Milk	1 pt.	2.13/gal.
Eggs Whole	8 each	.79 doz
Ground Beef	13 lbs.	1.49/lb.
Seasoning		

Eggs Hard Cooked 1½ doz.

Finely chop celery and onions and saute in butter. ADD: Bread crumbs, milk, whole eggs, ground beef, and seasoning and mix thoroughly.

Weigh into three (3) equal amounts. For each loaf, spread ½" of meat mix into the bottom of a loaf pan. Place six (6) hard boiled eggs end to end down the middle of the meat mixture. Cover eggs with remaining meat. Bake.

STANDARD RECIPE CARD

When a menu item is prepared, using the same recipe and procedure each time, the product will be consistent, which is very important. When a menu item is not quite to the liking of a restaurant, the operation should modify the recipe, writing down all changes. When all modifications have been made to produce a satisfactory item, the revised recipe is then distributed for use and becomes the standard recipe.

After the standard recipes are given final approval, the cost for each menu item can be calculated. The ingredients, measurements, production methods, and portion sizes used must be standardized to ensure a consistent cost for the menu item.

Before reviewing the recipe card, remember that, in Lesson 6, the final portion size (cut from the primary piece) was used to determine the standard portion cost. The portion cost derived from a butcher's yield test/cooking loss test is basically the same as the portion cost obtained from a standardized recipe card.

There are three parts to the recipe card: (1) the heading, (2) the body or ingredient list, and (3) the preparation/service section. A standard recipe card is shown in Figure 7–2.

FIGURE 7–2 Standard Recipe Card—Basic Format

DATE: _____

STANDARD RECIPE CARD

ITEM _____ AMOUNT PRODUCED _____ COST PER _____

NUMBER OF PORTIONS _____ PORTION SIZE _____ PORTION COST _____

Qty	Unit	INGREDIENTS	Purch. Price	Unit price	Total Cost	Qty	Unit	INGREDIENTS	Purch. Price	Unit price	Total Cost

PREPARATION AND SERVICE

METHOD: (Procedure, time, temperature, remarks)

_____

_____

_____

_____

_____

_____

_____

_____

_____

_____

_____

_____

_____

Heading Section

The top or heading section of the recipe card provides the following information:

- **Item**—the name of the menu item being standardized, for example, beef stew. The recipe for the item could be obtained from a text, a family file handed down from generation to generation, or an original or modified recipe.

- **Amount produced**—the total quantity of the menu item generated by the recipe. The amount produced can be expressed in the following measurements: pounds, ounces, gallons, quarts, pints, cups, or fluid ounces. A measurement, whether expressed in pounds and ounces or just ounces for liquids, can also be expressed in decimal equivalents, as explained in Lesson 6. An important detail to remember is that an item like soup is usually expressed in gallons or quarts, or in another unit of liquid measurement. Items like beef stew, which are partially liquid but the bulk of whose ingredients are measured in pounds, should be expressed in pounds.

- **Cost per**—the total cost of producing the entire recipe. The cost, which is recorded, should also be broken down into the cost of a pound, if produced in pounds, or in gallons produced, if a liquid measurement is used. The cost is then calculated for the individual portion, using ounces for weight and fluid ounces for liquid measurements. Another way the portion cost should be expressed is in a decimal equivalent. To convert the cost into the decimal equivalent, calculate the total cost of all ingredients and extend the total four decimal places. To help in understanding this conversion, imagine that when an apple is weighed on a digital scale in a supermarket, it weighs one ounce over a pound. The weight would be recorded as 1.0625 times the price. If the price of apples is \$.50 per pound, then the cost of 17 ounces expressed in the decimal equivalent would be \$.5312 ($1.0625 \times \$.50 = \$.5312$). Therefore, if 17 ounces was the total amount produced, the value would be \$.5312, accounting for the total cost. You can then charge for any fraction and you can always recover the total cost of .5312.

- **Number of portions**—the total number of portions produced by the recipe. Most recipes' portions are expressed in straightforward numbers such as 50 or 100 portions. Sometimes, the total number of portions is expressed differently, such as 25 portions per pan, and the recipe produces 4 pans, totaling 100 portions.

- **Portion size**—the single serving size; usually noted for a recipe, such as 8-ounce portions of soup. The portion size should be an edible and salable single portion; otherwise, the accuracy of the amount produced or the number of portions needs to be checked.

■ ***Portion cost***—the cost of one serving, found by using the following formula:

$$\frac{\text{Total cost}}{\text{Total number of portions}} = \text{Portion cost}$$

If the cost per ounce and the portion size are known, the following formula could be used:

$$\text{Portion} \times \text{Cost per ounce} = \text{Portion cost}$$

■ **Hint** _____

When the cost per ounce and the portion size are known, either one of the mathematical formulas could be used to find the portion cost. The easier and superior formula uses division. (In the previous lessons, the best calculation methods used either multiplcation or addition, as opposed to division or subtraction.) Division is recommended because of the use of rounded numbers. Study these examples:

$$\begin{array}{r} \$\ \ .1575 \text{ portion cost} \\ 70 \text{ portions } \overline{)\$11.0251 \text{ total cost}} \end{array}$$

or

$$\begin{array}{r} 2.9285 \text{ oz. portion size} \\ 70 \text{ portions } \overline{)205 \text{ oz.}} \end{array}$$

or

Portion size (oz.)	2.9285
× Cost per ounce	× $.0537
= Cost per portion	$.1572

The portion cost of $.1575 almost duplicates the portion cost of $.1572. When rounding numbers, and going four places to the right of the decimal point, you should opt for the simpler method of dividing, although keep in mind that it is not incorrect to use the other procedure.

Ingredient Section

The second part of the recipe card is the ingredient section. Explanations of the terms listed in the body or ingredient portion follow:

- ***Quantity***—the total amount of the ingredient used. Most of these quantity amounts will be whole, fraction, or decimal equivalent amounts.
- ***Unit***—a single quantity regarded as a whole in a calculation. The unit information is obtained from the priced-out ingredient and is used to multiply the quantity times the unit price. Standards of measurement in this column include pounds, ounces, gallons, quarts, pints, fluid ounces, each, can, dozen, and so on.
- ***Ingredients***—the actual items used in a recipe, for example, carrots, onions, celery, flour, tomatoes (canned), water, and eggs.
- ***Purchase price***—the cost of a bulk item bought. Purchasing was addressed in Lesson 3 and is used again in this lesson for control purposes. For example, onions are purchased in 50-pound bags but are listed in recipes by the pound. Therefore, if a bag of onions is $8.00, the cost of a pound must be determined, and that unit price is used in calculating the total cost of the recipe. It is very important to know how to break down bulk packaging into smaller units for pricing out a standard recipe. Figure 7–3 shows the bulk purchase prices for a recipe's ingredients.
- ***Unit price***—the cost of a single quantity of a bulk item. As explained in defining purchase price, bulk packaging is broken down into smaller amounts or units. Using the earlier example, to break down into units a 50-pound bag of onions costing $8.00, the following formula is used: $8.00 ÷ 50 = $.16 the unit price per lb. for onions. (See Figure 7–4.)
- ***Total cost***—the final price of an item, calculated by multiplying the quantity times the unit price, which equals the total cost. (See Figure 7–5.) Remember that you have to multiply like-quantity units times the like-quantity unit price, which will then equal the total cost for the correct like units. As an example, 15 each × $.30 = $4.50.

Another point should be mentioned regarding ingredients. Because many recipes contain numerous spices, a common practice in the industry is to charge a 2% to 5% cost to the entire recipe for spices, rather than to price out each spice individually. In Figure 7–6, a 2% charge has been entered for seasoning. Some recipes may list spices as a major portion of the ingredients; in those cases, the spices should be given an actual cost by multiplying the quantity times the unit price to get the total cost.

Figure 7–7 shows how the portion cost is identified by reducing all ingredients (except the seasoning) to ounces, dividing the total cost by the total number of ounces to get the cost per ounce, and then multiplying each item's weight by the cost per ounce. The amount produced is stated in (1) ounces, (2) pounds plus ounces, and (3) pounds plus decimal equivalent of ounces.

FIGURE 7–3   Standard Recipe Card—Bulk Purchase Prices

DATE: _____

STANDARD RECIPE CARD

ITEM _Stuffed Baked Meatloaf Viennese Style_ AMOUNT PRODUCED _____ COST PER _____

NUMBER OF PORTIONS _15 portions per loaf_ PORTION SIZE _____ PORTION COST _____

Qty	Unit	INGREDIENTS	Purch. Price	Unit price	Total Cost	Qty	Unit	INGREDIENTS	Purch. Price	Unit price	Total Cost
3	lbs.	Onions	8.00 / 50 LBS								
1	lb.	Celery	.60 / 2 LBS								
8	oz.	Butter	1.71 / LB								
1 1/2	lbs.	Flav Brd Crumbs	.15 / LB								
1	pt.	Milk	2.13 / GAL								
8	ea.	Whole Eggs	.79 / DZ.								
13	lbs.	Ground Beef	1.49 / LB								
1 1/2	doz.	Hard Boiled Eggs	.79 / DZ.								

PREPARATION AND SERVICE

METHOD: (Procedure, time, temperature, remarks)

_____

_____

_____

_____

_____

_____

_____

_____

_____

_____

_____

_____

_____

_____

FIGURE 7–4 Standard Recipe Card—Unit Price

DATE: _____

STANDARD RECIPE CARD

ITEM _Stuffed Baked Meatloaf Viennese Style_ AMOUNT PRODUCED _____ COST PER _____

NUMBER OF PORTIONS _15 portions per loaf_ PORTION SIZE _____ PORTION COST _____

Qty	Unit	INGREDIENTS	Purch. Price	Unit price	Total Cost	Qty	Unit	INGREDIENTS	Purch. Price	Unit price	Total Cost
3	lbs.	Onions	8.00 / 50 LBS	1600							
1	lb.	Celery	.60 / 2 LBS	3000							
8	oz.	Butter	1.71 / LB	1068							
1 1/2	lbs.	Flav Brd Crumbs	.15 / LB	1500							
1	pt.	Milk	2.13 / GAL	2612							
8	ea.	Whole Eggs	.79 / DZ	0658							
13	lbs.	Ground Beef	1.49 / LB	1	4900						
1 1/2	doz.	Hard Boiled Eggs	.79 / DZ	0658							

PREPARATION AND SERVICE

METHOD: (Procedure, time, temperature, remarks)

_____

_____

_____

_____

_____

_____

_____

_____

_____

_____

_____

_____

_____

FIGURE 7–5   Standard Recipe Card—Total Cost per Item

DATE: _____

STANDARD RECIPE CARD

ITEM _Stuffed Baked Meatloaf Viennese Style_   AMOUNT PRODUCED _____ COST PER _____

NUMBER OF PORTIONS _15 portions per loaf_ PORTION SIZE _____ PORTION COST _____

Qty	Unit	INGREDIENTS	Purch. Price	Unit price	Total Cost	Qty	Unit	INGREDIENTS	Purch. Price	Unit price	Total Cost
3	lbs.	Onions	8.00 / 50 LBS	1600	.4800						
1	lb.	Celery	.60 / 2 LBS	3000	.3000						
8	oz.	Butter	1.71 / LB	1068	.8544						
1 1/2	lbs.	Flav Brd Crumbs	.15 / LB	1500	.2250						
1	pt.	Milk	2.13 / GAL	2612	.2662						
8	ea.	Whole Eggs	.79 / DZ	0658	.5264						
13	lbs.	Ground Beef	1.49 / LB	1 4900	19 3700						
1 1/2	doz.	Hard Boiled Eggs	.79 / DZ	0658	1 1844						

PREPARATION AND SERVICE

METHOD: (Procedure, time, temperature, remarks)

_____

_____

_____

_____

_____

_____

_____

_____

_____

_____

_____

_____

_____

FIGURE 7–6 Standard Recipe Card—Cost of Seasoning

DATE: _____

STANDARD RECIPE CARD

ITEM <u>Stuffed Baked Meatloaf Viennese Style</u> AMOUNT PRODUCED _____ COST PER _____

NUMBER OF PORTIONS <u>15 portions per loaf</u> PORTION SIZE _____ PORTION COST _____

Qty	Unit	INGREDIENTS	Purch. Price	Unit price		Total Cost		Qty	Unit	INGREDIENTS	Purch. Price	Unit price	Total Cost
3	lbs.	Onions	8.00 / 50LBS		1600		.4800						
1	lb.	Celery	.60 / 2 LBS		3000		.3000						
8	oz.	Butter	1.71 / LB		1068		.8544						
1½	lbs.	Flav Brd Crumbs	.15 / LB		1500		.2250						
1	pt.	Milk	2.13 / GAL		2612		.2262						
8	ea.	Whole Eggs	.79 / DZ		0658		.5264						
13	lbs.	Ground Beef	1.49 / LB	1	4900	19	3700						
		Seasoning +2%					4408						
1½	doz.	Hard Boiled Eggs	.79 / DZ		0658	1	1844						

PREPARATION AND SERVICE

METHOD: (Procedure, time, temperature, remarks)

_____

_____

_____

_____

_____

_____

_____

_____

_____

_____

_____

_____

_____

_____

FIGURE 7–7   Standard Recipe Card—Portion Cost

DATE: _____

STANDARD RECIPE CARD

OZ 372
LB 23LB 4oz

ITEM _Stuffed Baked Meatloaf Viennese Style_ AMOUNT PRODUCED _DEC. 23.2500_ COST PER

TOTAL COST $23.6468
OZ.   .0635
LB.   1.0160
DEC.   1.0178

NUMBER OF PORTIONS _15 portions per loaf_ PORTION SIZE _8.2666 oz_ PORTION COST _.5260_

	Qty	Unit	INGREDIENTS	Purch. Price	Unit price	Total Cost	Qty	Unit	INGREDIENTS	Purch. Price	Unit price	Total Cost
3x16=48	3	lbs.	Onions	8.00 / 50LBS	1600	4800						
1x16=16	1	lb.	Celery	.60 / 2 LBS	3000	3000						
8x1=8	8	oz.	Butter	1.71 / LB	1068	8544						
1 1/2x16=24	1 1/2	lbs.	Flav Brd Crumbs	.15 / LB	1500	2250	22.0220					
1x16=16	1	pt.	Milk	2.13 / GAL	2612	2262						
8x2=16	8	ea.	Whole Eggs	.79 / DZ	0658	5264						
13x16=208	13	lbs.	Ground Beef	1.49 / LB	1 4900	19 3700						
			Seasoning +2%			4408						
18x2=36	1 1/2	doz.	Hard Boiled Eggs	.79 / DZ	0058	1 1844						
372oz												
						23 6468						

PREPARATION AND SERVICE

METHOD: (Procedure, time, temperature, remarks)

_____
_____
_____
_____
_____
_____
_____
_____
_____
_____
_____
_____
_____
_____

Preparation and Service Procedures Section

The last part of a standard recipe card describes the method of preparation and the service procedures. Method is summarized as: *procedure, time, temperature,* and *remarks*. This part of the recipe card should not be taken any less seriously than the other two sections. All three sections help in better understanding the portion cost analysis.

The preparation and service section of the recipe card states the most logical sequence of the steps for cooking. Following the recipe sequence for the combination of ingredients ensures that the recipe will turn out as expected. This section also describes the cut suggested for the ingredient; for example, large dice, small dice, minced, or grated. The suggested temperature or cooking method should also be included; for example, boiling, simmering, or cooking 5 minutes at 100 degrees. Handling procedures are stated—for example, chill, or refrigerate overnight. Details are given on how to portion out the recipe and what size dish or bowl to use; for example, "Ladle chilled soup in an 8-ounce portion into a 9-ounce bowl and top with a teaspoon of sour cream." The garnish should also be stated in the recipe and given a cost as part of the ingredients.

Before turning to the spreadsheet information, remember that this lesson has several formulas that are based on information you already have. There will be two possible ways to find the same totals, not just one way of finding the answer.

■ SPREADSHEET OBJECTIVES

Upon completion of Lesson 7, you should be able to:

1. Calculate total cost per recipe and cost per portion.
2. Calculate portion size based on changing variables (for example, number of portions, increased cost).
3. Use various formulas to conduct portion cost analysis.

SPREADSHEET INFORMATION

Review the supplied fact sheet; you will need it to complete the spreadsheet. To be able to complete the totals, you must first find the missing numbers by using the calculations you learned in this lesson.

Figure 7–8 shows the basic format of the spreadsheet.

The amount produced is one of the numbers that must be found. To discover the missing number, take the quantity of each item and break it

Spreadsheet Information ■ 173

FIGURE 7–8   Standard Recipe Card Spreadsheet—Basic Format

```
FOODSERVICE COST CONTROL USING MICROSOFT EXCEL          PG 1 OF 1
STUDENT NAME:          {NAME}          RESTAURANT NAME:
DATE:                  {DATE}          {NAME}
```

STANDARD RECIPE CARD

```
ITEM:       {ENTER ITEM NAME}
AMOUNT PRODUCED:          {AMOUNT} OUNCES (eg: 164 OUNCES)
                         {AMOUNT} POUNDS (eg: 10 POUNDS 4 OUNCES)
                         {AMOUNT} POUNDS/OUNCES
                                  (DECIMAL EQUIVALENT eg: 10.2500 POUNDS)
COST PER OUNCE:          $0.0000
COST PER POUND:          $0.0000
DEC. RECIPE COST:        $0.0000

NO. OF PORTIONS:         {AMOUNT}
PORTION SIZE:            0.0000
PORTION COST:            $0.0000
```

	A	B	C	D	E
	QUANTITY	UNIT	INGREDIENT	PURCHASE PRICE	UNIT PRICE	TOTAL COST
	0.0000	{UNIT}	{INGREDIENT}	$0.00	$0.0000	$0.0000
	0.0000	{UNIT}	{INGREDIENT}	$0.00	$0.0000	$0.0000
	0.0000	{UNIT}	{INGREDIENT}	$0.00	$0.0000	$0.0000
	0.0000	{UNIT}	{INGREDIENT}	$0.00	$0.0000	$0.0000
	0.0000	{UNIT}	{INGREDIENT}	$0.00	$0.0000	$0.0000
	0.0000	{UNIT}	{INGREDIENT}	$0.00	$0.0000	$0.0000
	0.0000	{UNIT}	{INGREDIENT}	$0.00	$0.0000	$0.0000
	0.0000	{UNIT}	{INGREDIENT}	$0.00	$0.0000	$0.0000
	0.0000	{UNIT}	{INGREDIENT}	$0.00	$0.0000	$0.0000
	0.0000	{UNIT}	{INGREDIENT}	$0.00	$0.0000	$0.0000
	0.0000	{UNIT}	{INGREDIENT}	$0.00	$0.0000	$0.0000
	0.0000	{UNIT}	{INGREDIENT}	$0.00	$0.0000	$0.0000
	0.0000	{UNIT}	{INGREDIENT}	$0.00	$0.0000	$0.0000
	0.0000	{UNIT}	{INGREDIENT}	$0.00	$0.0000	$0.0000
	0.0000	{UNIT}	{INGREDIENT}	$0.00	$0.0000	$0.0000
	0.0000	{UNIT}	{INGREDIENT}	$0.00	$0.0000	$0.0000
	0.0000	{UNIT}	{INGREDIENT}	$0.00	$0.0000	$0.0000
	0.0000	{UNIT}	{INGREDIENT}	$0.00	$0.0000	$0.0000
	0.0000	{UNIT}	{INGREDIENT}	$0.00	$0.0000	$0.0000
	0.0000	{UNIT}	{INGREDIENT}	$0.00	$0.0000	$0.0000

```
                                                  TOTAL COST    $0.0000
```

down into a smaller dry or liquid measurement. In the meatloaf recipe, the common measurement is ounces:

3 lbs. onions	3×16 oz. =	48
1 lb. celery	1×16 oz. =	16
1 pt. water	1×16 oz. =	16
2 ea. eggs	2×2 oz. =	4
	Total	= 84 oz.

With the ingredients broken down into ounces, 1 pound (1 lb.) equals 16 ounces (16 oz.); 1 pint (1 pt.) of water (liquid measurement) equals 16 ounces; and 1 each (ea.) egg (large) weighs 2 ounces, therefore, 2 eggs × 2 ounces 4 ounces. The total weight of this recipe at preparation is 84 ounces. The recipe will *not actually produce* 84 ounces because of evaporation. Most standardized recipes will provide the evaporation or percent of loss obtained from the cooking loss test. Using 84 ounces as an example, the amount produced is:

Oz.	84
Lb.	5 lbs. 4 oz.
Decimal equivalent	5.2500 lbs.

The next missing number to find is the total cost, which appears after entering all quantities, multiplied by the unit price of the ingredients. When all are totaled, the result equals the total cost.

Now that we have the amount produced and the total cost, the cost per ounce, pound, and decimal equivalent can be figured, as follows:

$$\text{Cost per oz.} = \frac{\text{Total value}}{\text{Total ounces}}$$

$$\text{Cost per lb.} = \text{Cost per oz.} \times 16 \text{ (number of ounces per lb.)}$$

$$\text{Cost per quart} = \text{Cost per fluid oz.} \times 32 \text{ (number of ounces per quart)}$$

$$\text{Cost per decimal equivalent} = \frac{\text{Total value}}{\text{Total decimal equivalent}}$$

The next missing number to find is the portion size, which is sometimes given instead of the number of portions. The formula for finding the portion size is:

$$\frac{\text{Amount produced (oz.)}}{\text{Total number of portions}} = \text{Portion size}$$

Keep in mind that an edible portion size is judged as acceptable for an average person, not a prizefighter and not a dieter.

If the portion size was provided and not the number of portions, the number of portions could be found by using the following formula:

$$\frac{\text{Amount produced (oz.)}}{\text{Portion size}} = \text{Number of portions}$$

The last missing number to find is the portion cost. If all the other information is completed, there are two ways of finding the portion cost:

1. Recommended method:

$$\frac{\text{Total cost}}{\text{Number of portions}} = \text{Portion cost}$$

2. Alternate method = Cost per ounce × Portion size = Portion cost (see Figure 7–9)

FIGURE 7–9   Standard Recipe Card—Portion Cost

```
FOODSERVICE COST CONTROL USING MICROSOFT EXCEL          PG 1 OF 1
STUDENT NAME:           {NAME}        RESTAURANT:
DATE:                   {DATE}        {NAME}
================================================================

                    STANDARD RECIPE CARD
================================================================

  ITEM:      STUFFED BAKED MEATLOAF VIENNESE STYLE
  AMOUNT PRODUCED:    372          OUNCES (eg: 164 OUNCES)
                      23 LBS. 4 OZS.   POUNDS (eg: 10 POUNDS 4 OUNCES)
                      23.2500      POUNDS/OUNCES
                                   (DECIMAL EQUIVALENT eg: 10.2500 POUNDS)

  COST PER OUNCE:              $0.0635
  COST PER POUND:             $1.0160
  DEC. RECIPE COST:           $1.0170

  NO. OF PORTIONS:                  45
  PORTION SIZE:               8.2666
  PORTION COST:               $0.5254
```

	A	B	C	D	E
QUANTITY	UNIT	INGREDIENT	PURCHASE PRICE	UNIT PRICE	TOTAL COST
3.0000	LBS	ONIONS	$8.00	$0.1600	$0.4800
1.0000	LBS	CELERY	$0.60	$0.3000	$0.3000
8.0000	OZ	BUTTER	$1.71	$0.1068	$0.8544
1.5000	LBS	FLAV BRD CRUMBS	$0.15	$0.1500	$0.2250
1.0000	PT	MILK	$2.13	$0.2662	$0.2662
8.0000	EA	WHOLE EGGS	$0.79	$0.0658	$0.5264
13.0000	LBS	GROUND BEEF	$1.49	$1.4900	$19.3700
1.0000	EA	SEASONINGS	$0.00	$0.4404	$0.4404
18.0000	EA	EGGS - GARNISH	$0.79	$0.0658	$1.1844
					$0.0000
					$0.0000
					$0.0000
					$0.0000
					$0.0000
					$0.0000
					$0.0000
					$0.0000
					$0.0000
					$0.0000
					$0.0000

TOTAL COST $23.6468

FIGURE 7–10   Portion Cost Analysis Spreadsheet—Basic Format

| FOODSERVICE COST CONTROL USING MICROSOFT EXCEL | | | | PG 1 OF 2 LEFT SIDE | |

| STUDENT NAME: | {NAME} | | RESTAURANT NAME: | {RESTAURANT NAME} | |
| DATE: | {DATE} | | | | |

RECIPE / PORTION COST ANALYSIS

A	B	C	D		E		F
ITEM NAME	PORTION SIZE OZ.	NUMBER OF PORTIONS	QUANTITY PREPARED		UNIT COST		TOTAL COST
NAME	0.0000	0.0000		0 OZ	0.0000 OZ		0.0000
			0 LBS	0 OZ	0.0000 LB		
			0.0000 LBS		0.0000 DEC		
NAME	0.0000	0.0000		0 OZ	0.0000 OZ		0.0000
			0 LBS	0 OZ	0.0000 LB		
			0.0000 LBS		0.0000 DEC		
NAME	0.0000	0.0000		0 OZ	0.0000 OZ		0.0000
			0 LBS	0 OZ	0.0000 LB		
			0.0000 LBS		0.0000 DEC		
NAME	0.0000	0.0000		0 OZ	0.0000 OZ		0.0000
			0 LBS	0 OZ	0.0000 LB		
			0.0000 LBS		0.0000 DEC		
NAME	0.0000	0.0000		0 OZ	0.0000 OZ		0.0000
			0 LBS	0 OZ	0.0000 LB		
			0.0000 LBS		0.0000 DEC		
NAME	0.0000	0.0000		0 OZ	0.0000 OZ		0.0000
			0 LBS	0 OZ	0.0000 LB		
			0.0000 LBS		0.0000 DEC		
NAME	0.0000	0.0000		0 OZ	0.0000 OZ		0.0000
			0 LBS	0 OZ	0.0000 LB		
			0.0000 LBS		0.0000 DEC		
NAME	0.0000	0.0000		0 OZ	0.0000 OZ		0.0000
			0 LBS	0 OZ	0.0000 LB		
			0.0000 LBS		0.0000 DEC		

This concludes the information needed to complete the three sections of the standard recipe card. The information obtained from the calculations will now be used for the next part of this lesson, which is the portion cost analysis. All the information is recorded in a particular section of the spreadsheet.

PORTION COST ANALYSIS

The second part of this lesson utilizes the completed recipe card. The spreadsheet used in this section is titled Portion Cost Analysis (Figure 7–10) and is described here in detail above.

FIGURE 7–10   (Continued)

FOODSERVICE COST CONTROL USING MICROSOFT EXCEL

STUDENT NAME: {NAME}   RESTAURANT NAME:
DATE: {DATE}   {RESTAURANT NAME}

==

REC./PORT. COST ANALYSIS

G	H	I	J
DESIRED GROSS FC	PORTION COST	SELLING PRICE/ITEM	TOTAL SALES POTENTIAL
32.0000%	0.0000	0.0000	0.0000
32.0000%	0.0000	0.0000	0.0000
32.0000%	0.0000	0.0000	0.0000
0.0000%	0.0000	0.0000	0.0000
0.0000%	0.0000	0.0000	0.0000
0.0000%	0.0000	0.0000	0.0000
0.0000%	0.0000	0.0000	0.0000
0.0000%	0.0000	0.0000	0.0000

FIGURE 7–11   Portion Cost Analysis Spreadsheet—Entries from Recipe Card

FOODSERVICE COST CONTROL USING MICROSOFT EXCEL   PG 1 OF 2
LEFT SIDE

STUDENT NAME: {NAME}   RESTAURANT NAME:
DATE: {DATE}   {RESTAURANT NAME}

RECIPE / PORTION COST ANALYSIS

A	B	C	D		E	F
ITEM NAME	PORTION SIZE OZ.	NUMBER OF PORTIONS	QUANTITY PREPARED		UNIT COST	TOTAL COST
BAKED MEATLOAF	8.2666	45.0000		372 OZ	0.0635 OZ	23.6468
			23 LBS	4 OZ	1.0160 LB	
			23.2500 LBS		1.0170 DEC	
BAKED MEATLOAF	0.0000	0.0000		372 OZ	0.0635 OZ	23.6468
			23 LBS	4 OZ	1.0160 LB	
			23.2500 LBS		1.0170 DEC	
BAKED MEATLOAF	0.0000	0.0000		372 OZ	0.0000 OZ	0.0000
			23 LBS	4 OZ	0.0000 LB	
			23.2500 LBS		0.0000 DEC	
NAME	0.0000	0.0000		0 OZ	0.0000 OZ	0.0000
			0 LBS	0 OZ	0.0000 LB	
			0.0000 LBS		0.0000 DEC	
NAME	0.0000	0.0000		0 OZ	0.0000 OZ	0.0000
			0 LBS	0 OZ	0.0000 LB	
			0.0000 LBS		0.0000 DEC	
NAME	0.0000	0.0000		0 OZ	0.0000 OZ	0.0000
			0 LBS	0 OZ	0.0000 LB	
			0.0000 LBS		0.0000 DEC	
NAME	0.0000	0.0000		0 OZ	0.0000 OZ	0.0000
			0 LBS	0 OZ	0.0000 LB	
			0.0000 LBS		0.0000 DEC	
NAME	0.0000	0.0000		0 OZ	0.0000 OZ	0.0000
			0 LBS	0 OZ	0.0000 LB	
			0.0000 LBS		0.0000 DEC	

FIGURE 7–11   (Continued)

FOODSERVICE COST CONTROL USING MICROSOFT EXCEL

PG 2 OF 2
LEFT SIDE

STUDENT NAME: {NAME}   RESTAURANT NAME:
DATE: {DATE}   {RESTAURANT NAME}

===

REC./PORT. COST ANALYSIS

G	H	I	J
DESIRED GROSS FC	PORTION COST	SELLING PRICE/ITEM	TOTAL SALES POTENTIAL
32.0000%	0.5254	1.6418	73.8810
32.0000%	0.0000	0.0000	0.0000
32.0000%	0.0000	0.0000	0.0000
0.0000%	0.0000	0.0000	0.0000
0.0000%	0.0000	0.0000	0.0000
0.0000%	0.0000	0.0000	0.0000
0.0000%	0.0000	0.0000	0.0000
0.0000%	0.0000	0.0000	0.0000

■ Column A begins with the item name (for example, Beef Stew), which is obtained from the recipe card.

■ Column B starts with portion size ounces, also obtained from the recipe card and inserted in that spot. (Refer to the recipe card for formulas used in this section.)

■ Column C, number of portions, is taken from the recipe card heading.

■ Column D, quantity prepared, also comes from the recipe card. It is important to state the quantity prepared in ounces, pounds plus ounces, and pounds plus decimal equivalent on all three forms, using all three methods if necessary.

■ Column E, unit cost, and Column F, total cost, are also taken from the recipe card.

■ Column G, desired food cost percent, is a set number (in this case, 32%) and is used to start the spreadsheet at line 1. The desired food cost percent is locked in and cannot be changed.

■ Column H, portion cost, is taken from the recipe card.

■ Column I, the selling price for the item, is calculated by using the formula:

$$\frac{\text{Cost}}{\text{Cost percent (c\%)}} = \text{Sales (s)}$$

This number will automatically be calculated for you, provided you have entered portion cost in column H. The fixed number (32%) from column G will calculate the sales for this item.

■ Column J is total sales potential. The formula used for this column is number of portions (column C) multiplied by selling price for the item (column I). The formula looks like this:

Number of portions × Selling price for the item = Total sales potential

Notice that to complete the first line of the portion cost analysis, you are using numbers that you already calculated for the recipe card. All you have to do is insert the numbers from the recipe card into columns A through F and column H. (The number in column G is fixed and given.) After completing those columns, columns I and J self-calculate, providing all the numbers are in the appropriate columns. (See Figure 7–11.)

EXERCISES

Most of the exercises can be completed on the spreadsheet; among the "Check Your Understanding" questions, question 7 is completed on the second line of the spreadsheet and question 9 is completed on the third line. If you are daring, you can attempt to do other analyses that are not protected in any manner, from lines 4 to 8 on the spreadsheet. To complete line 2 on the spreadsheet and to answer question 7, you will enter new numbers in columns B, C, and H. The spreadsheet allows you to work left-to-right when you enter the data from the recipe cards. You will be replacing the existing numbers with new ones that allow you to do an analysis. For question 7, you enter the new number of portions, which in turn changes the portion size and portion cost. To fully understand the math involved, review all the formulas used for calculating the recipe card. Keep in mind that (1) even though some formulas are multiplied for a recipe card, the analysis may require dividing a number, and (2) we have been working with numbers from left to right on the worksheet and we have used formulas that multiply or divide. It may happen that you can work from right to left instead, and divide and multiply, based on the number you want to substitute for analysis purposes.

Figure 7–12 shows the effect of varying the number of portions.

Question 9 of the "Check Your Understanding" section asks: if the original recipe cost is increased by 14% but the selling price and cost percent remain the same, what would be the new portion size? Your portion cost analysis must then determine which columns remain the same with this information and which numbers change.

Look carefully at line 3 on the spreadsheet in Figure 7–13, to help you answer question 9. The total cost will increase by 14%; therefore, you must take the original total cost and multiply it by 14%. After that amount is determined, it is added to the original amount to come up with the new total cost. When you have a new total cost, you realize that the desired gross food cost percent remains the same as the original, which means that the selling price per item must remain the same. You should then realize that the portion cost also has to remain the same. These numbers remain the same because you are using three basic formulas:

1. $$\frac{\text{Portion cost}}{\text{Desired gross food cost percent}} = \text{Selling price per item}$$

If desired gross food cost percent and selling price per item remain the same, then you need to find the cost. The solution would be:

FIGURE 7–12 Portion Cost Analysis Spreadsheet—Varying Number of Portions

FOODSERVICE COST CONTROL USING MICROSOFT EXCEL

PG 1 OF 2
LEFT SIDE

STUDENT NAME: {NAME}   RESTAURANT NAME:
DATE: {DATE}   {RESTAURANT NAME}

RECIPE / PORTION COST ANALYSIS

A	B	C	D			E		F
ITEM NAME	PORTION SIZE OZ.	NUMBER OF PORTIONS	QUANTITY PREPARED			UNIT COST		TOTAL COST
BAKED MEATLOAF	8.2666	45.0000			372 OZ	0.0635	OZ	23.6468
			23 LBS	4 OZ		1.0160	LB	
			23.2500 LBS			1.0170	DEC	
BAKED MEATLOAF	5.3142	70.0000			372 OZ	0.0635	OZ	23.6468
			23 LBS	4 OZ		1.0160	LB	
			23.2500 LBS			1.0170	DEC	
BAKED MEATLOAF	0.0000	0.0000			372 OZ	0.0000	OZ	0.0000
			23 LBS	4 OZ		0.0000	LB	
			23.2500 LBS			0.0000	DEC	
NAME	0.0000	0.0000			0 OZ	0.0000	OZ	0.0000
			0 LBS	0 OZ		0.0000	LB	
			0.0000 LBS			0.0000	DEC	
NAME	0.0000	0.0000			0 OZ	0.0000	OZ	0.0000
			0 LBS	0 OZ		0.0000	LB	
			0.0000 LBS			0.0000	DEC	
NAME	0.0000	0.0000			0 OZ	0.0000	OZ	0.0000
			0 LBS	0 OZ		0.0000	LB	
			0.0000 LBS			0.0000	DEC	
NAME	0.0000	0.0000			0 OZ	0.0000	OZ	0.0000
			0 LBŚ	0 OZ		0.0000	LB	
			0.0000 LBS			0.0000	DEC	
NAME	0.0000	0.0000			0 OZ	0.0000	OZ	0.0000
			0 LBS	0 OZ		0.0000	LB	
			0.0000 LBS			0.0000	DEC	

Desired gross food cost percent
$\times$ Selling price per item
$=$ Portion cost

All the numbers are used to find the same answers, based on which numbers are given.

2. $\dfrac{\text{Total cost}}{\text{Portion cost}}$ $=$ Number of portions

FIGURE 7–12 (Continued)

FOODSERVICE COST CONTROL USING MICROSOFT EXCEL   PG 2 OF 2
LEFT SIDE

STUDENT NAME: {NAME}   RESTAURANT NAME:
DATE: {DATE}   {RESTAURANT NAME}

REC./PORT. COST ANALYSIS

G	H	I	J
DESIRED GROSS FC	PORTION COST	SELLING PRICE/ITEM	TOTAL SALES POTENTIAL
32.0000%	0.5254	1.6418	73.8810
32.0000%	0.3378	1.0556	73.8920
32.0000%	0.0000	0.0000	0.0000
0.0000%	0.0000	0.0000	0.0000
0.0000%	0.0000	0.0000	0.0000
0.0000%	0.0000	0.0000	0.0000
0.0000%	0.0000	0.0000	0.0000
0.0000%	0.0000	0.0000	0.0000

is your second formula. Once you have concluded that all numbers remained the same as the original numbers in columns G, H, and I in Figure 7–13, you can then proceed to work backward on the spreadsheet to come up with the new portion size. You can conclude that if the portion cost is a certain amount and you have the total cost of the recipe, you can calculate the number of portions.

3. $\dfrac{\text{Quantity prepared}}{\text{Number of portions}} = \text{Portion size}$

FIGURE 7–13   Portion Cost Analysis Spreadsheet—Gross Food Cost Percent

FOODSERVICE COST CONTROL USING MICROSOFT EXCEL

PG 1 OF 2
LEFT SIDE

STUDENT NAME: {NAME}
DATE: {DATE}

RESTAURANT NAME:
{RESTAURANT NAME}

RECIPE / PORTION COST ANALYSIS

A	B	C	D		E	F
ITEM NAME	PORTION SIZE OZ.	NUMBER OF PORTIONS	QUANTITY PREPARED		UNIT COST	TOTAL COST
BAKED MEATLOAF	8.2666	45.0000	23 LBS 23.2500 LBS	372 OZ 4 OZ	0.0635 OZ 1.0160 LB 1.0170 DEC	23.6468
BAKED MEATLOAF	0.0000	0.0000	23 LBS 23.2500 LBS	372 OZ 4 OZ	0.0635 OZ 1.0160 LB 1.0170 DEC	23.6468
BAKED MEATLOAF	7.2503	51.3081	23 LBS 23.2500 LBS	372 OZ 4 OZ	0.0724 OZ 1.1584 LB 1.1594 DEC	26.9573
NAME	0.0000	0.0000	0 LBS 0.0000 LBS	0 OZ 0 OZ	0.0000 OZ 0.0000 LB 0.0000 DEC	0.0000
NAME	0.0000	0.0000	0 LBS 0.0000 LBS	0 OZ 0 OZ	0.0000 OZ 0.0000 LB 0.0000 DEC	0.0000
NAME	0.0000	0.0000	0 LBS 0.0000 LBS	0 OZ 0 OZ	0.0000 OZ 0.0000 LB 0.0000 DEC	0.0000
NAME	0.0000	0.0000	0 LBS 0.0000 LBS	0 OZ 0 OZ	0.0000 OZ 0.0000 LB 0.0000 DEC	0.0000
NAME	0.0000	0.0000	0 LBS 0.0000 LBS	0 OZ 0 OZ	0.0000 OZ 0.0000 LB 0.0000 DEC	0.0000

After calculating the number of portions, you calculate the portion size by dividing the quantity prepared, in ounces, by the number of portions.

You have now found the new portion size and also the answer for question 9 in "Check Your Understanding." Another way to find the portion size, without working through the spreadsheet, would be:

Multiply the number of portions by a 14% increase, which will increase the number of portions. Next, divide the number of portions into the quantity prepared, in ounces, to arrive at your new portion size. This gives you the same answer as with the other method. By rounding and going four decimal places to the right, the answers are as close as possible. This shows that there are several methods to obtain an answer for the portion cost analysis.

FIGURE 7–13 (Continued)

FOODSERVICE COST CONTROL USING MICROSOFT EXCEL

PG 2 OF 2
RIGHT SIDE

STUDENT NAME: {NAME}　　　　RESTAURANT NAME:
DATE:　　　　　{DATE}　　　　　　{RESTAURANT NAME}

REC./PORT. COST ANALYSIS

G	H	I	J
DESIRED GROSS FC	PORTION COST	SELLING PRICE/ITEM	TOTAL SALES POTENTIAL
32.0000%	0.5254	1.6418	73.8810
32.0000%	0.0000	0.0000	0.0000
32.0000%	0.5254	1.6418	84.2376
0.0000%	0.0000	0.0000	0.0000
0.0000%	0.0000	0.0000	0.0000
0.0000%	0.0000	0.0000	0.0000
0.0000%	0.0000	0.0000	0.0000
0.0000%	0.0000	0.0000	0.0000

The answers to questions 6 and 8 of "Check Your Understanding" have not been covered and do not originate from the spreadsheet. Question 6 is information pertaining to a recipe factor. This is obtained in the following manner:

$$\text{Original recipe (number of portions)} \overline{)\text{Number of portions needed}} \quad \text{Recipe factor}$$

For example:

$$20\overline{)40} \quad 2 \quad \text{(40 divided by 20 equals 2, which is the recipe factor)}$$

You would then multiply by 2 all quantities of ingredients in the original recipe, to create a recipe for 40 portions.

For example:

Original recipe × Recipe factor = New recipe
Flour 1 lb × 2 (recipe factor) = 2 lbs.
Water 4 qts. × 2 (recipe factor) = 8 qts. or 2 gals.

When you want a smaller amount than the original recipe, the recipe factor will be a decimal, not a whole number. For example, suppose the recipe is scaled for 20 portions and you need only 10. The formula would be the same as above, but the factor would be .5:

$$20\overline{)10.0}^{\,.5}$$

Original recipe   × Recipe factor = New recipe
Flour 1 lb. = 16 oz. × .5   = 8.0 oz. or ½ lb.
Water 4 qts. = 128 oz. × .5   = 64.0 oz. or 2 qts.

Using this formula, you will be able to complete question 6.

The last question involving numbers is question 8 of "Check Your Understanding." To answer this question, you would apply one of the three basic formulas mentioned throughout the book:

$$\frac{\text{Portion cost}}{\text{Gross food cost percent}} = \text{Selling price per item}$$

There is a final question for you to consider regarding portion cost analysis: Can you make the necessary portion changes to a recipe without damaging the original recipe? If you must use a large recipe factor and the quantities are greatly increased, what ingredients might you substitute to lower the cost of the new recipe without changing the quality, intent, or success of the original recipe?

CHECK YOUR UNDERSTANDING

Using the information and costs provided on pages 187 and 188 for the recipes from the Red Woodpecker Grill (R.W.G.) and the Terrace Garden Restaurant (T.G.R.), fill out standard recipe cards.

Standardize the recipes by conversion.

Add 2% of the total cost for seasoning, and use a standard 32% food cost.

Answer the following questions:

	R.WG.	T.G.R.
1. Total amount produced	_____	_____
2. Cost per unit	_____	_____
3. Number of portions	_____	_____
4. Portion size	_____	_____
5. Portion cost	_____	_____

6. What is the recipe factor needed to produce 30 portions?

_____

7. If 70 portions are produced from the original recipe, what is the new portion cost?

_____

8. Based on the answer to question 5, what would the selling price per portion be at 30% food cost?

_____

9. If the total cost of the original recipe is raised 14% but the selling price and cost percent remain the same, what must the new portion size be?

_____

10. What ingredients could be substituted to bring the cost down without changing the quality?

_____

_____

_____

Red Woodpecker Grill

Baked Stuffed Pork Chops

25 portions

	Quantity/Units	Cost	
Bread Stuffing	1½ lbs.	7.15	3.5.1b./box
Pork Chops (8 oz.)	12½ bs.	1.65 lb.	
Oil	1 pt.	6.63	5 qt./container
Salt			
White Pepper			
Water	8 oz.		
Brown Sauce	3½ pts.	7.27	2 lb./for 2 gal. sauce
Sherry	2 oz.	8.51	liter/33.8 oz.

1. Cut pockets in the pork chops.
2. Fill the pockets equally with stuffing. Secure the openings with picks or skewers.
3 Oil a bake pan and place chops in it. Brush them with oil and season with salt and pepper.
4. Place the chops under the broiler until lightly browned.
5. Transfer the pan to a preheated 350°F oven and bake for about ½ hour until chops are cooked through.
6. Remove the chops from pan and place in hotel pan for holding. Remove picks.
7. Deglaze the bake pan with the water, degrease, and strain it into the hot brown sauce.
8. Bring the sauce to a boil and reduce slightly to bring to proper consistency.
9. Add sherry and adjust seasonings.
10. Serve 1 chop per portion with 2 oz. gravy.

Terrace Garden Restaurant

Breaded Veal Cutlets

24 portions

	Quantity/Units	Cost	
Veal Cutlets	6 lbs.	7.19 lb.	
Salt			
White Pepper			
Flour	12 oz.	18.99	100/lbs.
Eggs	8 each	14.40	15 doz./½ cs.
Milk	8 oz.	1.99 gal.	
Bread Crumbs	2.5 lbs.	2.63	5 lb./bag
Oil	8 oz.	6.63	5 qt./container

---

1. Lightly flatten each piece of veal with a meat mallet. Do not pound too hard or you may tear the meat.
2. Season the meat with salt and pepper.
3. Pass through Standard Breading Procedure.
4. Heat about ¼ inch of oil. Place cutlets in the pan and fry until golden brown. Turn and brown the other side. Remove from pan and place on hot plates.

CRITICAL THINKING QUESTIONS

1. After increasing the number of portions in a recipe for the Red Woodpecker Grill or the Terrace Garden Restaurant, what is your opinion of the results?

    _____

    _____

    _____

    _____

    _____

2. You should be aware of ingredient substitutions for the Red Woodpecker Grill and Terrace Garden Restaurant recipes. For each ingredient, indicate a method or item that can be substituted.

    _____

    _____

    _____

    _____

3. When increasing the total price of all ingredients for the Red Woodpecker Grill and Terrace Garden Restaurant, you are instructed to keep the food cost percent and the selling price the same. Indicate what is affected by increases and decreases on the spreadsheet for portion cost analysis.

    _____

    _____

    _____

    _____

MENU ENGINEERING

■ **OBJECTIVES**

Upon completing Lesson 8, you should be able to:

1. Understand the "menu engineering" concept.
2. Make menu adjustments that enhance profit.
3. Calculate food costs for table d'hôte, du jour, and à la carte menus.
4. Manipulate food items and their menu frames for ultimate profitability.
5. Decide when to add new items

■ **KEY TERMS**

Table d'Hôte	Menu Frame
American Plan	Menu Engineering
Full American Plan	Contribution Margin
Modified American Plan	Menu Mix Percent

■ **CONCEPT REVIEW**

The objective of this lesson is to show how to price out a menu, making it attractive to customers. The final result of this lesson should be that you understand how menu cost and menu choices can be manipulated, keeping one underlying principle in mind: You are always trying to make a profit. The major exercise will incorporate principles called ***menu engineering***, a concept or method of calculations designed by Michael L. Kasavana and Donald J. Smith. Details of menu engineering will be supplied after preliminary topics like menu types and menu frames are discussed.

Lesson 8 includes material from *Menu Engineering*, 2nd edition, by Michael L. Kasavana and Donald J. Smith, copyright © 1990, Hospitality Publications, Inc., P.O. Box 448, Okemos, MI 48805, and used with permission.

First, let's cover the three different types of menus: (1) table d'hôte, (2) du jour, and (3) à la carte.

Whatever type of menu is used for an establishment, the bottom line is that the menu must make a profit. A table d'hôte menu is limited; the offerings should not exceed 15 selections. Most table d'hôte menus offer between 5 and 15 entrees. The du jour menu usually offers 1 to 3 items. The à la carte menu, the most extensive list, offers between 15 and 45 selections.

Restaurants often combine parts of one type of menu with another, sometimes offering more or fewer items than a typical standard menu. Whatever method is used for a menu is fine as long as the ultimate objective is kept in mind: make a profit. No restaurant is in business to lose money.

Menu Types

Table d'Hôte

The first type of menu, **table d'hôte**, is also known as *bill of fare, standard house menu*, or, in the hotel business, **American Plan** (AP), meaning it includes a meal with an overnight stay at a hotel. **Full American Plan** (FAP) includes three meals (breakfast, lunch, and dinner) with an overnight stay at a hotel. Another meal plan is the **Modified American Plan** (MAP), which includes breakfast and dinner with an overnight stay at a hotel. Table d'hôte menus contain a number of selections that are sold at the same selling price but have different costs. It is very difficult to cost these items because the customers have the option of choice. Solutions among today's types of service include buffets, salad bars, dessert bars, all-you-can-eat specials, and family or early-bird specials.

Knowing the definition and concepts helps in understanding how the table d'hôte menu is priced out to make a profit. The mathematical formula for determining a table d'hôte menu price is:

$$\frac{\text{Cost}}{\text{Sales}} = \text{Food cost percent}$$

This formula was reviewed in Lesson 1 and is essential in food cost control. The amount of profit made on a menu item cannot be determined until after the fact, however, because this formula is based on history. After the day's sales are completed, you will know your actual cost and the amount of sales generated. You can then compare the actual versus the desired food cost percent.

Du Jour

The second type of menu is ***du jour*** (of the day), also known as *chef's specials*, *blue plate specials*, or *manager's specials*. The term blue plate special originated years ago, when the daily specials were served on blue plates different from the regular plates used in the restaurant.

The terms du jour, blue plate, or special can be interpreted two ways: (1) the restaurant has purchased a limited amount of key ingredients for a particular recipe or an event such as a Friday Fish Fry special, or has taken advantage of an item that is in season, like melons or soft shell crabs; or (2) a special has been created because a regular menu item-for example, calves' liver—is not selling, and management wants to use the item before it spoils. The chef could then devise a special for the day using the calves' liver. Specials can also be produced from by-products remaining from the butcher's yield test or the cooking loss test (see Lesson 6). A good example of using by-products for a special would be to take reserved beef bones (by-products) from the freezer, bake them, apply barbecue sauce, and offer a special or barbecued ribs. A du jour menu has limitations, not an endless supply, so it is acceptable to run out of a special.

Good forecasting for future planning is essential in understanding this lesson. The mathematical formula (from Lesson 1) for finding the cost of a du jour menu item is:

$$\text{Sales} \times \text{Food cost percent} = \text{Cost}$$

This formula represents the present. You should have a target price for a du jour special, and a desired food cost percent that will enable you to know exactly how much to spend on the special. Remember that the final objective of a special is to make a profit.

À la Carte

The third type of menu, ***à la carte***, means, literally, off the cart; the customer pays for each item ordered separately. If a customer orders soup, salad, a main entrée, a side vegetable, a side of pasta, beverages, and dessert from an à la carte menu, each item would be priced out separately on the check. The mathematical formula for finding the cost of menu items from an à la carte menu is:

$$\frac{\text{Cost}}{\text{Food cost percent}} = \text{Sales}$$

This formula (from Lesson 1) represents the future and is also known as precosting because you know the cost and you know the food establishment's desired food cost percent. Therefore, by using the above formula, you can determine the sales figure. Using this method, you will always make a profit.

MENU FRAMES

Connected with the types of menus used is a concept called a **menu frame**, the cost of the items surrounding the entrée. It is very easy for a restaurant to determine the actual cost of a main entrée. For example, by going back to the butcher's yield test (Lesson 6), you can easily find the cost for an 8-oz. portion of filet of beef. An area that you can't always calculate, but for which you need to find the cost, is the surrounding cost of an entrée, or the menu frame. In Lesson 7, you found the cost for one portion of Beef Stew. Using Beef Stew as an example, what should the menu frame be? If bread and butter or margarine are served with the meal, along with a glass of water with a wedge of lemon in it, these costs need to be determined. If you were to combine Beef Stew with a salad for one price, would it be sensible? Remember: the cost of the salad must include the cost of salad dressing, which could be limited to oil and vinegar, French, or Italian, or, for an extra charge, Blue Cheese. What if you were to serve breadsticks instead of bread with the salad? These examples should help you to realize that surrounding costs or menu frames can add up quickly and must be considered when pricing out a menu item in order to make a profit.

Think for a minute about the last time you went to a pancake restaurant with a friend. Pancakes were $1.95. How much butter and syrup did you put on your pancakes? How about your friend—did he or she go crazy with the syrup while you used it sparingly? What about your coffee? How much cream or milk, sugar or Equal did you put in your coffee? The menu frame or surrounding costs of a menu item can seem endless; therefore, when pricing out any of the three menu types, the menu frame must be calculated also.

There are three types of menu frames: (1) high cost, (2) medium cost, and (3) low cost. Because menu frames vary, consumers can negotiate menu prices on banquets at hotels and restaurants. The range of items allows people with different budgets an opportunity to enjoy the same facility. Figure 8–1 gives examples of assorted menu choices and prices for a low cost menu frame. Figure 8–2 shows examples of items that justify a high cost menu frame.

It is important to understand the concepts of menu frames. Costs vary from low to high and that is acceptable. You should be able to "mix and match" or combine assorted food items that have various costs, to

FIGURE 8–1 Low Cost Menu Frame

(a) Menu choices

LOW COST MENU FRAME

APPETIZER OR SOUP CUP:	Tomato Juice Fruit Cup Consomme or	Stuffed Egg Vegetable Juice Cream Soup	
ENTREES:			
	(1) A		
	(2) B		
	(3) C		
	(4) D		
	(5) E		
VEGETABLES:	String Beans Potatoes (Boiled - French Fried - O'Brien)	Peas	Carrots
DESSERTS:	Ice Cream	Rice Pudding	Fruit Jello
BEVERAGES:	Coffee Rolls and Butter	Tea	Milk

(b) Cost per serving

LOW COST MENU FRAME

Appetizers
(1) .06   (2) .05   (3) .06

Soups
(2) .06

Entrees
(1) .05

Salads
(1) .06   (2) .06   (3) .07

Desserts
(1) .05   (2) .07   (3) .06

Beverages
(1) .06   (2) .06   (3) .07

Rolls and Butter .10

Cost Range: $ .37 to $ .43   Median $ .40

All entrees are not sold at the same cost %. Many low cost items have higher mark-ups than some high cost items (Reasons for this are labor costs and competitive factors.) These frames can be used for:

Table D'Hote Menus
A La Carte Menus
Banquet Menus

These worksheets are not for patron viewing.

FIGURE 8–2 High Cost Menu Frame

(a) Menu choices

HIGH COST MENU FRAME

APPETIZER:	Fruit Supreme	½ Cantalope	Hors D-Oeuvres
SOUP (Plate)	Vichyssoise	Petit Marmite	Green Turtle
RELISH:	Hearts of Celery	Ripe and Green Olives	
	Salted Almonds and Pecans		
ENTREES:			
VEGETABLES:	Broccoli	Asparagus	Cauliflower
	Bouquettiere of Fresh Vegetables		
	Potatoes (Parisiene Au Gratin		
	Candied Sweet Potato)		
SALAD:	Avocado	Half Bartlett Pear	French Endive
DESSERTS:	Baked Alaska	Pecan Pie	
	Frozen French Vanilla Ice Cream		
BEVERAGES:	Coffee	Tea	Milk
	Rolls and Butter		

(b) Cost per serving

HIGH COST MENU FRAME

Appetizers
(1) .25   (2) .75   (3) 1.50

Soups
(2) 1.00

Entrees
(1) .50
(1) A
(2) B
(3) C
(4) D
(5) E

Salads
(1) .25   (2) .50   (3) .80

Desserts
(1) .35   (2) .55   (3) 1.00

Beverages
(1) .06   (2) .25   (3) .50

Rolls and Butter .25

Cost Range: $1.75 to $5.10   Median $3.45

All entrees are not sold at the same cost %. Many low cost items have higher mark-ups than some high cost items (Reasons for this are labor costs and competitive factors.) These frames can be used for:

Table D'Hote Menus
A La Carte Menus
Banquet Menus

These worksheets are not for patron viewing.

195

produce your cost goal. When you apply the three basic formulas to your cost goal, a profit is realized. Generating a profit is a result of combining the concepts of menus and menu frames.

The following example will clarify how to price out a menu item to produce a profit.

Cost Analysis

Main entrée	Steak	$2.83	per 8-oz. portion
Menu frame	Salad	.1000	
	Dressing	.0300	
	Bread	.0200	
	Butter	.0100	
	Potato	.1000	
	Vegetable	.0800	
	Menu frame total	.3400	
Total cost of meal =		$3.17	

Using the formula below, you can plug in the total cost of the meal ($3.17) to determine the price to charge for this meal on an à la carte menu.

$$\frac{\text{Total cost}}{\text{Desired food cost percent}} = \text{Sales} \qquad \frac{\$3.17}{35\% \,(.35)} = \$9.0571$$

A decision can now be made as to whether this steak with surrounding food should sell for $9.05. If you did not want the steak dinner to sell for $9.05, you could reduce the surrounding cost (menu frame) of the steak. You would not eliminate the bread, starch, or vegetable; instead, you would choose a lower cost bread, starch, and vegetable. If the surrounding food costs (menu frame) were reduced to $.15, the price formula for the steak dinner would be:

$$\$2.83 + \$.15 = \$2.98$$

$$\frac{\$2.98}{.35} = \$8.5142$$

The price of the steak dinner is now $8.51. Will that price fit acceptably into most consumers' budget for a banquet dinner? If the price is acceptable, you can book the function. On the same night, two functions may be held at the same time in different sections of the restaurant, with both groups enjoying steak dinners. One group may pay $9.05 for their dinners while the other group pays $8.51. The restaurant still makes its desired profit because it has changed the items within the menu frame. The restaurant does not lose money on either function.

When booking group meals at a restaurant or hotel, you will notice that the menus are printed on different colored sheets of paper. In effect, they are trying to make you mix and match by color coding their menus. It may not be obvious to you, but the restaurant may have mapped out the menu exactly as shown in Figures 8–1 and 8–2.

MENU ENGINEERING

The concept of *menu engineering* unites the two previous concepts in this lesson: (1) types of menus and (2) menu frames. Because the concept of menu engineering is common and is included in most cost control texts and many food and beverage texts, it will not be covered in depth here. Menu engineering will be demonstrated through examples and application to the exercises in this lesson. For more detailed information on menu engineering, consult other texts for food management courses or check with your library. A typical menu engineering worksheet is shown in Figure 8–3.

For complete understanding of the menu engineering concepts, parts of this lesson should be performed twice. First, determine the ideal food cost percent. Divide the total costs by the total sales of an item to find the ideal food cost percent. The formula is as follows:

$$\frac{\text{Cost}}{\text{Sales}} = \text{Ideal food cost percent}$$

If you came up with the following numbers, what would they tell you?

$$\frac{\$20.00}{\$30.00} = 66.6666\%$$

You would be correct if you said that the ideal food cost percent is far too high. Why is that so and what can be done? When the food costs are too high, you are not making a profit. The average food cost percent should be about 40% or lower. Make sure the calculation is correct, and see whether any changes in the makeup of the cost can be made so that, when cost and sales are divided, the food cost percent will be in line. In most instances, all items combined should be in the range of 40% or lower. If you understand this concept, look at the three menu items on the menu engineering worksheet shown in Figure 8–4.

FIGURE 8-3 Typical Worksheet for Menu Engineering

MENU ENGINEERING WORKSHEET

Restaurant: _____

Date: _____

Meal Period: _____

(A) Menu Item Name	(B) Number Sold	(C) Menu Mix (MM%)	(D) Item Food Cost	(E) Item Selling Price	(F) Item CM (E−D)	(G) Menu Cost (D×B)	(H) Menu Revenues (E×B)	(L) Menu CM (F×B)	(P) CM Category	(R) MM% Category	(S) Menu Item Classification
Column Totals:	N					I	J	M			

K = I/J   O = M/N   Q = (100% items)(70%)

CM = Contribution Margin

FIGURE 8-4 Worksheet for Menu Engineering—Sample Entries

MENU ENGINEERING WORKSHEET

Restaurant: _____

Date: _____

Meal Period: _____

(A) Menu Item Name	(B) Number Sold	(C) Menu Mix (MM%)	(D) Item Food Cost	(E) Item Selling Price	(F) Item CM (E−D)	(G) Menu Cost (D×B)	(H) Menu Revenues (E×B)	(L) Menu CM (F×B)	(P) CM Category	(R) MM% Category	(S) Menu Item Classification
1/2 CHICKEN	1	33.3333	1.20	4.50	3.30	1.20	4.50	3.30			
10 oz. STEAK	1	33.3333	3.20	8.00	4.80	3.20	8.00	4.80			
12 oz. STEAK	1	33.3333	3.84	8.95	5.11	3.84	8.95	5.11			
SUBTOTALS	3	100.0000	8.24	21.45	15.21	8.25	21.45	13.21			
	N										
Column Totals:						I	J	M			
						K = I/J		O = M/N	Q = (100% items)(70%)		

CM = Contribution Margin

199

In Figure 8–4, the ideal food cost percent for this menu is:

$$\frac{\$8.24}{\$21.45} = 38.4149\%$$

From your earlier calculation and information, you know that this food cost percent is acceptable. But is it the best available food cost percent? To answer that question, you need to know the contribution margin (CM) of each item.

Item Contribution Margin

Contribution margin (CM) refers to the amount you get when you subtract the cost of an item from its selling price, giving you the actual dollars and cents of profit made on an item. In Figure 8–4, the total CM for the three menu offerings is $13.21. Divide $13.21 by 3, which gives you a contribution margin average of $4.4033 per offering.

Until now, you have dealt with the ideal food cost percent. In the second part of this lesson on menu engineering concepts, you will record the actual number of menu items sold.

New quantities and related numbers have been entered on the menu engineering worksheet shown in Figure 8–5. Columns A through L follow the procedures shown earlier, but reflect actual items sold. We need to define and explain columns P, R, and S.

To determine the average contribution margin (CM), the following formula is used:

$$\frac{\text{Total contribution margin (column L totals)}}{\text{Total number of items sold (column B totals)}} = \text{Average CM}$$

$$\frac{\$240.25}{50} = \$4.8050$$

After finding the CM average, you can compare this amount to each item's CM (column F). If an item's CM is above $4.8050, it would fall into the *high* category and if it is below $4.8050, it would fall into the *low* category.

Menu Mix Percent

The next column to calculate is the menu mix percent (MM%). This number is plotted on a basic X–Y graph and measured against a breakeven line, drawn across the X–Y graph, that separates profit from loss in the restaurant business. Your **menu mix percent** determines whether you are in a breakeven situation: it should not be less than 30%. (See Figure 8–6.)

FIGURE 8–5 Worksheet for Menu Engineering—Menu Item Classification

MENU ENGINEERING WORKSHEET

Restaurant: _____

Date: _____

Meal Period: _____

(A) Menu Item Name	(B) Number Sold	(C) Menu Mix (MM%)	(D) Item Food Cost	(E) Item Selling Price	(F) Item CM (E–D)	(G) Menu Cost (D×E)	(H) Menu Revenues (E×B)	(L) Menu CM (F×B)	(P) CM Category	(R) MM% Category	(S) Menu Item Classification
1/2 CHICKEN	5	10.0000	1.20	4.50	3.30	6.00	22.50	16.50	Low 3.30	Low	DOG
10 oz. STEAK	20	40.0000	3.20	8.00	4.80	64.00	160.00	96.00	High 4.80	High	STAR
12 oz. STEAK	25	50.0000	3.84	8.95	5.11	96.00	223.75	127.75	High 5.11	High	STAR
SUBTOTALS	50	100.0000	8.24	21.45	13.21	166.00	406.25	240.25			
							I	M			
Column Totals:	N						J				

CM = Contribution Margin

K = I/J   O = M/N   Q = (100% items)(70%)

FIGURE 8–6   Menu Engineering Graph

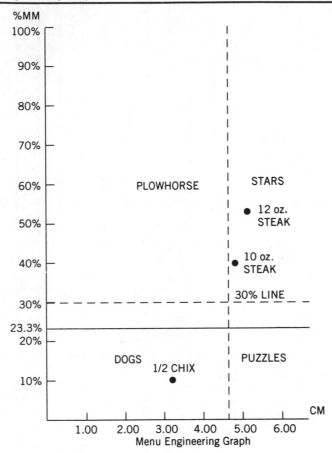

You will see the figure of 70% in the formula below, The authors of *Menu Engineering*, Michael L. Kasavana and Donald J. Smith, chose 70% after many alternate calculations, and it seems the most logical choice. The formula for the menu mix percent is:

$$(100/\text{items on menu}) \times 70\% = \text{Menu mix percent}$$

$$(100/3) \times .70 = 23.3333\%$$

This figure is then compared to column C, the menu mix percent. Any number above the column C figure is described in column R as *high*, and any number below that figure is described in column R as *low*.

Menu Item Classification

The last column, menu item classification, compares two columns, column P and column R. There are four possibilities; the ratings of high or low in the CM and MM categories earn the menu item classification of plowhorse, star, puzzle, or dog:

CM Category	MM Category	Menu Item Classification
1. Low	High	Plowhorse
2. High	High	Star
3. High	Low	Puzzle
4. Low	Low	Dog

These classifications are presented graphically in Figures 8–6 and 8–7.

Stars. These are the most popular and profitable items on a menu and may be a restaurant's prestige or *signature items* (products that are proprietary (noncompetitive) to a foodservice establishment). Decision actions appropriate for star items are:

1. Maintain rigid specifications for quality, portion size, and presentation.
2. Locate these items in a highly visible position on the menu.
3. Test for price elasticity.

"Superstars," the highest margined stars, may be less sensitive to price changes than any other items on the menu. If this situation exists, then these items can be sold at a higher CM by bumping their selling price. This increase will contribute greatly to covering a restaurant's ever-increasing costs (food, production, labor).

Plowhorses. These items are relatively popular; however, they yield lower CMs than the menu's average CM. Plowhorse items are often demand generators and are important to a restaurant's appeal to the price-conscience market segment. For this reason, they are often referred to as "leader" menu items. Decision actions for these items include:

1. Test for price sensitivity. If an item is highly price elastic (sensitive), only pass minimal cost-of-goods increases for this item on to a "Superstar." Closely monitor any negative effect on demand. Price increases can be accomplished in stages, particularly if "odd pricing" opportunities exist—for example, increases from $4.55 to $4.75, and eventually to $4.95. It is important to note that, at times, restaurants are more resistant to price increases than consumers are.

FIGURE 8–7   Menu Engineering Matrix

2. Relocate nonsignature, plowhorse items to a low profile position on the menu.

3. Consider combining plowhorse items with lower cost products to achieve a greater CM. In essence, merchandise highly popular items by packaging them with lower cost foods, to increase the items' overall CM without reducing their strong MM% appeal. For example, a highly popular 12-ounce Top Sirloin Steak may be replaced by an 8-ounce cut when a low cost enchilada is added to this menu item.

4. Consider a portion reduction, as long as the change doesn't produce a noticeable change in demand for the item.

5. Determine the direct labor factor, to establish the item's labor and skill intensiveness. If the item is highly skill- or labor-intensive, consider price increases or substitution, to achieve CM parity.

Puzzles. These items yield high contribution margins but are low in popularity. The appropriate decision actions suggested for puzzles are:

1. Take the items off the menu, particularly if they are very low in the menu mix, are labor-intensive, or have poor shelf life. This action is especially warranted when the puzzle items are not the restaurant's image enhancers.

2. Reposition and feature these items in a more popular location on the menu.

3. Rename the items. Often, food items' popularity can be affected by the assignment of a familiar name or trendy phrasing.

4. Decrease the price. Puzzle items that have too high a contribution margin may be overpriced and should be repriced in such a manner that their demand level is enhanced.

5. Enhance these items MM% by promoting them through merchandising. Increase their visual presentation, have the sales staff recommend them, and/or offer them as "specialty" items.

6. Limit the total number of puzzles allowed on the menu. Do this especially if they create quality, consistency, production, or inventory problems.

Dogs. These items are the menu's "losers"—they are unpopular and provide a low contribution margin. Dog decision actions are:

1. Eliminate the items from the menu. It is not unusual to discover a number of highly unpopular menu items, often with little, if any,

relation to other popular, more profitable items held in inventory. An operator should not be afraid to terminate dog items, especially those unrelated to other menu items.

2. Raise the items' prices, to achieve at least puzzle status. The more popular dog items often have some market potential and could possibly be converted to puzzles with a price increase.

3. Carry the items in inventory (assuming they have a reasonable shelf life) but do not list them on the menu. The availability of an item via only special request or reservation for certain influential guests may well turn a dog from a loser to a winner.

New Menu Item Development

Development of new menu items should be carefully considered and pre-tested before addition to the menu. When deciding whether to add new menu items that may be currently held in inventory, look for the following characteristics:

1. Low skill and labor intensity;
2. High popularity or growth potential;
3. Relatively stable cost;
4. Not easily prepared at home (i.e., roasts or fish);
5. Low cost and good plate merchandising;
6. High contribution margins.

There are two major reasons for adding new menu items:

1. *Increase Demand*. Add menu items with a relatively high degree of popularity, to increase frequency and/or broaden a market segment. For example, salad bars have become high-appeal entrées among lighter eaters and have been effective in almost all restaurant operations. Add items that have or can create greater market share, prestige, and visibility for the restaurant. Signature items are especially successful new items. These are items that simply cannot be gotten elsewhere.

2. *Increase Contribution Margin*. Add items that have high contribution margins, particularly if they do not require any additional inventory items. For example: a 20-oz. Prime Rib sold also in smaller cuts could increase the menu's overall CM.

The decision of whether to retain, reposition, reprice, or replace a menu item can be made intelligently, based on the classification of each menu item according to its relative popularity (menu mix percent) and contribution margin (CM).

The classification of menu items is broken down into four categories:

1. *Stars*—menu items high in menu mix (popularity) and high in contribution margin.
2. *Plowhorses*—menu items high in menu mix and low in contribution margin.
3. *Puzzles*—menu items low in menu mix and high in contribution margin.
4. *Dogs*—menu items low in menu mix and low in contribution margin.

The ranking of menu items as high or low according to MM% and CM classification should be followed by a thorough decision analysis for each of the four categories.

■ SPREADSHEET OBJECTIVES

Upon completion of Lesson 8, you should be able to:

1. Calculate menu mix percent and contribution margin in order to clarify the profit performance and popularity of menu items.
2. Make menu engineering decisions based on your calculations.

You now have three concepts to help in your understanding of menu engineering: (1) contribution margin, (2) menu mix %, and (3) menu item classification. You have the information necessary to correct, make adjustments to, or improve a menu, and thereby to increase the profit for your operation.

SPREADSHEET INFORMATION

The two spreadsheets designed for this lesson on menu engineering have no major special column. The only "real" task is the work prior to entering the data—calculation of the individual menu items, which will be explained later in the exercises.

In Figure 8–8, just enter the item number and then, in column A, the item name. Enter the number sold, in column B. In the first spread

FIGURE 8–8 Spreadsheet for Menu Engineering—Basic Format

FOODSERVICE COST CONTROL USING MICROSOFT EXCEL   PG 1 of 1
STUDENT NAME: {NAME}   RESTAURANT NAME:
DATE: {DATE}   {NAME}

MENU COSTING PERCENTAGES

ITEM ##	A ITEM NAME	B ## SOLD	C MENU MIX %	D ITEM FOOD COST	E ITEM SELL PRICE	F ITEM CM (E-D)	G MENU COST (D*B)	H MENU REVS (E*B)	L MENU CM (F*B)
1	NAME	0	ERR	0.0000	0.00	0.0000	0.0000	0.00	0.0000
2	NAME	0	ERR	0.0000	0.00	0.0000	0.0000	0.00	0.0000
3	NAME	0	ERR	0.0000	0.00	0.0000	0.0000	0.00	0.0000
4	NAME	0	ERR	0.0000	0.00	0.0000	0.0000	0.00	0.0000
5	NAME	0	ERR	0.0000	0.00	0.0000	0.0000	0.00	0.0000
6	NAME	0	ERR	0.0000	0.00	0.0000	0.0000	0.00	0.0000
7	NAME	0	ERR	0.0000	0.00	0.0000	0.0000	0.00	0.0000
8	NAME	0	ERR	0.0000	0.00	0.0000	0.0000	0.00	0.0000
9	NAME	0	ERR	0.0000	0.00	0.0000	0.0000	0.00	0.0000
10	NAME	0	ERR	0.0000	0.00	0.0000	0.0000	0.00	0.0000
11	NAME	0	ERR	0.0000	0.00	0.0000	0.0000	0.00	0.0000
12	NAME	0	ERR	0.0000	0.00	0.0000	0.0000	0.00	0.0000
TOTALS:		0	ERR				$0.00	$0.00	$0.0000

AVERAGE FOOD COST PER ITEM = $0.0000
FOOD COST PERCENTAGE =   0.0000%

FIGURE 8-9 Spreadsheet for Menu Engineering—Contribution Margins

FOODSERVICE COST CONTROL USING MICROSOFT EXCEL

STUDENT NAME: {NAME} RESTAURANT NAME: {NAME}

DATE: {DATE}

MENU COSTING PERCENTAGES

	A	B	C	D	E	F	G	H	L
ITEM ##	ITEM NAME	## SOLD	MENU MIX %	ITEM FOOD COST	ITEM SELL PRICE	ITEM CM (E-D)	MENU COST (D*B)	MENU REVS (E*B)	MENU CM (F*B)
1	HALF CHICKEN	1	33.3333%	1.2000	4.50	3.3000	1.2000	4.50	3.3000
2	10 oz. STEAK	1	33.3333%	3.2000	8.00	4.3000	3.2000	8.00	4.8000
3	12 oz. STEAK	1	33.3333%	3.8400	8.95	5.1100	3.8400	8.95	5.1100
4		0	0.0000%	0.0000	0.00	0.0000	0.0000	0.00	0.0000
5		0	0.0000%	0.0000	0.00	0.0000	0.0000	0.00	0.0000
6		0	0.0000%	0.0000	0.00	0.0000	0.0000	0.00	0.0000
7		0	0.0000%	0.0000	0.00	0.0000	0.0000	0.00	0.0000
8		0	0.0000%	0.0000	0.00	0.0000	0.0000	0.00	0.0000
9		0	0.0000%	0.0000	0.00	0.0000	0.0000	0.00	0.0000
10		0	0.0000%	0.0000	0.00	0.0000	0.0000	0.00	0.0000
11		0	0.0000%	0.0000	0.00	0.0000	0.0000	0.00	0.0000
12		0	0.0000%	0.0000	0.00	0.0000	0.0000	0.00	0.0000
TOTALS:		3	100.000%				$8.24	$21.45	$13.2100

AVERAGE FOOD COST PER ITEM = $2.7466

FOOD COST PERCENTAGE = 38.4149%

you will be calculating, the number will be 1, because you will be using the ideal food cost percent method. The menu mix (column C) will be automatically calculated for you; the total has to equal 100.0000%. The individual item sold formula is:

$$\frac{\text{Individual item sold}}{\text{Total items sold}} = MM\%$$

Keep in mind that when you divide the total items sold by the individual items sold, this number has to equal 100.0000% in all cases.

Here is how you should approach Figure 8–9:

FIGURE 8–10—Spreadsheet for Menu Engineering—Actual Sales

FOODSERVICE COST CONTROL USING MICROSOFT EXCEL   PG 1 OF 1
STUDENT NAME: {NAME}   RESTAURANT NAME:
DATE: {DATE}   {NAME}

MENU COSTING PERCENTAGES

	A	B	C	D	E	F
ITEM ##	ITEM NAME	## SOLD	MENU MIX %	ITEM FOOD COST	ITEM SELL PRICE	ITEM CM (E-D)
1	HALF CHICKEN	5	10.0000%	1.2000	4.50	3.3000
2	10 oz. STEAK	20	40.0000%	3.2000	8.00	4.8000
3	12 oz. STEAK	25	50.0000%	3.8400	8.95	5.1100
4		0	0.0000%	0.0000	0.00	0.0000
5		0	0.0000%	0.0000	0.00	0.0000
6		0	0.0000%	0.0000	0.00	0.0000
7		0	0.0000%	0.0000	0.00	0.0000
8		0	0.0000%	0.0000	0.00	0.0000
9		0	0.0000%	0.0000	0.00	0.0000
10		0	0.0000%	0.0000	0.00	0.0000
11		0	0.0000%	0.0000	0.00	0.0000
12		0	0.0000%	0.0000	0.00	0.0000
TOTALS:		50	100.000%			

AVERAGE FOOD COST PER ITEM = $3.3200
FOOD COST PERCENTAGE =   40.8615%

- For column D, item food cost, enter the menu cost that you have calculated for each item.
- For column E, enter the item selling price that has been given to you.
- For column F, the calculation formula is given and is automatically calculated; that is, item selling price minus item food cost equals item contribution margin (CM), the profit made per menu item.
- Column G is calculated for you; the total item food cost times the number sold equals the total menu cost for that item.
- Column H is also calculated for you; the total menu item times the number sold equals the total revenues for that item.
- In column L, this is calculated for you; you get the item contribution margin (CM), which is the profit made per item.
- Column F times the number of items sold equals the total profit of each category of items, which will now equal the total menu contribution margin per item.

FIGURE 8–10   (Continued)

G	H	L	P	R	S
MENU COST (D*B)	MENU REVS (E*B)	MENU CM (F*B)	CM CATEGORY	MENU MIX % CAT	MENU ITEM CLASSIFICATION
6.0000	22.50	16.5000	LOW	LOW	DOG
64.0000	160.00	96.0000	LOW	HIGH	PLOWHOSE
96.0000	223.75	127.7500	HIGH	HIGH	STAR
0.0000	0.00	0.0000			
0.0000	0.00	0.0000			
0.0000	0.00	0.0000			
0.0000	0.00	0.0000			
0.0000	0.00	0.0000			
0.0000	0.00	0.0000			
0.0000	0.00	0.0000			
0.0000	0.00	0.0000			
0.0000	0.00	0.0000			
$166.00	$406.25	$240.2500			

You should find these first steps relatively easy; you will just be entering data that you calculated, using the information given.

Working with Figure 8–10 will be even easier because it repeats the numbers used in Figure 8–9. The only difference is that you are given actual numbers to enter in column B, number of items sold. These numbers will allow you to compare the actual sales shown in the previous spreadsheet for ideal food cost percent (Figure 8–9). By using the actual numbers this time, you can compare the restaurant's standard performance to the ideal food cost percent. This spreadsheet section includes columns A through L. For the remaining columns—P, R, and S—you must apply the techniques previously discussed in menu engineering:

Calculate the average CM so you can determine whether that number is high or low. Use the formula:

$$\frac{\text{Total CM}}{\text{Total number of items sold}} = \begin{array}{l}\text{Average CM (to be}\\\text{compared to item CM)}\end{array}$$

■ Calculate the menu mix percent category so you can determine whether that number is high or low. Use the formula:

$$(100/\text{Number of menu items}) \times 70\% = \text{Percent to compare to MM\%}$$

■ Determine, using the chart of classifications, whether a menu item will be a plowhorse, star, puzzle, or dog. Let's review this chart one more time:

CM Category	MM Category	Menu Item Classification
1. Low	High	Plowhorse
2. High	High	Star
3. High	Low	Puzzle
4. Low	Low	Dog

After you identify the classifications, you can make some decisions to redesign the cost structure, change the selling price of an item, or eliminate or develop a new product, all of which are options for menu engineering design.

EXERCISES

EXERCISE 8–1A   Red Woodpecker Grill—Breakfast Specials

Cost out the 12 Breakfast Specials offered by the Red Woodpecker Grill. The information given is gathered into three categories:

1.   The portion size information;

2.   The cost of the food items;

3.   The menu combinations

1.   *Portion Sizes*

*Juice—6 oz.
Milk—6 oz.
Coffee, Tea—5 oz. (1 lb. of coffee makes 3 gallons)
Coffee Lite—½ oz.
Eggs—Large
Muffins—standard 1 each
Croissant—standard 1 each
Danish—standard 1 each
Bread—Pullman 2 slices (30 slices per loaf)
Texas Toast—½ loaf
Melon—½ of melon
Grapefruit—½ of grapefruit
Granola—6 oz.
Canadian Bacon—3 oz.
Hollandaise Sauce (1.5 lb. can makes 1 gal.) 2 oz. portion
New York Strip—7 oz.
Hash Browns—6 oz. potato (frozen portion)
Pancake—6 oz. of mix = 6 pancakes
Maple Syrup—3 oz.
Butter—2 oz.
Egg Batter—2 whole eggs
Belgium Waffle Mix—1 oz. makes 1 waffle
Ham—3 oz.
Blended Cheese—2 oz. 2 oz. Swiss 2 oz. Cheddar
Choice of Cheese—portion size 2 oz.
Green Pepper—3 oz.
Spanish Onion—2 oz.
Ground Sausage—3 oz.
Jalapeno Peppers—¼ oz.
Salsa Sauce—2 oz.
French Toast—2 eggs, ½ loaf of bread

* Juice on menu is choice of Orange, Pineapple, Apple, Grapefruit, or Tomato.

2. Cost of Food Items

Milk	1.69	per gal.
Coffee	2.54	per #
Tea	2.48	per 100 ct.
Coffee Lite	1.02	per 64 oz.
Eggs	.87	per dozen
Muffins	.20	ea.
English Muffins	.25	ea.
Croissants	.30	ea.
Danish	.24	ea.
Bread—Pullman Sliced	.90	per loaf
Texas Toast Bread	1.25	per loaf
Melon	1.30	each
Grapefruit	.34	each
Granola	2.12	per lb.
Hash Browns	8.10	96/3 oz.
Hollandaise Sauce	6.54	per 1.5 lb. can
Canadian Bacon	3.19	per lb.
N.Y. Strip Steak	3.77	per lb.
Ham	2.35	per #
Ground Sausage	1.62	per lb.
Green Peppers	.48	per lb.
Spanish Onions	.36	per lb.
Jalapeno Peppers	4.62	per gal.
Swiss Cheese	1.90	per lb.
Cheddar Cheese	1.90	per lb.
Salsa Sauce	7.57	per gal.
Butter	1.70	lb.
Pancake Mix (Buttermilk)	.52	per lb.
Waffle Mix	5.72	per lb.
Pancake Syrup	3.22	per gal.
Juices: Orange	.51	per qt.
Pineapple	.79	per 46 oz.
Apple	.64	per 46 oz.
Grapefruit	1.14	per qt.
Tomato	.78	per 46 oz.

Find the cost and cost percent of each menu combination. Enter these figures in the spaces provided beneath each menu combination.

3. Menu Combinations—Breakfast Specials

No. 1: $4.95
Choice of two:
Muffin, Croissant, Danish, or Toast
Coffee, Tea, or Small Milk
COST _____ FOOD COST % _____

No. 2: $5.25
½ Fresh Melon or Grapefruit
Bowl of Granola
Orange Juice
Coffee, Tea, or Small Milk
COST _____ FOOD COST % _____

No. 3: $5.95
Two Eggs, poached; served on English Muffin with Canadian Bacon
and Hollandaise Sauce
COST _____ FOOD COST % _____

No. 4: $8.95
Charbroiled New York Strip
Two Eggs
Hash Browns
Toast
Coffee, Tea, or Small Milk
COST _____ FOOD COST % _____

* Items 5 thru 8 served with Creamy Fresh Butter & Maple Syrup

* No. 5: $3.50
Buttermilk Pancakes (3)
COST _____ FOOD COST % _____

* No. 6: $2.95
Short Stack (2)
(Buttermilk Pancakes)
COST _____ FOOD COST % _____

* No. 7: $3.25
French Style Texas Toast
Extra Thick Slice Bread, Dipped in a Rich Egg Batter
COST _____ FOOD COST % _____

* No. 8: $3.95
Belgium Waffle
COST _____ FOOD COST % _____

No. 9: $4.25
Ham and Cheese Omelette
Three Eggs, Diced Ham, Blended Cheese
COST _____ FOOD COST % _____

No. 10: $3.25
Three Egg Omelette
Your choice of plain or cheese
COST _____ FOOD COST % _____

No. 11: $4.25
Western Omelette
Three Eggs, Green Peppers, Ham, and Diced Onions
COST _____ FOOD COST % _____

No. 12: $4.50
Spanish Omelette
Three Eggs, Ground Sausage, Jalapeno Peppers, Cheese, and Salsa
Sauce
COST _____ FOOD COST % _____

EXERCISE 8–1B   Terrace Garden Restaurant

Cost out the 12 Breakfast Specials offered by the Terrace Garden
Restaurant.
The information given is gathered into three categories:

1. The portion size information;

2. The cost of the food items;

3. The menu combinations

1. *Portion Sizes*

*Juice—4 oz.
 Milk—4 oz.
 Coffee, Tea—5 oz. (1 lb. of coffee makes 3 gallons)
 Coffee Lite—½ oz.
 Eggs—Large
 Muffins—standard 1 each
 Rolls—standard 1 each
 Bread—Pullman 2 slices
 Home Fries—2 oz. of potato
 Pancake—3 oz. of mix = 6 pancakes
 Maple Syrup—1 oz.
 Butter Chips—#90 ct. 2 each
 Bacon—20 ct. 2 slices each
 Sausace—1 oz. 2 each
 Ham—1 oz. per order
 French Toast—1 egg, 2 slices of bread.

*Juice on menu is choice of Orange, Pineapple, Apple, Grapefruit, or
 Tomato.

2. Cost of Food Items

Milk .51 per qt.
Coffee 2.54 per #
Tea 1.88 per 100 ct.
Coffee Lite 1.69 per ½ gal.
Eggs .84 per dozen
Muffins 1.32 per doz.
Rolls 1.56 per doz.
Bread Pullman sliced .71 per loaf 22 slices
Potato .14 per #
Pancake Mix .31 per #
Maple Syrup 2.39 for 24 oz.
Butter Chips 1.93 per #
Bacon 1.55 per #
Sausage 1.35 per #
Ham 2.87 per #
Juices: Orange .84 per qt.
         Pineapple .96 per 46 oz.
         Apple .77 per qt.
         Grapefruit .90 per qt.
         Tomato .83 per 46 oz.

Find the cost and cost percent of each menu combination. Enter these figures in the spaces provided beneath each menu combination.

3. Menu Combinations—Breakfast Specials

No. 1: $.79
English Muffin
Coffee, Tea, or Small Milk
COST _____ FOOD COST % _____

No. 2: $.79
Fried Egg on a Hard Roll
Coffee, Tea, or Small Milk
COST _____ FOOD COST % _____

No. 3: $.89
2 Eggs any Style,
Home Fries, Toast
Coffee, Tea, or Small Milk
COST _____ FOOD COST % _____

No. 4: $.99
1 Egg, 2 Pancakes,
2 Strips of Bacon
Coffee, Tea, or Small Milk
COST _____ FOOD COST % _____

No. 5: $1.39
3 Golden Brown Wheat Cakes,
Butter, Maple Syrup
Coffee, Tea, or Small Milk
COST _____ FOOD COST % _____

No. 6: $1.39
Juice, French Toast,
Butter, Maple Syrup
Coffee, Tea, or Small Milk
COST _____ FOOD COST % _____

No. 7: $.30
Single Egg Any Style
COST _____ FOOD COST % _____

No. 8: $.55
Two Eggs Any Style
COST _____ FOOD COST % _____

No. 9: $.75
Three Eggs Any Style
COST _____ FOOD COST % _____

No. 10: $1.95
Juice, 2 Eggs with Choice of Bacon, Ham, or Sausage
Home Fries, Toast, Coffee
COST _____ FOOD COST % _____

No. 11: $1.99
3 Pancakes, 3 Sausages,
Butter, Maple Syrup
Coffee, Tea, or Small Milk
COST _____ FOOD COST % _____

No. 12: $1.19
Grapefruit Juice,
1 Poached Egg, Dry Toast
Coffee, Tea, or Small Milk
COST _____ FOOD COST % _____

CHECK YOUR UNDERSTANDING

1. What is the food cost percent for each menu item? (Fill out right on menu page.)

   _____

   _____

2. If one of each menu combination was sold, what would the average food cost percent be?

   _____

   _____

3. If you had to make any changes in the menu at this point, what items would you change? Why?

   _____

   _____

EXERCISE 8–2

Now that you know the cost of the individual Breakfast Specials, use the following sales figures, reported for the day, to indicate the highs and lows.

Number Sold	Red Woodpecker Grill Breakfast Special	High/Low
10	No. 1	
45	2	
12	3	
32	4	
0	5	
0	6	
62	7	
10	8	
33	9	
16	10	
12	11	
18	12	

Terrace Garden Restaurant
Breakfast

Number Sold	Special	High/Low
13	1	
16	2	
11	3	
25	4	
12	5	
10	6	
0	7	
0	8	
0	9	
15	10	
12	11	
11	12	

CHECK YOUR UNDERSTANDING

1. What is the actual food cost percent?

   _____

   _____

2. Based on the information you have, and acting as a cost controller, which Breakfast Specials, if any, would you eliminate or restructure? Why?

   _____

   _____

   _____

   _____

   _____

CRITICAL THINKING

1. Redo Exercise 8–2, adjusting the information on the Red Woodpecker Grill specials as follows:

Breakfast Special	Number Sold	High/Low
No. 7	15	
8	5	
9	18	

Adjust the information on the Terrace Garden Restaurant specials as follows:

Breakfast Special	Number Sold	High/Low
5	35	
6	10	

After entering these new numbers and recalculating, adjust for the menu classifications. Comment on how you view the menus now.

_____

_____

2. Take at least one menu item with the highest food cost percent for both the Red Woodpecker Grill and Terrace Garden Restaurant, and adjust the cost of the item. Re-enter this cost on the immediately previous configuration (question 1), and recalculate the figures to determine the new menu classifications. Comment on how you view these new menu calculations or explain what you would have to adjust to come up with a better menu.

_____

_____

_____

_____

_____

_____

LABOR

■ **OBJECTIVES**

Upon completing Lesson 9, you should be able to:

1. Calculate labor percent using a register tape reading.

2. Monitor labor control using various restaurant performance variables.

■ **KEY TERM**

Register tape reading

Many people claim that labor is a topic that a manager should be most concerned with and that perhaps a whole course should be devoted to labor in the foodservice industry. Most texts emphasize human resources, but do they cover labor control? What information on the topic of labor could be included to make the subject more interesting and relevant?

Some experts in labor control, working in the fast-food industry, have fine-tuned labor control. If you frequent fast-food restaurants, you may have been inconvenienced for a few minutes while the manager, assistant manager, or crew manager ran a ***register tape reading***—a procedure used to develop labor control for a particular operation. The manager takes a register reading every hour or half hour, to view the total sales in dollars that occurred in a set time period.

CALCULATING LABOR PERCENT

How can running a register tape reading every hour have an influence on labor? Several things are revealed on the register tape; for example, total payroll cost for the employees working during that hour could indicate the labor percent for that time period:

$$\frac{\text{Cost}}{\text{Sales}} = \text{Labor percent} \qquad \frac{\$500.00}{\$1,500.00} = 33.3333\%$$

Register readings can also help in determining how many employees are needed in each position to obtain a $500.00 cost for an hour; for example, 3 cooks, 2 cashiers, 1 busperson, and 1 cleanup person. Would it be necessary to have this many employees, to achieve $1,500.00 in sales? You would need to get some feedback (1) from customers, regarding how they would rate the service they received, and (2) from employees, regarding their position and work distribution. Could this operation have done $3,000.00 in sales with the same labor cost? With a labor cost of $500.00 and sales at $3,000.00, the labor percent would be 16.6666%.

The questions for the person controlling labor are: Could you have done $1,500.00 in sales with half the labor and half the cost? Is a cost of $250.00 appropriate when sales are $1,500.00? Were the customers satisfied and did employees feel their work load was appropriate? Your questions might be: "How do I learn this? What is the great secret? Is that all there is to labor control?" The concept of labor control, once understood, calculated, and monitored vigorously, will give you a true knowledge of your labor cost percent, enabling you to aim for a bottom-line profit. The key words for controlling labor are *calculate, monitor* and *aim for a profit or goal*. In the income statement in Lesson 1, one of the break-down items was labor.)

It is difficult to give an actual cost-of-labor percentage that an operation should aim for. The operation has to know its other costs and its projected sales. With that information, guidelines can be established for projecting income on a daily basis. Once the daily sales are calculated, management must determine the number of employees needed to work each position during each shift, and the rate of pay needed to meet the anticipated sales.

This brief explanation has given a simplistic outlook on labor control. You should consult all available information on the subject of labor control through texts or library research.

CONTROL USING RESTAURANT PERFORMANCE VARIABLES

When calculating labor control, you must have all the restaurant "facts" that were covered throughout the lessons of this book. Use the following checklist to review your labor control situation:

- What was the number of operating hours?
- What were the average sales per person?

■ What was the number of people served per meal period?

■ What are the guidelines or projections of the average number of meals each staff person can handle?

■ What was the average number of hours allotted for serving customers, based on meals served?

■ What is the projected labor cost for producing a profit?

■ What is the forecasted cost of food and beverages combined?

■ What is the overall cost percentage for the restaurant? (If all costs, including food and beverage and labor, are projected to be, say, 60%, your profit prior to overhead would yield approximately 40% gross profit percentage.)

■ What is the average rate per hour that you pay your staff? (Assorted rates are paid to various employees for different levels of skill and responsibility.)

■ What is the turnover rate for the restaurant?

Along with the checklist, which covers much information, it is important to remember that you must continually calculate, monitor, and aim for a goal, and repeat the process again and again.

■ SPREADSHEET OBJECTIVES

Upon completion of Lesson 9, you should be able to:

1. Calculate daily cost of labor based on total sales and total employee hours.

2. Recap sales, costs, and profits based on data gleaned from previous spreadsheets.

SPREADSHEET INFORMATION

Careful reading and complete understanding of the data given must be ac-complished prior to entering any data on the spreadsheet. The format has been set up for a five-day workweek, Monday through Friday, and the hours of operation have been preset. (See Figure 9–1.) You will be given (1) the number of covers the restaurant anticipates serving on each of the days and (2) the average cover. You can then calculate the total sales for the day by multiplying the number of covers forecasted by the average cover. The formula is:

$$\text{Cover forecasted} \times \text{Average cover} = \text{Total sales}$$
$$100 \quad \times \quad \$10 \quad = \$1,000$$

Several workers in each category of the various payroll positions are listed for scheduling purposes, based on the previous information on day of the week, covers, and sales. Always take into account the five days of activity that contribute to the weekly payroll target, the projected income to meet the budget, or the projected profit. Enter all the above information, supplied on your fact sheet, onto the spreadsheet (see Figure 9–1).

FIGURE 9–1   Labor Control Spreadsheet—Basic Format

FOODSERVICE COST CONTROL USING MICROSOFT EXCEL   PAGE
RESTAURANT NAME: {NAME}   1
STUDENT NAME: {NAME}
DATE: {DATE}

DAY: MONDAY			DATE:	{DATE}		COVERS FORCASTED:	{###}				TOTAL SALES: $	0.00
HOURS	10-11	11-12	12-1	1-2	2-3	6-7	7-8	8-9	9-10	10-11	11-12	12-1	TOT HRS
WAITER													0.00
WAITER													0.00
WAITER													0.00
BAR													0.00
BUSSER													0.00
BUSSER													0.00
BUSSER													0.00
COOK													0.00
COOK													0.00
COOK													0.00
TOTAL	0.00	0.00	0.00	0.00	0.00	0.00	0.00	0.00	0.00	0.00	0.00	0.00	0.00

	WAITER	WAITER	WAITER	BAR	BUSSER	BUSSER	BUSSER	COOK	COOK	COOK	TOTAL
HOURS	0.00	0.00	0.00	0.00	0.00	0.00	0.00	0.00	0.00	0.00	0.00
RATE	0.00	0.00	0.00	0.00	0.00	0.00	0.00	0.00	0.00	0.00	XXXXXX
TOTAL	0.00	0.00	0.00	0.00	0.00	0.00	0.00	0.00	0.00	0.00	0.00

After you have determined the number of hours you want to schedule for an employee, enter on the spreadsheet, for each day, a 1 for a full hour or .5 for a half hour. This will allow you to calculate the number of hours to schedule for each position during the hours of operation. You will then have the number of hours needed for each position, the total hours worked per employee for the day, and the total hours for all employees for the day.

When you have the number of daily hours needed for each position and the total for the day, you will be instructed to summarize that information and calculate the cost of labor for the day. The different positions are separated on the spreadsheet. The number of hours for each position is calculated for you. After you enter the rate of pay for each employee, the total pay for each position will be calculated for you. For double-checking, the spreadsheet will give you the total number of hours for the day and the total dollar amount for labor for the day. You are to do this for all five days. Make sure that you take productivity and service into consideration when scheduling labor.

The next spreadsheet for this exercise is best described as a recap of sales, costs, and profits. (See Figure 9–2.)

For each category, you will need the dollars and percentages. You have already calculated some of the costs and entered them onto the daily schedule of labor. Now, you simply enter the data for the five days onto the recap spreadsheet. The items obtained from previous spreadsheets are covers forecasted, sales forecasted, number of labor hours, and labor cost

FIGURE 9–2   Labor Control Spreadsheet—Sales, Cost, and Profit Forecasts

FOODSERVICE COST CONTROL USING MICROSOFT EXCEL
RESTAURANT NAME: {NAME}
STUDENT NAME: {NAME}
DATE: {DATE}

RECAPITULATION OF SALES, COSTS, AND PROFITS				WEEK OF:	{FROM}	- {TO}
DATE:	MONDAY	TUESDAY	WEDNEDSAY	THURSDAY	FRIDAY	TOTAL
SALES FORECAST $						0.00
COVERS FORECAST #						0
LABOR HOURS						0
LABOR COST $						0.00
LABOR COST %						0.0000%
FOOD & BEV COST $						0.00
GROSS PROFIT $						0.00
GROSS PROFIT %						0.0000%

in dollars. The labor cost percent can then be calculated using the following formula:

$$\frac{\text{Payroll for day}}{\text{Sales for day}} = \text{Labor cost percent} \qquad \frac{\$120.00}{\$1,000.00} = 12.0000\%$$

You then calculate the food and beverage cost, which is a certain percent given to you, multiplied by the sales for the day, for each of the five days. For example, if food and beverage cost was 45% and sales $1,000.00, then 45% × $1,000.00 = $450.00.

The next column is gross profit, which is obtained by subtracting from sales the labor cost and the food and beverage cost, calculated for the five days and totaled for the week. For example:

	$1,000.00	Sales
−	120.00	Labor cost
=	880.00	Subtotal
−	450.00	Food and beverage cost
	$430.00	Gross profit for the day

The last column is gross profit percent. Use the same formula as was used to find all other percents:

$$\frac{\text{Gross profit}}{\text{Gross sales}} = \text{Gross profit percent} \qquad \frac{\$450.00}{\$1,000.00} = 45\%$$

On the recap spreadsheet, you are calculating the total of the columns for the week, across the five days. When calculating percent, you are calculating from top to bottom. Keep in mind that you are aiming for certain targets that are given to you in the original data for the lesson.

Figures 9–3 and 9–4 are examples of worksheets—a blank form and a form completed by hand, respectively.

FIGURE 9–3 Labor Control Worksheet—Basic Form

DAY: _MONDAY_

DATE: _4/10/89_

COVERS FORECASTED _____

TOTAL SALES $ _____

HOURS	10–11	11–12	12–1	1–2	2–3	6–7	7–8	8–9	9–10	10–11	11–12	12–1
WAITER												
WAITER												
WAITER												
BARTENDER												
BUSPERSON												
BUSPERSON												
BUSPERSON												
COOK												
COOK												

HOURLY LABOR COST WORKSHEET

POSITION	HOURS WORKED	NO. OF HOURS	RATE/HR	TOTAL
WAITER				
WAITER				
WAITER				
BARTENDER				
BUSPERSON				
BUSPERSON				
BUSPERSON				
COOK				
COOK				
COOK				
	TOTAL HOURS		TOTAL WAGES	

FIGURE 9-4   Labor Control Worksheet—Daily Schedule

DAY: __THURSDAY__
DATE: __3/21/87__

HOURS	10–11	11–12	12–1	1–2	2–3	6–7	7–8	8–9	9–10	10–11	11–12	12–1
POSITION												
WAITER		▨	▨	▨	▨		▨	▨	▨	▨	▨	
WAITER			▨	▨	▨		▨	▨	▨	▨		
WAITER			▨	▨					▨	▨		
BARTENDER	▨	▨	▨	▨	▨	▨	▨	▨	▨	▨	▨	
BUSPERSON												
BUSPERSON			▨	▨					▨	▨		
BUSPERSON							▨	▨	▨	▨		
COOK												
COOK	▨	▨	▨	▨	▨		▨	▨	▨			
COOK		▨	▨	▨		▨	▨	▨	▨	▨		

HOURLY LABOR COST WORKSHEET

POSITION	HOURS WORKED	NO. OF HOURS	RATE/HR	TOTAL
WAITER	11–3 / 7^{30}–11^{30}	8	2.20	17.60
WAITER	11^{30}–2^{30} / 7–11	7	2.20	15.40
WAITER	12–2 / 8–10	4	2.20	8.80
BARTENDER	10^{30}–2^{30} / 6^{30}–11^{30}	9	4.00	36.00
BUSPERSON	12–2 / 8–10	4	2.20	8.80
BUSPERSON	7^{30}–10^{30}	3	2.20	6.60
BUSPERSON				
COOK	10–3 / 7–10	8	4.75	38.00
COOK	11–2 / 6–11	8	4.75	38.00
COOK				
	TOTAL HOURS	51	TOTAL WAGES	169.20

EXERCISES

Choose *one* of the following exercises, and complete the staff schedule and related costs.

Exercise 9–1A   Red Woodpecker Grill

Given below are the standard labor hour requirements relating to the 60-seat Red Woodpecker Grill. The restaurant is medium priced, and caters to business and company executives for lunch (11:30 A.M.–2:30 P.M.), and family dining at night (7:30 P.M.–11:30 P.M.). The average guest check is $12.50, and all labor requirements are scheduled on an hourly basis. The bar services as a holding area, to stagger business and aid in the cover turnover of the restaurant.

Because of a change in the management, you are hired as the new Restaurant Manager and will be responsible for the hiring and scheduling of employees and for control of related costs for the operation.

Labor costs of the restaurant are not to exceed 15% of sales. Your salary is not to be included in the labor cost because you are retained on a contract basis by the management. Because you were hired for job completion and not for the number of hours of work put in, you are to exclude yourself from the schedule you plan to prepare.

Combined food and beverage costs are forecasted and are not to exceed 48% of total sales, so as to have an overall variable cost percentage of 63%. The restaurant is closed on Saturdays and Sundays.

The following guide serves as a reference on labor staffing for each labor position in the restaurant.

Variable Labor Staffing Guide (Information Only)

	Number of Meals				
	50	75	100	125	150
Hours required:					
Waiter	8.5	9.5	16.0	16.0	19.0
Bartender	9.0	9.0	9.0	9.0	9.0
Cook	7.0	14.0	14.0	14.0	14.0
Busperson		2.0	4.0	5.0	7.0

The figures represent labor hours, not persons. For example, 8.5 hours could be assigned to one waiter hired for an 8.5-hour duration, or to two waiters (working 4 hours and 4.5 hours, respectively), thereby dividing the labor hour requirement set for the forecasted 50 covers.

The hourly rates for each labor position are:

1. Waiter $2.90/hr
2. Bartender $5.00/hr
3. Busperson $2.90/hr
4. Cook $5.75/hr

You are given the following forecast for the 5 days during which you are required to schedule staff:

Monday, April 10   45 covers
Tuesday, April 11   70 covers
Wednesday, April 12   ˙105 covers
Thursday, April 13   145 covers
Friday, April 14   120 covers

Complete the schedule worksheets.

Exercise 9–1B   Terrace Garden Restaurant

Given below are the standard labor hour requirements relating to the 80-seat Terrace Garden Restaurant. The restaurant is medium priced, and caters to business and company executives for lunch (11:30 A.M.–2:30 P.M.), and family dining at night (7:30 P.M.–11:30 P.M.). The average guest check is $12.50, and all labor requirements are scheduled on an hourly basis. The bar serves as a holding area, to stagger business and aid in the cover turnover of the restaurant.

Because of a change in the management, you are hired as the new Restaurant Manager and will be responsible for the hiring and scheduling of employees and for control of related costs for the operation.

Labor costs of the restaurant are not to exceed 15% of sales. Your salary is not to be included in the labor cost because you are retained on a contract basis by the management. Because you were hired for job completion and not for the number of hours of work put in, you are to exclude yourself from the schedule you plan to prepare.

Combined food and beverage costs are forecasted and are not to exceed 48% of total sales, so as to have an overall variable cost percentage of 63%. The restaurant is closed on Saturdays and Sundays.

The following guide serves as a reference on labor staffing for each labor position in the restaurant.

Variable Labor Staffing Guide (Information Only)

	Number of Meals				
	50	*75*	*100*	*125*	*150*
Hours required:					
Waiter	8.5	9.5	16.0	16.0	19.0
Bartender	9.0	9.0	9.0	9.0	9.0
Cook	7.0	14.0	14.0	14.0	14.0
Busperson		2.0	4.0	5.0	7.0

The figures represent labor hours, not persons. For example, 8.5 hours could be assigned to one waiter hired for an 8.5-hour duration, or to two waiters (working 4 hours and 4.5 hours, respectively), thereby dividing the labor hour requirement set for the forecasted 50 covers.

The hourly rates for each labor position are:

1. Waiter $2.90/hr
2. Bartender $6.00/hr
3. Busperson $2.90/hr
4. Cook $6.50/hr

You are given the following forecast for the 5 days during which you are required to schedule staff:

Monday, April 10   150 covers
Tuesday, April 11   100 covers
Wednesday, April 12   175 covers
Thursday, April 13   250 covers
Friday, April 14   285 covers

Complete the schedule worksheets.

CHECK YOUR UNDERSTANDING

Using the information for the restaurant you selected in Exercise 9–1, fill in the blanks.

1. Total forecasted sales _____
2. Total labor cost in $ _____
3. Labor cost percent _____
4. Food and beverage costs in $ _____
5. Turnover rate for the room _____
6. Gross profit in $ _____
7. Gross profit percent _____
8. Average rate per hour for labor _____
9. If you were to propose that management adopt a mix of full-time and part-time staffing, would the total labor cost go up or down? Why?

_____
_____
_____
_____

CRITICAL THINKING QUESTIONS

1. If you had to create new positions other than the ones on the list given to you, what would the positions and job descriptions be for the Red Woodpecker Grill and Terrace Garden Restaurant?

_____

_____

_____

_____

2. What wage would you recommend for the above positions at both the Red Woodpecker Grill and the Terrace Garden Restaurant?

_____

_____

_____

3. Compare the average hourly rate of pay at the Red Woodpecker Grill to the rate at the Terrace Garden Restaurant. Can you suggest how both operations could be somewhat alike?

_____

_____

_____

_____

4. If you were to adjust the food and beverage percent, what number would make your restaurant more profitable? Suggest ways of accomplishing profitability.

_____

_____

_____

_____

5. Comparing the gross food percent of the Red Woodpecker Grill to that of the Terrace Garden Restaurant, which one is better? If income were to increase by 25% in both restaurants, how much profit in dollars would the Red Woodpecker Grill and the Terrace Garden Restaurant produce?

_____

_____

_____

_____

APPENDIX

Conversion Tables

Fractions - Decimals		Ounces - Decimals		Ounces - Decimals	
½	.50	16	1.00	8	.50
⅓	.333	15	.9375	7	.4375
¼	.25	14	.8750	6	.375
⅕	.20	13	.8125	5	.3125
⅙	.1667	12	.75	4	.25
1/7	.1428	11	.6875	3	.1875
⅛	.1250	10	.6250	2	.1250
1/9	.1111	9	.5625	1	.0625
1/10	.10				
1/16	.0625				
1/32	.03125				

Pounds

1/16	=	1 oz.	=	.0625		
2/16	=	2 oz.	=	.1250		
3/16	=	3 oz.	=	.1875		
4/16	=	4 oz.	=	.25	=	¼ lb.
5/16	=	5 oz.	=	.3125		
6/16	=	6 oz.	=	.3750		
7/16	=	7 oz.	=	.4375		
½	=	8 oz.	=	.50	=	½ lb.
9/16	=	9 oz.	=	.5625		
10/16	=	10 oz.	=	.6250		
11/16	=	11 oz.	=	.6875		
12/16	=	12 oz.	=	.75	=	¾ lb.
13/16	=	13 oz.	=	.8125		
14/16	=	14 oz.	=	.8750		
15/16	=	15 oz.	=	.9375		
16/16	=	16 oz.	=	1.	=	1 lb.
. . . .						
1.2 oz.			=	.03125		

Drinks

Size in oz.	Decimal Equivalent	Fifth	Quart
½	.50	51.20	64.00
¾	.75	34.13	42.67
⅞	.875	29.26	36.57
1	1.	25.6	32.
1⅛	1.125	22.76	28.44
1¼	1.25	20.48	25.6
1⅜	1.375	18.62	23.27
1½	1.5	17.07	21.33
1⅝	1.625	15.75	19.69
1¾	1.75	14.63	18.28
1⅞	1.875	13.65	17.07
2	2.	12.8	16.

INDEX